YOUR PRETTY FACE
IS GOING TO HELL

YOUR PRETTY FACE
IS GOING TO HELL

THE DANGEROUS GLITTER OF
DAVID BOWIE, IGGY POP, AND LOU REED

Dave Thompson

An Imprint of Hal Leonard Corporation
New York

Frontispiece: David Bowie, Iggy Pop, and Lou Reed (with MainMan boss Tony Defries laughing in the background) at the Dorchester Hotel, 1972.

Published in 2009 by Backbeat Books
An Imprint of Hal Leonard Corporation
7777 West Bluemound Road
Milwaukee, WI 53213

Trade Book Division Editorial Offices
19 West 21st Street, New York, NY 10010

Printed in the United States of America

Book design by David Ursone
Typography by UB Communications

Library of Congress Cataloging-in-Publication Data

Thompson, Dave, 1960 Jan. 3-
    Your pretty face is going to hell : the dangerous glitter of David Bowie, Iggy Pop, and Lou Reed / Dave Thompson. — 1st paperback ed.
        p. cm.
    Includes bibliographical references and discography.
    ISBN 978-0-87930-985-5 (alk. paper)
    1. Bowie, David. 2. Pop, Iggy, 1947-3. Reed, Lou. 4. Rock musicians—England—Biography. 5. Punk rock musicians—United States—Biography.
I. Title.
    ML400.T47 2009
    782.42166092'2—dc22
                                        2009036966
www.backbeatbooks.com

For Robert Dean Hanson
(1932–2009)

CONTENTS

PROLOGUE

Nico was in Paris, France, when she first met Andy Warhol.

It was May 1965, and Warhol—spindly, blotchy, awkward, and shy—was visiting the city for the second time in little more than a year, triumphantly returning to the gallery where his electric chair portraits had introduced him to Europe.

Under the banner of Pop Art Américaine, a series of screen prints depicting the establishment's preferred method of execution had excited nothing but controversy back home, where Warhol was still best regarded as the weirdo pop artist who painted Campbell's soup cans. France, too, was uncertain, but American poet John Ashbery and French writer Jean-Jacques Lebel praised his work in the exhibition brochure, and gallery owner Ileana Sonnabend (who had once been married to Warhol's agent, Leo Castelli) knew that her countrymen were fascinated despite themselves. She had barely waved the artist off one chilly morning in February 1964 before she was scheming his return.

This time Warhol was exhibiting his screen-printed poppies, gaudy and vivid, primary colors pregnant with childish exuberance, and alive with the promise of the spring that was just breaking over Paris. May 1965 was as warm as the season could ever be: the sidewalk cafés were alive with the sound of the city breaking its hibernation, and the nightclubs were bubbling their own intoxicating brew.

Nico was there with Willy Maywald, the German-born photographer who was her constant escort during her visits to France. Old enough to be her father, a role that she gratefully placed upon him, Maywald had tirelessly pushed Nico forward in her first role as a fashion model, sat back somewhat when she moved into movies, and watched indulgently as a brief fling with Bob Dylan pinballed her toward a musical career. The pair holidayed in Greece together, Nico and Dylan; it was there that he wrote a song for her, the timelessly charming "I'll Keep It with Mine," but she frowned when she was asked if they ever sang it together. "He didn't like it when I tried to sing along with him," she told her biographer, Richard Witts. "I thought he was . . . a little annoyed that I could sing properly, at least in tune, so he made me more determined to sing to other people."

Since that time, she had visited New York and performed at the Blue Angel; flown to England and seduced Brian Jones; encountered Andrew Loog Oldham, and hatched plans to make a record with him. Now she was in Paris, and she met Andy Warhol. As Maywald understated in his memoir, "She had the gift of ferreting out interesting people."

Warhol's table at the Chez Castel nightclub, on rue Princesse, glittered as only his inner sanctum could. The movie *What's New Pussycat* had just wrapped shooting at the club, and the place, Warhol told his diary, was popping with stars—Terence Stamp, Ursula Andress, Peter Sellers, Woody Allen, Romy Schneider.

Warhol was a star too, and he caught people's eye, if only because it was so hard not to stare at him. But it was his companion Edie Sedgwick who conquered their hearts, elfin and boyish, wide-eyed but not yet the legless tragedy of future legend, bubbling with charm and the innocent beauty that so enraptured Warhol that he wound up destroying it. The previous evening, dining with Salvador Dalí at the Crazy Horse Saloon, it was Edie who broke the ice between the artists when she leaned over to the grandfather of surrealism and asked, "How does it feel to be such a famous writer?"

Edie was irresistible. "Twenty-two, white-haired with anthracite-black eyes and legs to swoon over," mooned *Vogue* magazine, and that was when she was in New York. "In Paris," the article continued, "Warhol's gang startled the dancers at Chez Castel by appearing with fifteen rabbits and Edie Sedgwick in a black leotard and a white mink coat."

"It's all I have to wear," she sighed softly.

Nico watched her like a hawk. "She was so lovely," she recalled twenty years later. "Like a little bird that you wanted to hold in your hand." She barely noticed the rest of the entourage, Warhol's assistant Gerard Malanga, all whiplash grace and tousled hair; Edie's friend Chuck Wein, bearded and bulky, and so eager to please (but please whom? That was the sting in *his* tail); but then her gaze fell on a familiar face and an old friend, Denis Deegan, an American in Paris in true Gene Kelly style.

Nico caught Deegan's eye, joined the group and, when Warhol's curiosity could stand no more tension (but only then—like Edie, Nico not only knew how but when to make an entrance), introduced herself by discussing her friends. Some were real, some were assumed, a few were probably imaginary—Nico never allowed reality to stand on the toes of her self-mythology. But the names William Burroughs, Lee Strasberg, Marilyn Monroe, Federico Fellini, Coco Chanel, Bob Dylan, and Brian Jones fell from her lips, and she knew she had her audience's attention.

Edie, she recalled, was "too preoccupied with her lipstick" to pay the newcomer much mind, except to ask Nico how she kept her hair so blonde. But Malanga told her about the silver-enshrined studio where the master did his work, and suggested that she visit someday; Warhol's mind worked more methodically, and he quietly grilled her about her movie career, second-guessing her interest in the Rolling Stones.

"Is it true that Mick Jagger has a huge cock?"

He never let on that pasted in his scrapbook was one of the advertisements Nico had shot for London Fog raincoats. They parted that evening with promises to meet again.

Nico returned to London and her assignation with Andrew Oldham, as he kick-started his Immediate record label. They toyed with recording her Dylan song and, because its author was in town as well, the pair of them wound up in a little demo studio in central London, Dylan pounding drunken piano while Nico sang "I'll Keep It with Mine."

But Oldham shrugged away their one-take acetate and suggested Nico go with Gordon Lightfoot's "I'm Not Saying" instead. Through the remainder of the summer, she lived the life of an Immediate pop star, scarcely bothering the charts with her music, but a familiar face on the swinging city scene nonetheless. Then, tiring of the looming London winter, she flew to New York to hook up with Brian Jones again. They would visit Andy Warhol together.

All the way to the Factory, Nico imagined the splendor in which Warhol must exist—for how else could he surround himself with so much beauty and talent? Even as they turned onto East Forty-seventh Street, the warehouse district that struggled for light beneath the shadow of the Empire State Building, she refused to let the shit-toned stonework chase away her dreams. But then they clambered into the rickety elevator that creaked and groaned its way to the fourth floor, and reality screamed out at her in all its sordid grime.

Yes, the Factory was cloaked in silver. But it was silver foil, supermarket aluminum, and there were rips and tears in it, revealing the dull dishpan paintwork that cowered underneath. Yes, its denizens were beautiful. But only if you took your solace in ugliness, inhaled through the fug of smoke and sex and fast-food morsels that clung to every corner.

Not everybody struck her as useless, and Nico swiftly assigned people roles in her own mind—the ones she should listen to, the ones she could laugh with, and the ones that did not exist.

Essential. Paul Morrissey, sharp and suave, keen-eyed and acid-tongued, Warhol's business manager and the true directorial power behind the throne of Warhol's movie empire.

Essential. Gerard Malanga. She considered him her first friend at the Factory, and the most important as well. "It was Gerard who gave me the Factory phone number. I met up with him again when I had my record out in London; he was looking for a gallery for Andy to exhibit in and we met. I always loved Gerard." The feeling was mutual. "If there exists beauty so universal as to be unquestionable," he once said, "Nico possesses it."

Mary Woronov. A Cornell University student who hopped a Greyhound to New York; not quite a fixture, but no stranger either. Plus she and Gerard looked so beautiful together. *Essential.*

Richie Berlin. A junkie whose father ran the Hearst Corporation. *Decorative.*

Brigid Polk, so named because she kept po(l)king herself. Richie's sister. Generally plump, oft-times naked. But *decorative.*

Ondine. A junkie. Maybe *decorative.*

Paul America. A decoration. *Dispensable.*

Billy Name. Andy's odd-job man. Great if you needed a lightbulb changed. Otherwise, *dispensable.*

Edie. She wasn't sure what she made of Edie.

And so Nico went on, checking out each of the figures who sat nodding out on the furniture, utterly oblivious to the hive of inactive activity that exploded around them. She studied them all, watching the ones who rode the most recent amphetamine rush across however many hours it took to come down, as they stared in turn at the shriveled dicks that were the most immediate legacy of their sulfate haze, and wondered why they couldn't get it on like the other couples in the room, the ones who fucked and sucked and licked and flicked like so many living art installations.

All of them, she decided, were shameless and loveless, acting up because they could, because nobody told them not to, because they thought it was what Andy wanted. But Andy kept his thoughts to himself until something or someone came along that intrigued him.

Nico intrigued him, especially after she handed him a copy of her record, then stood patiently smiling while he spun it on the tiny gramophone that sat in one corner of the Factory. Wordlessly, he ushered her to a chair, up against a plain plywood background, and adjusted the lights, illuminating one side of her face while leaving the other in shadow. Wordlessly, too, Malanga stepped over, camera at the ready, and focused unblinkingly on her face for four and a half minutes, until he deemed that her "screen test" was over.

It was a ritual that every visitor to the Factory underwent. That same chair and much the same background had hosted poet John Giorno and actor Dennis Hopper, drag queen Mario Montez and filmmaker Barbara Rubin, superstar Baby Jane Holzer and Queen Edie, alongside every one of the Factory regulars, past and present. Through these short movies— or stillies, as Warhol called them, because so many of his subjects froze before the motionless camera—the artist would ultimately build up an unparalleled portrait of the New York avant-garde of the mid-1960s: Dylan, Donovan, and Dalí; Ginsberg and Burroughs—189 different faces floated before his cameras, some just once, some on several occasions. One day he would decide what he wanted to do with them.

Her first screen test over, Nico underwent her second moments later. But whereas her first film caught her all but immobile, with just the occasional smirk and, once, a hand raised to blot out the harsh lighting, to shatter the photographic stillness, her second was a riot of action, the camera dancing around her while she sat or stood as she saw fit. And days later, Nico was invited to make her debut in a Warhol movie, standing in a cupboard with Randy Bourscheidt for an hour and six minutes, one small part in the sprawling masterpiece that Warhol was compiling around the theme of *Chelsea Girls*.

Nico would make at least nine movies for Warhol, intriguing shorts and bewildering marathons alike. She might even have made many more—she admitted that the one-take, ad-libbed scenarios were scarcely a drain on anything more than her patience—had Warhol and Morrissey not placed her in an even more audacious situation, playing her Immediate single to a pop group they had recently brought under their wing. Then, when the members bemusedly acknowledged that yes, this Nico person did sound as good as she looked, Morrissey informed them that she was their new singer. And Nico just smiled when she heard the news, as she did whenever she was presented with any fresh surprise. She would become a member of the Velvet Underground.

"Andy suggested we use Nico as a vocalist," guitarist Sterling Morrison said. Her single wasn't bad, he thought, "sort of like early Marianne Faithfull [another Andrew Oldham discovery]. So we said fine, she looks great, and just gradually tried to work her in." It was the way her entire life had played out. All good things come to those who radiate beauty.

In fact, Warhol and the band scarcely knew one another at that point, but if anything about Warhol's universe could be termed haphazard, the Velvet Underground's arrival in the Factory was it.

The saga began when Warhol and Morrissey were approached by a businessman keen to append the artist's name to a new discothèque he was opening. The pair agreed, but only if the club would also showcase their band. "Fine, what's their name?" asked the entrepreneur, and Morrissey had to hang up the phone there, because not only did he not have a clue, he didn't have a band, either. He'd just suggested it so that Warhol might get something more than money out of the venture; it could also become a part of his art. After all, Cocteau had once managed a boxer, Panamanian prizefighter Al Brown.

The search was on and ended almost immediately. It might even have been that same day that Gerard Malanga asked if he could borrow Warhol's Bolex camera for an evening, to film a band that Barbara Rubin was interested in. One of *her* friends, a Freeport-out-of-Brooklyn guy named Lewis Reed, was their singer and guitarist, and had just landed a three-day residency at the Café Bizarre in the East Village.

Curious, Morrissey handed over the camera. He also volunteered to tag along to help Malanga work the light meter and load the film. He wasn't certain precisely what he was expecting to see that evening, but it would probably be something cut in a post-Byrds folk-rock mode, because that summed up almost everything playing in the city right then. Or it would be some squeaky-keen pop group that thought it could outflank the Fab Four. The Beatles or the Byrds. You could turn turn turn all you liked, but you still wound up facing in the same direction. Only the Velvet Underground, and the very select handful of fans they'd accumulated along the way, knew just how mistaken he would be.

Part

PERFORMANCE

1

A GHOST BLOODED COUNTRY
ALL COVERED WITH SLEEP

Detroit and New York, 1975

"Sticks and stones may break my bones but words will never hurt me."

Whoever it was first coined that rejoinder had obviously never met Lou Reed.

"Lou Reed," wrote journalist Lester Bangs in 1975, "is a completely depraved pervert and pathetic death dwarf and everything else you want to think he is. On top of that, he's a liar, a wasted talent, an artist continually in flux and a huckster selling pounds of his own flesh. A panderer living off the dumbbell nihilism of a seventies generation that doesn't have the energy to commit suicide."

"Aw, all Lester wants to do is suck Lou Reed's cock," hit back an unnamed musician whom a similarly anonymous girlfriend was managing at the time. And that was Bangs's girlfriend, not Reed's. Reed did not have girlfriends. He had a steady stream of companions, whose omnipresence left his entourage feeling even more unnerved than he did, not because of what they said and did, but because anybody who could spend that much time with Reed had to have the psyche of a cybernaut and skin as thick as the planet's crust.

Reed was acidic and acerbic, merciless and mean; even his friends admitted there were days when they didn't want to hang with him. Some blamed the drugs that even strangers assumed had been his constant companions since at least his early twenties.

Others blamed his childhood, the parents who tried so hard to keep him on the straight and narrow that they committed him to electric shock therapy when it became clear they had failed. In those days, when such things were considered medical maladies, he'd been diagnosed as suffering from mood swings and homosexual tendencies, so the doctors tried to fry them out of his

brain. Few of Reed's subsequent friends or biographers have possessed the nec-
essary psychiatric qualifications to truly understand how the process affected
him, but it's unlikely that it effected a cure.

The Velvet Underground was not Reed's first band. Already midway through his twenties, he had served his songwriting apprenticeship in the Pickwick Records neo-hit factory, a sub–Brill Building monolith where aspiring young writers, musicians, and arrangers were thrown together in increasingly random combinations in the hopes that one of them might strike gold. But Reed was never really going to do that, if only because the sense of humor that sometimes left even his cowriters—Jerry Vance and Terry Phillips, mostly—staring blankly was never going to let him.

In early sixties America, dance songs were all the rage. There was Chubby Checker swiveling the twist, there was someone doing the swim, and someone else preparing the locomotion, and so on and so forth until you only needed to think of a distinctive arm or leg movement, and somebody was setting it to music. But only Reed could have read a fashion mag report on how ostrich feathers were about to become the next big thing on the catwalks of the city and then designed a dance to accompany them, one in which you place your head on the dance floor and somebody else comes and steps on it.

He wrote constantly. The all-girl Foxes sang his "Soul City"; the Beachnuts cut his "Cycle Annie" and "I've Got a Tiger in My Tank"; the Jades recorded "Leave Her for Me" and "So Blue." The Roughnecks warned "You're Driving Me Insane," and Reed himself cut a solo single, "Your Love" and "Merry Go Round," although it was never released. But "The Ostrich" was just so far out there, so absurd (and, absurdly, so danceable) that the powers of Pickwick figured they might even have a shot at a hit. A band was thrust together.

The Primitives included Reed on vocals and guitar, violinist Tony Conrad, artist Walter De Maria, and, slumming it on bass, a Welshman named John Cale, raised in Swansea, schooled at Tanglewood, taught by Iannis Xenakis, and last seen playing alongside La Monte Young (and Conrad) in the über-minimalist Dream Syndicate.

He was scarcely pop star material. "They would never let me perform my pieces at Tanglewood," Cale lamented, "because they were so violent.

Eventually they did let me. I didn't tell them what I was going to do. There was a table and another pianist, I was working away inside the piano and I just took an axe and…right in the middle of the table. People were running out of there, but I also had the acolytes who came backstage afterward in tears. I got all the reactions. It was the element of surprise. It's very important for me to be able to keep leading people up the garden path and then turn around, *boing!*"

Meeting Reed, the "boing" was mutual. Neither expected to encounter a kindred spirit at Pickwick, much less to be thrown together with one in a band whose entire existence revolved around a minor local hit single and a solitary appearance on *American Bandstand*. And, just as Reed never expected to meet somebody there who'd worked alongside La Monte Young, so Cale was astonished to meet someone whose Syracuse poetry teacher was Delmore Schwartz. Slam those two influences together and what do you get?

The first song Reed and Cale ever wrote together was called "Why Don't You Smile Now?" which was then recorded by a Syracuse band called the All Night Workers. It was good enough that British Invaders the Downliners Sect covered it on their 1966 album *The Rock Sect's In*, without having any idea (for who did at that time?) of its cowriters' import. But, by the time the record actually came out, its composers had already stepped far away.

"Being in a rock 'n' roll band," Cale explained, "was my fantasy that I couldn't live out in Wales. It was important that it was different." He had learned viola at school: "It was an allocation orchestra; they had clarinets ands flutes and stuff. Everyone else got the clarinets and flutes—all I got was the viola." Now he put it to good use, an ethereal backdrop that punished the listener, scratching hauntingly behind whichever lyrics Reed—now determinedly introducing himself as Lou, as he sought to distance himself from his Pickwick past—brought to the fore.

"I didn't like [Lou's] folk songs," Cale shuddered. "I hated Joan Baez and Dylan—every song was a fucking question. But Lou had these songs where there was an element of character assassination going on. He had strong identification with the characters he was portraying. It was method acting in song. The melodies weren't great, so we put arrangements around them." They were, he laughed, "trying to get that grandiose Phil Spector feeling," without having anything close to Spector's resources.

Despite the relatively steady work coming in from the song factory, money was tight. "We used to eat oatmeal all day and all night and give blood and pose for these nickel or fifteen-cent tabloids they have every week," Reed reflected. "And when I posed for them, my picture came out and it said I was a sex maniac that had killed fourteen children and tape recorded it and played it in a barn in Kansas at midnight. And when John's picture came out in the paper, it said he had killed his [male] lover because his lover was going to marry his sister and he didn't want his sister to marry a fag."

By mid-1965, Reed, Cale, and a guy they met on the subway, a guitarist named Sterling Morrison, were regularly convening at Cale's Ludlow Street apartment to work through songs and play with names.

With a percussively minded artist named Angus MacLise on drums, they were the Warlocks for a time, and then the Falling Spikes. They settled upon the Velvet Underground after Tony Conrad came around with a book he'd found on the street, Michael Leigh's S&M sexploitation novel *The Velvet Underground*. "There were whips and chains on the cover, but it was basically about wife-swapping in suburbia," Morrison remarked disappointedly, although nobody had any need to read it. The title gave them all they needed, "because it sounded nice and it alluded to the underground in cinema." Plus, it blended perfectly with a song that Reed could never have taken to Pickwick, the gently balladic "Venus in Furs," idly drifting on acoustic guitar while an angelically elucidating Cale sang the ode to shiny boots of leather.

Cale took the lead, too, on "Wrap Your Troubles in Dreams," its tender lyric belied by the metronomic persistence with which MacLise tapped time, and a sparse guitar that barely punctuated the funereal still-ness that hung between the verses.

But only Reed could handle the riffless urban blues of "Waiting for the Man" and "Heroin," already fully formed and fearful, and needing only a handful of lyrical twists to seal the deal.

Cale's pronounced dislike of Dylan and folk, meanwhile, was shredded by "Prominent Men." Another Cale-Reed cowrite, it not only rode a weary harmonica and a nasal Reed vocal, but it swaggered beneath a lyric that so vividly echoed Dylan at his most acerbic that it could almost have been a put-on.

They had the repertoire, then, but attempts to land gigs were doomed to failure. "We tried to play clubs in Harlem, but they wouldn't let us in,"

Cale admitted. They did manage a show or two at the oddly named Larry's Love Nest, but the bulk of the band's public appearances took place on whichever stretch of sidewalk could accommodate two or three acoustic guitarists, playing for whatever small change the passersby might throw their way. "We made more money on the sidewalks than anywhere else," Cale shrugged.

In July 1965, the trio put themselves on tape for the first time, tracing the metamorphosis of songs from their folkiest first takes to the sporadic violence that interrupted later run-throughs, and toyed vaguely with using it to try and attract attention. One copy got as far as Marianne Faithfull, after Cale turned up on her doorstep one day while visiting London, but it probably traveled no further; another was entrusted to his old college English tutor; and a third somehow found its way into the possession of director Michelangelo Antonioni as he plotted and cast his next movie, *Blow-Up*.

There, Antonioni heard enough to visualize the Velvet Underground in the explosive near-finale to the film, grinding some yet unwritten mantric ode to auto-destruction, while the audience cowered in vicarious terror. But his budget balked at the expense of flying the foursome to London, and his schedule shuddered to think of the red tape he'd be faced with, simply landing work permits and union papers for the group. He turned instead to someone closer at hand, the Yardbirds, and the Velvet Underground looked elsewhere for their celluloid debut—the grandly named Film-Makers' Cinematheque.

New York was littered with subterranean hangouts in those days, darkened basements and tenements where artists, filmmakers, musicians, and politicos thrashed out their dreams of world domination. Most of them faded away unnoticed. Before they did so, however, they might be lucky enough to wind up at the Cinematheque.

The Film-Makers' Cooperative, as it was originally known, was launched in 1962 by a darkly glowering Lithuanian refugee named Jonas Mekas, as a home for the city's independent filmmakers, a venue where they could screen their work to an audience of their peers. Since then, it had spent much of its lifetime drifting nomadically around the city, forever keeping one step ahead of both the police and public opinion. It was common in those days for film processing labs to confiscate stock that they considered a violation of one public decency law or another, while New York's Finest regularly visited the cooperative in search of filth.

In 1965, the cooperative occupied a 199-seat space in the basement of the Wurlitzer Building on West Forty-first Street. There, the swarthy-lipped Italian filmmaker and poet Piero Heliczer would project his latest creation, *The Launching of the Dream Weapon*, onto a screen, while the Velvet Underground provided the sound track unseen.

It was drummer MacLise who brought the Velvet Underground into Heliczer's orbit. Almost a decade earlier, MacLise had contributed to Heliczer's underground classic *A Pulp Magazine for the Dead Generation*. He knew, and his bandmates excitedly agreed, that the Italian's patronage could only advance the group's own ambitions. Even Andy Warhol appeared in his *Joan of Arc* movie, while a screening of Heliczer's *Satisfaction* so enraged one Cinematheque regular that he knocked the projector over and attacked other members of the audience.

Heliczer promised to make regular use of the Velvet Underground, encouraging them to dispense with any pretense at acoustic niceties and to start assaulting Reed's imagery with all the amplification at their disposal. *The Launching of the Dream Weapon* was quickly followed by a string of other installations, before November 1965 saw him unveil his masterpiece, *Venus in Furs*—named for the song and sound tracked by the Velvet Underground. Even more thrillingly, a news crew from television's *Walter Cronkite Presents* was on hand to capture both band and filmmaker for *The Making of an Underground Film*—a short piece that turned out to be the only network television exposure either band or filmmaker would ever receive.

MacLise departed before the cameras arrived, inching out gradually as he realized that the band had ambitions beyond its artistic potential, and finally resigning after they accepted a booking at a high school in New Jersey that would pay them seventy-five dollars. True artists did not get paid.

With the old purist went the unique polyrhythms that he beat out on his tablas and hand drums, but in his place came Maureen "Mo" Tucker, whose brother Jim had roomed with Morrison at Syracuse. Her kit was scarcely more advanced than her predecessor's: a snare, a bass drum, a floor tom, and a single battered cymbal, but she also had an amplifier that her new bandmates desperately craved.

She made her debut at a rudely curtailed gig before a bewildered Summit High School audience on November 11, 1965. The band's set lasted just three numbers. They opened with "There She Goes Again," slid into "Venus in Furs," and wound up with "Heroin." "The murmur of surprise that greeted our appearance as the curtain went up increased to a roar of disbelief once we started to play 'Venus' and swelled to a mighty howl of outrage and disbelief by the end of 'Heroin,'" Morrison proudly related. But Tucker was sold on the band's delights regardless. By the time CBS TV's cameras descended upon the Film-Makers' Cinematheque, she was firmly in place, lining up alongside her body-painted bandmates and Heliczer's own freak-show entourage to pound tambourine in blindfold and prom dress, while a nurse cavorted to the din of the band, Heliczer jammed on saxophone, and a host of other players chimed in on the racket.

Gerard Malanga's friend Barbara Rubin met the Velvet Underground for the first time at the Cinematheque, and when they lined up for a marathon residency at the Café Bizarre in Greenwich Village, six sets a night for three nights around Christmas, she knew she had to capture them on film. Enter Malanga with his borrowed Bolex camera, enter Paul Morrissey with his eye for opportunity, and enter Andy Warhol.

The Café Bizarre engagement was a disaster. Occasionally the band would slip into a song that the audience—on the occasions that there was an audience—might recognize, "Bright Lights Big City," perhaps, or something from the Chuck Berry songbook. But they concentrated on their own compositions, and swiftly discovered that the club's owner was not a big fan of theirs—or of their dissonance.

"The Black Angel's Death Song"—in which viola keened over percolating guitar while Reed's vocals clashed staccato poetics with nightmarish vision—was especially objectionable, and finally the owner laid out an ultimatum. If they played that song once more, they would be fired on the spot. "So we started the next set with it," Morrison laughed, "the all-time version"—and sure enough, they were fired. And hired almost immediately. Warhol, stung to curiosity by Malanga and Morrison's enthusiasm, was in the audience that evening. "He saw us," Reed said. "He thought it was great."

2

THEY WORE THE CLOTHES,
THEY SAID THE THINGS

"The original Velvet Underground. What a magnificent beginning that was for a career. I can't possibly imagine improving on it. I was thrilled and honored to be playing with those people. I loved John and Maureen and Sterling; I miss Nico and Andy and the rest of it. What a magnificent way to start—it couldn't have been more fun. I was very, very, lucky to be with such great people, such great musicians, right off the bat. Isn't that astonishing? Who would have believed it?"

—Lou Reed in conversation with the author, 1996

As always, where Warhol was concerned, it was Paul Morrissey who made the initial approach. "How would you like Andy Warhol as your manager? We are looking for a band, we can guarantee employment, we can open you in a big discotheque with lots of publicity, we'll sign a contract with you and find you a record deal."

Warhol, for his part, simply stood back and watched. Asked what he thought of their performance, he simply replied, "I love that word *Underground* in their name." Pressed harder, he said that he liked them. But, as Morrissey frequently pointed out, Warhol always said that he liked things. It was the easiest way to make something happen, and it was only as he got to know his new charges that Warhol perhaps realized just how appropriate the Velvet Underground were.

Two years earlier, Warhol had tried to form his own rock 'n' roll group, from within a circle of fellow artists—Claes Oldenburg, Lucas Samaras, Jasper Johns, and two of Reed and Cale's former bandmates, La Monte Young and Walter De Maria. Of course, coincidence can only stretch so far, and within the tight-knit world in which they moved, it is no surprise that Warhol and his new charges should have found friends in common. But at least he was assured that this project would prove a little longer lived than that one. The art supergroup managed ten loosely termed rehearsals and then disbanded.

The Velvet Underground visited the Factory for the first time the day after the Café Bizarre show, chatting and staring at the regulars (who happily stared back at them) while they waited their turn in the chair in the corner. It was a stance all four would soon become accustomed to, as Warhol shot stillie after stillie to splice into the films he intended projecting onto their live performance, but the first time was nerve-racking all the same; a white-turtlenecked Tucker staring solemnly back at the lens and only once breaking into a smile; Morrison in a polka-dirt shirt looking tired and uncertain; Cale staring with unbroken intensity until the light beside him flickered off and then on.

Reed was the most nervous of them all. Looking almost ridiculously boyish, he feigned disinterest, boredom, contempt. But his gaze was everywhere but into the camera and only at the end, perhaps as someone put on a record to try and break the awful silence, did he relax, nodding his head in time to the beat and leaning forward just enough to fall out of focus.

Even more discomforting was his second stillie, shot just minutes later. This time, he was being directed, turning to face first one way and then the other, as if displaying his profile for some unheard auteur. And all the while, he looked terrified. It was all a far cry from the stillies that he would shoot in the future, in which he eats an apple and drinks a Coke, cool and collected behind impenetrable shades; or another, in which he slowly opens and gnaws on a Hershey bar, in one of a series of mock commercials that Warhol had decided to create.

Only when the camera finally looked away was Reed able to relax and take in his surroundings. "I thought I'd gone to heaven. I couldn't have been in a righter place at a righter time. You know, without Andy, I probably wouldn't have had a career. He was right there saying, What you do—everything that you do—is fine; don't let anybody change it and keep it exactly as it is. And that was Andy Warhol saying that, so that was enough for me. Andy said it was okay, so it was."

As their friendship deepened, Warhol would occasionally harass Reed. "How many songs did you write today, Lou?" he'd ask, and when Reed shot back, "Five," Andy would ask why he didn't write ten, and then supply his own answer. "You're so lazy, Lou." But Reed rarely took offense. Andy was usually right about most things.

Warhol was determined from the outset that Nico should join the Velvet Underground, and John Cale agreed with Morrison's assertion that the splice was more or less painless. "We were stunned by Andy's suggestion to include her in the Velvet Underground. No one knew what to make of her, but we were far too self-concerned to either argue or refuse. Here was this formidable woman, the world's first supermodel. We were awed by her style—something that we were just beginning to taste the fruits of ourselves, with Kenneth J. Lane jewelry and Betsey Johnson designs. Of course we'd seen her in Fellini's *La Dolce Vita*—the first time you see her on-screen she is introduced as 'that German cow.' She was quintessentially the person that Andy used to make us aware of another dimension to music: publicity and image making."

Nico, too, recalled a seamless union. Just days after she met the group for the first time, she joined them in accompanying Warhol's inner circle—Edie Sedgwick, Paul Morrissey, and Gerard Malanga—on an excursion uptown to Harlem to catch the Apollo Theater's New Year's Eve bash, then arranged to see them all again just a couple of days later to begin rehearsals.

Only Morrissey appeared to have detected any resentment. "Right away that sour little Lou Reed bristled. He was hostile to Nico from the start"—but not so hostile that the pair did not quickly ignite a personal relationship, nor that Reed could resist writing what Warhol described as "the greatest songs for her to sing."

"Her voice, the words and the sounds the Velvets made were all so magical together," Warhol insisted, while Cale continued, "Lou fell madly in love with her." She was, he said, "exactly what Lou...was looking for. I was always suspicious of blondes; Lou was not. The band had no idea how to deal with her—the timing, the accent—but Lou rose to the occasion. His songs for her...are some of the most beautiful ballads he has written."

Three songs are indelibly associated with Nico's tenure with the Velvet Underground, but only one, "I'll Be Your Mirror," could be said to have reflected Reed's own feelings for her. Of the others, "Femme

Fatale" was written for Edie Sedgwick, after Warhol pulled Reed aside one day and told him to do precisely that. "I said, 'Like what?' and he said, 'Oh, don't you think she's a femme fatale, Lou?' So I wrote 'Femme Fatale.'" "All Tomorrow's Parties," meanwhile, had been around since the previous summer at least, when it lined up alongside "Prominent Men" as another of the band's folky rockers, all Weaver-like harmonies and, again, a distinctly nasal Reed delivery.

But so impersonally bland was Reed's attempt at singing these songs that one can easily understand Morrissey's insistence that the group was in desperate need of a new singer. "He's got no personality and nobody pays the slightest attention to him," Morrissey told Warhol, and at that point in time, he may have been correct.

Nico, on the other hand, constantly attracted attention, and not all of it welcome. *Playboy* once described her as "the most ethereal and lovely of Warhol's superstars; seeing her in her floor-length cloak and listening to her musical, remote talk, one gets the impression of a medieval German Madonna glimpsed in a dream full of images of spring and sunlight."

Offstage, however, she could be ferocious. Andrew Oldham, reflecting upon his time in her orbit, shivered, "She was no doormat. She was a lethal woman." The drugs and darkness for which she later became so renowned were still off in the future. Both in London with the Loog, and at least through her first months in New York with the Velvet Underground, she was grace and elegance personified, "and wonderful for it." But still, Oldham observed, "she was one of a new breed of woman, like Anita Pallenberg and Yoko Ono, who could have been a man. Like Carla Bruni is today. Far better that than the silly little English teacups around at that time."

Far more violent, too. Visiting an after-hours bar one night, Reed watched a man being beaten to death after "Nico threw a glass that shattered in a mob guy's face. He thought the man in back of me did it. I loved after-hours bars...." In fact, flying glasses seem to have been an occupational hazard around Nico. John Cale recalled another bar, another night, and a woman nearby telling all who would listen about how much she had suffered. "Suffering?" Nico shot back. "You don't know what suffering is," and her glass flew unerringly into the woman's face. "I can't remember whether Nico told me she intended only to throw the drink and not the glass," Cale reflected. "But anyway…"

Attempts to place Nico at the forefront of the Velvet Underground's repertoire were doomed to failure. On January 3, 1966, she had her first ever rehearsal with the group at the Factory, during which the quartet played her their existing set, while Reed patiently attempted to teach her the lyrics. But she struggled to grasp "Venus in Furs," and the one song they did push all the way through, "There She Goes Again," continually broke down as both band and singer sought to find the correct key.

On other occasions, however, Nico fit like a glove. Onstage, she would harmonize sweetly during the extended improvisation of "Melody Laughter," while "The Nothing Song" came to showcase one of her most dramatic, if oddly underdocumented, performances. As befits its title, "The Nothing Song" was based around what was essentially another improvisation, and could stretch to thirty or more minutes in length. Through much of it, however, Nico was at the microphone, singing a haunted lyric that has no counterpart in either her or the group's repertoire, a feat not only of endurance but also invention that proves just how crucial she was to the band's early development, and how much her bandmates, Reed in particular, would learn from her presence.

Nico was also responsible for the inclusion in the set of *her* Dylan song, although this time, it was the band, not Nico, who could not seem to fathom the complexities of "I'll Keep It with Mine." In fact, for a long time, they simply refused to even try. Then, once she had worn them down with her insistence, they spent so long "learning" it that even Reed finally ran out of excuses as to why they couldn't introduce it to the live set. Finally, then, it was unveiled, "and it was performed poorly," Morrison laughed. "We never got any better at it, either, for some reason.

"There were problems from the very beginning, because there were only so many songs that were appropriate for Nico, and she wanted to sing them all," Morrison recalled. "'Waiting for the Man,' 'Heroin'—all of them." In later years, "Waiting for the Man" would emerge as an intrinsic part of the solo Nico's live catalog, as it did for Reed, Cale, and even Mo Tucker, and it is arguable that, of them all, Nico retained the firmest grasp upon both the subject matter and delivery. "I recorded it as a tribute to Lou, and because I wanted to sing rock 'n' roll . . . and it's such a great rock 'n roll song." But she also observed, "I always wanted to sing [it] but Lou wouldn't let me. Lou was the boss and was very bossy. Anyway, I know a little bit more about the subject now than I did then!"

Nico was living at the Chelsea Hotel when she first encountered Reed. Soon, however, she was subletting a small apartment on Jane Street, and he quickly "came to stay with me. [He] was very soft and lovely. Not aggressive at all. You could just cuddle him like a sweet person when I met him, and he always stayed that way. I used to make pancakes for him."

She was not alone. According to journalist Danny Fields, Edie Sedgwick's loft mate, "Everyone was . . . in love with him. Me, Edie, Andy, everyone. He was so sexy. Everyone just had this raging crush. . . . [H]e was the sexiest thing going."

A large part of Reed's appeal, nurtured and perfected through the earliest days of the Velvet Underground, was that he simply didn't seem to care. Laconic, louche, even lazy in his demeanor and delivery, Reed hid behind his jet-black shades, the epitome of cool even as he tortured fresh extremes from his lyrics and guitar. Almost a decade later, with the media tripping over itself to drape ever-more dissolute labels across the so-called Phantom of Rock, English journalist Nick Kent would insist, "I'd sussed all along that Lou was just another mixed-up, tenderhearted kid who was just pretending to be committed to writing songs about heroin and drag queens, while all the time he was set on his own private passionate quest for 'Miss Right.'"

Kent may or may not have nailed the Reed mystique, just as Nico may or may not have been Miss Right. But Cale reckoned Reed was "absolutely torn up" when their relationship ended, while Nico blamed the demise of their romance for cementing her ultimately ephemeral vocal role in the band. "He wouldn't let me sing some of his songs because we'd split."

Their parting, however, has become the subject of one of the most pernicious of all Nico legends. "She came into the Factory one time without him," Cale explained, "and Andy said, 'So where's Lou?' And she replied, after a silence, 'I cannot sleep with Jews anymore.'"

Today—and, indeed, for a number of years now—such a remark is tainted with the poison brush of anti-Semitism, especially when wielded by a German. But Cale told the *London Times*, "All the revisionist speculation about her being a racist is ridiculous." She told a joke, at least partially at the expense of her own national stereotype, and "people chuckled and got on with their chores."

The new-look Velvet Underground made their live debut ten days after that first rehearsal, appearing alongside Warhol amid the Park Avenue splendor of the Delmonico Hotel, taking over a stage at one end of the gold and white Grand Ballroom. The occasion, as countless past commentators have marveled, was the Annual Dinner of the New York Society for Clinical Psychiatry, and the following morning's *New York Times* carried reporter Grace Glueck's incredulous report on the event.

"The Chic Mystique of Andy Warhol, described by an associate of the painter as 'a kind of community action–underground–look at yourself–film project,' was billed as the evening's entertainment...and until the very last minute, neither group quite believed the other would show up. What 'the Chic Mystique' was, nobody really explained. The Warhol part of the program included a showing of his underground films as background for cocktail conversation and, at dinner, a concert by the rock 'n' roll group."

Warhol picked up the thread. "The Velvets started to blast and Nico started to wail," while three hundred psychiatrists winced in the face of the hurricane. Scurrying around the tables, Jonas Mekas and Barbara Rubin were interviewing the audience for a forthcoming Warhol movie, dropping the most obscene questions they could think of onto the menu, then demanding to know why their victims looked embarrassed. "You're a psychiatrist! You're not supposed to get embarrassed."

Edie Sedgwick joined the Velvet Underground onstage, adding her voice to the cacophony and looking tiny and excitable alongside the stately, Valkyrie-like Nico. Afterward, Gerard Malanga would tell Warhol that even though she was barely audible, it was apparent that Edie didn't have much of a voice. But Warhol simply smiled. It didn't concern him. No matter that, for a few minutes there, he'd had the two most beautiful women in his universe sharing a stage. Edie was last week's news. Nico was the new superstar.

For the assembled shrinks, the evening was unofficially billed a case study in the popularity of Warhol. "Creativity and the artist have always held a fascination for the serious student of human behavior," explained the program chairman, Dr. Robert Campbell, "and we're fascinated by the mass communications activities of Warhol and his group." But still, even he had to confess that the city's first ever exposure to the Velvet Underground featuring Nico was simply "a short-lived torture of cacophony."

"You want to do something for mental health?" another psychiatrist asked Glueck when she approached him for a quote. "Kill the story."

The silent footage that cameraman Danny Williams shot that evening, precious though it is as a historical document, reveals little of the Velvet Underground beyond a series of out-of-focus blurs that dwell far more on Malanga and Mary Woronov's dance routine than on the musicians. Even less can be discerned from another shoot, from April 8, 1966. What was irrefutable was that the camera adored Nico and she, for the most part, adored the opportunities with which the Velvet Underground presented her.

Rigid in blonde and white, she was never less than a dramatic contrast to her black-clad bandmates, yet she did not steal the limelight so much as absorb it. "Okay, we've got a statue in the band," Cale thought, watching as she either stood or, just as frequently, perched herself on a convenient stool to bang her tambourine.

But the so-called straight press seemed scarcely more tolerant of the group than the audience at their first show. A second *Times* report in February 1966 commented upon the band's appearance at the Cinematheque, alongside Warhol's latest movie, *More Milk, Yvette*. "They bang away at their electronic equipment, while random movies are thrown on the screen in back of them." Warhol's next production, the article ventured, could be called *For Crying Out Loud*.

Warhol began making tentative inquiries around the record labels on behalf of the Velvet Underground almost as soon as he met them, but he was scarcely enthused by the responses that he received. Understandably convinced that the cachet of his name would be enough to circumvent traditional music industry requirements (it worked in other worlds, after all), he was shocked to discover that the group was still expected to audition, or least turn in a demonstration disc of their sound.

Cut out the middleman. Now contemplating the possibility of releasing the music himself, or at least being able to present any interested label with a finished (and therefore tamperproof) album, Warhol hired

Norman Dolph, a sales rep at Columbia Records, but a longtime jack-of-all-trades on the New York art scene, to record the Velvet Underground. Dolph would not, Warhol explained, be credited as producer on the finished and released record. But he would be handsomely paid with a Warhol original painting.

By 1966, Scepter Studios was among the more decayed jewels in New York's musical crown. The scene of so much action during the doo-wop and early rock eras, the outfit had crumbled badly. When the Velvet Underground arrived on-site on April 18, they found themselves uncertain whether the studio was in the midst of a wholesale renovation or outright demolition. The scene was, Cale later remarked with only a hint of exaggeration, "postapocalyptic."

With engineer John Licata beside him, Dolph oversaw four days of sessions, during which the heart of the band's live repertoire was laid down: "European Son (To Delmore Schwartz)," Reed's purposefully discordant tribute to his recently deceased former tutor; the Café Bizarre–emptying "Black Angel's Death Song"; Nico's strident march through "All Tomorrow's Parties" and more tender invocations "I'll Be Your Mirror" and "Femme Fatale"; and a vividly compulsive "Run Run Run," all topped off by the three songs upon which the fledgling group's renown rose and fell: "Heroin," "Waiting for the Man," and "Venus in Furs."[1]

The disc was finished. But Columbia Records, the first label that Warhol (via Dolph's contacts) approached with the resultant acetate, dismissed it out of hand. Atlantic Records was intrigued for a while, but drew the line at releasing a record that included such sordid scenarios as "Waiting for the Man" and "Venus in Furs." (Ironically, Atlantic would sign the Velvet Underground at the end of their career.)

Elektra, too, shrugged the group off, with Sterling Morrison recalling one executive's greatest criticism: "This viola. Can't Cale play anything else?" Again ironically, by 1968 the same label would be employing Cale as an in-house producer, handing him albums by both Nico and the

---

[1] This session was the source of the acetate disc that, having been purchased at a flea market in 2002 for seventy-five cents, attracted worldwide attention five years later, when it apparently sold for $155,401 on eBay. The winning bid later turned out to be fake.

Stooges to oversee, and not saying a word as he brought his viola along to both of them.

The Velvet Underground's record, meanwhile, would ultimately be released by MGM, and it was clear that the Warhol connection was what excited the label heads the most. And the nine songs recorded during those four days not only became the bedrock of the band's eventual debut album, they did so with very little adornment. Five of Dolph's productions received nothing more than a fresh mix before being pressed onto vinyl, leaving just four songs to be rerecorded with Tom Wilson in Los Angeles later in the year: "Heroin" (which in any case had undergone some lyrical revisions since April), "Venus in Furs," "Waiting for the Man," and "European Son." As for Warhol's input on the project, his greatest contribution was to spark Reed's lyric for "Sunday Morning."

Reed was strumming a melody one day when Warhol stopped to listen and asked to hear more. "I didn't have the lyrics... and he said, 'Why don't you make it a song about paranoia?' I thought that was great, so I came up with 'watch out, the world is behind you...,' which I feel is the ultimate paranoid statement in that the world even cares enough to watch you."

Matched to the sweet, chiming melody and knickerbocker pop arrangement that, again, Tom Wilson grafted onto the song, that lyric remains one of Reed's most frighteningly potent. However, it was also written right around the time that Reed and Nico split up. "He wrote... [it] for her and wouldn't let her sing it," accused Paul Morrissey.

The Erupting Plastic Inevitable was a performance-art installation that Warhol designed almost exclusively around the Velvet Underground and launched in New York at the beginning of April.

Later enshrined as the *Exploding* Plastic Inevitable, a name Warhol adopted shortly after the original posters were printed, the EPI effectively marked the opening of the discotheque that Warhol and Morrissey were planning all along, although the original venture was abandoned when its promoter decided to use the Young Rascals as his house band instead. Warhol responded by subletting for a month a Polish social club on St. Marks Place, the Dom (Polish for "home"), and converting that into the Velvet Underground's home away from home.

DO YOU WANT TO DANCE AND BLOW YOUR MIND
WITH
THE EXPLODING PLASTIC INEVITABLE
live

ANDY WARHOL

THE VELVET UNDERGROUND
and
NICO

Live music, Dancing, Ultra Sounds, Visions, Lightworks by Daniel
Williams, Color Slides by Jackie Cassen, Discotheque, Refreshments, Ingrid
Superstar, Food, Celebrities, and Movies, including Vinyl, Sleep, Eat,
Kiss, Empire, Whips, Faces, Harlot, Hedy, Butch, Banana, *Etc, Etc,*
Etc.

ALL IN THE SAME PLACE AT THE SAME TIME

Other advertising described the venture as Andy Warhol's new Disco-Flicka-Theque, as "a presentation of the Silver Dream Factory," and as "Your Last Chance to Dance." And so broadly appealing did Warhol apparently consider the venture that there was even a matinee dance marathon on Saturday afternoons, "for Teenage, Tot, and Tillie Dropout," as the posters referred to the expected audience.

"As I don't really do painting anymore, I thought we had a nice chance to combine music and film and art all together," explained Warhol. "Twenty-one screens, three or four bands—it'll be the biggest discotheque in the world." It was certainly the biggest dance floor in Manhattan, and every evening the Velvet Underground would walk across from their new headquarters, a rented apartment on Third Street in the West Village, to play live shows that grew increasingly slick and brilliant as the weeks passed by.

Malanga and Woronov danced their nightlong interpretation of "Venus in Furs," all whips and chains and writhing flesh, bloodied by gelatin slides and given fresh manic momentum by the merciless strobes. Five movie projectors worked full time around them, five carousel projectors shooting a fresh image onto the stage every ten seconds, colored gels, spotlights, and a huge revolving mirror ball, one of the first seen in a New York club since the golden age of the speakeasies. And Warhol would be everywhere, sometimes watching from the balcony, other times taking a spin on the projectors, contributing his own vision to a madness that could almost have been called psychedelic, had anybody thought of applying the term to music at that time. It would be another few months before San Francisco stepped up to lead the field in mixed media light shows, but nobody who heard it ever forgot Paul Morrissey's first response to seeing the Jefferson Airplane in full visual flight the following month. "You call *that* a light show?"

Warhol admitted that he had no idea how successful (or otherwise) the Dom would prove, but he had little to fear. The Velvet Underground were scarcely any kind of draw at that time. It was Warhol's name in lights that drew the crowds—the curious and the curiouser, the deviants and the deviations, art professors and businessmen... and kids, an army of kids who may not have known Warhol as anything more than a name to be dropped because it already had a certain kind of shock value, but who were certainly getting their education now.

Neither was the madness confined to the confines of the Dom. Perched on the edge of Greenwich Village, St. Marks Place had long enjoyed a Bohemian flair, sustaining wave after wave of youthful invasion as jazz, blues, and folk successively moved their New York centers of operation into the district. Just a year or so before, however, the trendiest boutique sold little more than ragged jackets, checkered shirts, drab flat caps, and harmonica cases—everything you needed to look like Bob Dylan.

Now the mood was changing, velvets and furs, fringes and tassels. A military surplus store called Limbo opened up and did a roaring trade in army greens and camouflage, to kids who would never dream of donning such costumes in earnest. The military draft was creeping ever closer to a lot of them as the United States stepped up its suicidal intervention into Vietnamese politics, and cops were beginning to stop kids on the streets to check their identification papers.

It would be two or three years more before it became truly epidemic, but New York was already getting a reputation as a hideaway for the first draft dodgers. A vaguely smart demeanor and a flash of military uniform might occasionally persuade the law to look elsewhere for a victim, and it was only when the streets seemed full of camo-clad dropouts and detritus that the ruse was finally abandoned.

Canadian poet Leonard Cohen encountered the Velvet Underground for the first time at the Dom. Nico was the initial attraction—"I stumbled in one night and I saw this girl singing behind the bar. She was a sight to behold, I suppose the most beautiful woman I'd ever seen up to that moment. I just walked up and stood in front of her until people pushed me aside. I started writing songs for her then"... although he quickly discovered that she scarcely needed them. "She's a great songwriter."

Nico quickly introduced Cohen to her bandmates, and Lou Reed made an instant impression upon the older man. "He surprised me greatly because he had a book of my poems. I hadn't been published in America and I had a very small audience even in Canada. So when Lou Reed asked me to sign *Flowers for Hitler*, I thought it was an extremely friendly gesture of his."

In conversation, it turned out that Reed had also read, and adored, Cohen's *Beautiful Losers*. "In those days, I guess he wasn't getting very many compliments for his work, and I certainly wasn't. So we told each other how good we were. I liked him immediately, because Nico liked him."

In fact, Nico attracted admirers everywhere the band set down, including the traffic cops who pulled her over as she drove Warhol and Co. to the annual Ann Arbor Festival in Michigan, later in April, haphazardly weaving across sidewalks and lawns as she battled to remember which side of the road she was meant to be driving upon, the American left or the English right—or some undetermined combination of the two.

Ann Arbor fell beneath her spell too, especially once the party moved onto a gathering at journalist Anne Wehrer's house. There, said Warhol, awaited a young high school kid named Jimmy Osterberg, drummer with a garage band called the Iguanas, "just a kid in a band, still in high school. I thought he was cute." So did others among his entourage. Within a couple of years of this meeting, Nico was Osterberg's lover, journalist Danny Fields—an old New York friend now working in

Detroit—was his manager, John Cale was his producer, and Osterberg himself was Iggy Pop.

The Velvet Underground gigged on. At the end of April, they played the opening night of an even bigger venue, the Cheetah, on Broadway and Fifty-third. Then in early May, it was off to Los Angeles for the EPI's three-week residency at the Trip on Sunset Strip—which was curtailed after just three days when the venue became ensnared within an ugly marital dispute involving one of the owners and was shut down by the courts.

The party remained in L.A. anyway. Union rules stipulated that so long as a band remained available to fulfill a scheduled booking, then they should be paid as though it had actually taken place. The entire EPI entourage hunkered down, split between the Tropicana Hotel on Santa Monica Boulevard, and the Castle, an aptly named pile in the Hollywood Hills that commanded some of the most breathtaking views in Hollywood, and attracted some of the most storied names in show business.

It was relaxing—too relaxing. Just days into their enforced (if well-paid) vacation, the band was bored to distraction, and frustrated as well. Back in New York, the city media was finally beginning to pay attention. The Dom had done its duty and thrust both the Velvet Underground and the EPI into a spotlight almost as bright as Warhol's own, and even the artist admitted that "it was foolish to be away just at the time we could be rolling in all that publicity."

Warhol did step away from the *ennui* long enough to attend an exhibition of his Silver Pillows at the Ferus gallery on La Cienega, and there was some amusement to be had in baiting San Francisco promoter Bill Graham, who seemed to be calling (and sometimes visiting) on a daily basis, trying to persuade Warhol to take the show to the Fillmore West. But ultimately the month was nothing less than a waste of time; such a waste that, finally, Warhol acceded to Graham's blandishments and agreed for the Fillmore to host three nights of *Pop-Op Rock: Andy Warhol and His Plastic Inevitable*, the Velvet Underground and the Mothers of Invention at the end of May.

On paper, pairing the Velvet Underground and the Mothers was probably a good match. Not only were they destined to be labelmates—the Mothers, too, were newly signed to MGM—they were also the only other band, on the West Coast of America at least, whose antipathy to what was already a burgeoning freak scene could be said to match the New Yorkers'.

British journalist Barry Miles, visiting America a couple of years later, even suggested as much to Mothers leader Frank Zappa, only to have the idea "rejected . . . totally, and with some vehemence."

"I think Frank's approach to the Mothers did have some similarities to Warhol's Factory," Miles persisted. "Particularly with the first lineup, who were encouraged to act out spontaneous plays, improvise with broken dolls, dildos, vegetables, and generally freak out." Zappa's hatred of the Velvet Underground, however, prevented his tongue from ever flapping kind words in Warhol's direction.

The feeling was mutual. To the Velvet Underground, so confident in their coolness, their unknown and unheard support act simply looked, said Miles, "like country bumpkins in their gaudy flowery costumes and long hair." Neither did they appreciate the sight of Zappa making his way out into the audience for their performance, "[and] making fun of them onstage."

The two groups spent their entire three-night residency either glowering at one another whenever they met or informing passing audience members just how appalling the other group was.

Even worse, though, was the band that opened the show. The Jefferson Airplane were still gigging with pre–Grace Slick vocalist Signe Anderson at that time, and resembled little more than a hairy folk band with a clutch of pleasant sub-Byrdsy ballads. Reed loathed them with a passion. Back at the Dom, Paul Morrissey used to delight in enraging him by slipping cuts from the Airplane's recently released debut album, *Takes Off*, into the EPI soundtrack, and Reed would cringe at the self-conscious whimsy of it all.

But the reality of the band was beyond even his worst expectations.

A lot of the acrimony that erupted into open warfare between the Velvet Underground and their West Coast foes, Warhol believed, was "just the difference between New York and San Francisco attitudes"; the uptight coolness of the East Coast clattering into the laidback vibes of the west.

But there was more to it than that, a cultural dislocation so sharp that it could have drawn blood. "Our attitude to the West Coast was one of hate and derision," Cale confessed. "They were into being flower children and beautiful and all that; they were pansying around. It was like some kind of airy-fairy puritanism that was based on the suppression of all adult feelings about what was out there in the world. They were being evangelical about it, but they didn't really care. As far as we were concerned, we were just getting on with it."

3

SOUL RADIATION IN THE DEAD OF NIGHT

Douglas, GA, 1993

Maureen Tucker was holding forth on the nature of modern pop music for the benefit of Alternative Press *magazine. And she wasn't happy.*

"Lyrics today... God, they're so degrading, so violent, so explicit. I object to my kids listening to songs about killing people, or with profanities through the song: 'fuck you, fuck this, fuck that.'"

Which, I suggested, were odd sentiments to hear spilling from the mouth of a member of the Velvet Underground. Odd, because that group probably has the most sordid reputation in history. Sundry jumped-up Charlies may have snatched the crown away for a few weeks of tabloid fun and games. But none of them were capable of keeping it.

Tucker puckered, ready to respond, but I was on solid ground here. Just ask her old bandmates what they think?

"When Andy picked up on us," Lou Reed once noted, "there was nothing else like it going down. We used to have a whole theatrical trip, with whips and dancers and Andy or Paul Morrissey doing the lights." Indeed, had Reed had his way, the band's live spectacle might have been even more extreme. "Paul had some really weird films in those days, and I was always trying to get him to let us show them, but he wouldn't."

Nevertheless, the movies that were projected onto the band as they played, the celluloid imagery bright and bewildering across the darkness of their stage gear, were powerful enough. Warhol's entire celluloid canon was at their disposal, shorts such as Sleep, *in which the camera stares unblinkingly at a sleeping man:* Empire, *in which eight hours in the life of the Empire State Building are patiently documented;* Blow Job, *witnessing the changing facial expressions of a man as he receives one;* Harlot, The Shoplifter, Couch, Banana...

Such imagery cloaked the Velvet Underground with ease. Even Playboy *was to describe Warhol movies as a feast of "rape, male prostitution, and sado-masochism, bondage involving leather halters and torture masks," before going on to repeat some of the other commentaries aimed at his work. "Many establishment critics denounce . . . Warhol movies as 'seamy,' 'dirty,' 'half Bosch and half bosh,' 'sewage,' 'a peep show,' 'freakish,' 'physically filthy,' 'desperate,' 'gloomy,' 'decadent,' 'Dadaistic provocation,' 'travelogs of a modern hell' . . . " And so forth.*

Neither could Dante have designed a greater inferno of lost souls than that which accumulated around Warhol. Playboy *again: "Warhol doesn't supply drugs . . . [but] with or without his help, other members of the Factory have suffered from 'drug abuse' and two are acknowledged amphetamine addicts. Nervous breakdowns occur with alarming regularity. . . . [O]ne girl commits herself every summer to the psychiatric ward at Bellevue Hospital."*

In September 1966, the Velvet Underground lighting engineer, Danny Williams, drove out to the shore, undressed alongside his parked car, then walked out into the sea and drowned. A month later, Edie Sedgwick almost died when a lit cigarette torched her apartment while she lay in the arms of an overdose.

No band associated with such apparent perversity could hope to escape unscathed, and the Velvet Underground were no exception. But Maureen Tucker was a she-wolf in defense of their reputation. Not long into her early-1990s comeback as a touring musician, she remained more conscious of her full-time role as a mother than her reputation as the engine room behind the single most influential band in American musical history. And she was adamant: "The Velvets do have a certain sordid image. But it's a media misinterpretation. We weren't like that at all."

Oh.

"I'd let my kids listen to 'Heroin,'" Tucker continued. "There's nothing wrong with them hearing a song about a bad trip."

Well, you could look at it that way, although there's probably a couple of thousand smackheads out there who'd disagree. They used to go up to Reed during his seventies solo tours and tell him, "I shot up to your song," and Lou would go on stage the following evening, tie off his arm, and break out a syringe and . . . when the blood begins to flow, and it shoots up the dropper's neck . . .

Hey Mo, what about "Murder Mystery"—screw me in the daisies. What about "Black Angel's Death Song"—cut mouths, bleeding razors. And what about "Sister Ray"—still sucking on my ding-dong.

For many listeners, "Sister Ray" remains the ultimate test of the Velvet-loving mind, seventeen minutes on vinyl (it would wrap up their second album, White Light White Heat *in 1968), and anything up to forty minutes in concert, when it often erupted out of the improvised "Sweet Sister Ray" jam. But it is also the ultimate Velvet Underground performance, the consummation of all that their reputation insisted they were, a musical freak show that stepped out from where their earlier repertoire had left off, and then drove blindly forward from there.*

A mutant Bo Diddley riff built around a lyric littered with lines that made you pay attention, "'Sister Ray,'" Reed insisted, "was done as a joke—no, not as a joke—but it has eight characters in it and this guy gets killed and nobody does anything. It was built around this story that I wrote about this scene of total debauchery and decay. I like to think of 'Sister Ray' as a transvestite smack dealer. The situation is a bunch of drag queens taking some sailors home with them, shooting up on smack, and having this orgy when the police appear."

At last, Tucker reacts. "'Sister Ray' is the only Velvets song I don't play when the kids are in the room and it pisses me off, because I love that song. But Lou should just have thought of a different word."

Early in September 1966, Warhol and Paul Morrissey returned to the Dom to negotiate a fresh residency for the band, only to discover that Bob Dylan's manager, Albert Grossman, had taken over the venue and was in the process of renaming it the Balloon Farm. No matter. He was happy to book the Velvet Underground regardless, albeit in the much smaller upstairs rooms, and Warhol happily noted that "most people assumed it was a continuation of the EPI show from the spring... even though it wasn't our place anymore."

With the Dom and its attendant dreams of a Warhol-run nightclub now out of reach, the Factory required a new after-hours hangout. They soon found one. Club owner Mickey Ruskin opened Max's Kansas City in fall 1965, at an address on Park Avenue South, off Union Square. A year later, the Warhol crowd paid it their first visit.

Ruskin was no stranger to Warhol. His reputation as a club owner was at least partially constructed around his fascination with the downtown arts scene; he had encouraged artists and poets alike to visit, exhibit, and just contribute to the ambience of a succession of previous ventures... Les Deux Magots on East Seventh, the Ninth Circle in the Village, the Annex on Avenue B. Max's, though, was positively uptown compared to those past niteries, and Ruskin might well have been taking a chance shifting so far away from his traditional haunts. But his old clientele followed, and a new brigade began forming as well—particularly once word got around that Warhol was a regular visitor.

So was Lou Reed. "Mickey, thin, hawk-faced. Dark stringy hair severely parted and forever hanging over his right eye, was personally responsible for my survival for three years because he fed me every day," he wrote in his forward to *High on Rebellion*, Ruskin's widow Yvonne's memoir of Max's magical heyday. "It was... the tab that made it possible for me and a small army of other artists to exist just left of the line that defines more extreme modes of criminality." Warhol had long since realized that there was no way for the Factory to continue feeding the ever-growing coterie of friends, associates, and hangers-on that descended daily upon its premises. Max's, with its generous policy of free bar snacks, and Ruskin's happy provision of interest-free credit, solved that problem once and for all; although half a decade later, Lester Bangs reported that "the waitresses hate [Reed], because he never tips."

Food notwithstanding, the club's appeal was immediate. "The back room at Max's was pure theater," Elektra Records chief Paul Rothschild remembered. "People dressed for it. Those red fluorescent lights. The first really broad expression of homosexuality in New York City... embracing, kissing, great jealousies displayed for the world to see. Before, it had been a confused, almost proper kind of European homosexuality, but with the Warhol wave, it became very theatrical, direct and out-front. Then at the tables you saw the seedier side—people shooting up coke, speedballs, the great pill contest: 'How many could you drop at Max's and still walk out?'"

Max's became the after-hours roost that the Factory elite craved. "We used to practice at the Factory and hang out there every day for a couple of years," Sterling Morrison recalled in 1981. "We would arrive sometime in the afternoon, and every day would begin with the same question.

'What parties shall we go to tonight?'" Increasingly, the best ones were taking place at Max's.

They would descend en masse, six, twelve, twenty or more. Drugs were commonplace, sex was unremarkable. "I wish I had a nickel for everyone who got fucked in my phone booth," Mickey Ruskin once mused, and while he finally drew the line at a shabby lass who used to specialize in distributing blow jobs to any patron who looked even remotely famous, it was her appearance, not her behavior, that counted the hardest against her.

The Velvet Underground played there as often as they could, not quite treating the venue as a rehearsal space, but feeling relaxed enough that they could have. Even the fire that broke out one evening, shortly before they went onstage, could not faze them. While the smoke billowed up the stairs and the lights started flickering as the heat melted the wires, the musicians pitched in with the waitresses and staff, mopping up the water that the firemen were pouring onto the flames.

Max's was not only a party place—it was also a secure environment in which business could be discussed away from the business hours of the day. When Beatles manager Brian Epstein visited the Factory, at a time when there was at least a possibility (and certainly a rumor) that he might become the Velvet Underground's British manager, it was to Max's that he was whisked—and, continued Reed, it was "there [that] Epstein took me to his limo to tell me between drags of pot how, if he could 'only take three records to a desert island...,'" one of them would be by the Velvet Underground.

But Epstein was neither the only, nor even the first Anglo entrepreneur to be drawn to the Factory. Kenneth Pitt was a London-based agent whose career included stints in journalism and PR before moving into personal management. He handled Judy Garland during one of her U.K. visits, and Bob Dylan during one of his, and enjoyed periods managing Manfred Mann and "Pied Piper" hit maker Crispian St. Peters.

He arrived in New York in November 1966 to oversee the U.S. release of the debut LP by his latest client, a chirpy young singer-songwriter named David Bowie, when a friend asked him if he would be interested in working with Warhol. With the Velvet Underground's debut album on the cusp of release on both sides of the Atlantic, there was talk that the band might soon be needing a U.K. representative.

Pitt did not need to be asked twice. "I first heard about Andy Warhol in the early 1950s, when an American cousin of mine, a fellow art student, sent me examples of his work that appeared in newspapers. Needless to say, I particularly remember the shoe ads! Then I saw the screen prints, copies of which were beginning to appear in the U.K."

Denis Deegan made the arrangements. The meeting was to take place on November 10, Pitt's birthday, and Pitt recalled "feeling honored to have been invited to meet Warhol. A meeting with the president at the White House could not have impressed me more, and when Denis said that I had 'made it' with Andy, I realized that I had achieved an important breakthrough."

For all that, Warhol himself scarcely made an impression on Pitt. The man who believed that the art of conversation revolved specifically around people talking to *him* had never shied away from calling up friends in the early hours of the morning, desperately insisting that they needed to talk, and then demanding, "Well, say something." Pitt was ushered into Warhol's presence, and then silence fell. "[He] was everything I had expected, looking exactly as he did in the gossip column pictures, the shades, the polo neck, the mask. I cannot recall what was said, or even that anything was said at all.

"My meeting with Andy lasted only a matter of minutes, and then I was allowed to wander at will around the Factory, chatting to all and sundry." He spotted Nico, seated at a typewriter. They had met the previous year, "the day I responded to a knock on the door of Bob Dylan's suite at the Savoy Hotel to find it was [her] paying a visit." Warhol, however, had floated away and they never spoke again. Pitt returned to London a few days later, with just one souvenir of his visit, a white label pressing of the Velvet Underground's album. He intended to give it to Bowie and, decades later, Bowie admitted that one of the most important events in his entire professional career was receiving that gift. It would be pure hyperbole to say that record changed his life, but the fact of the matter is, it did.

Largely unspoken, but vivid regardless, one of the tenets of Warhol's philosophy was the belief that one does not become a leader by marching to the center of things and expecting the world to follow. You become a leader by stepping to one side, often far to one side, and waiting for the world to join you.

Warhol's personal odyssey, his transition from a competent commercial artist with a flair for drawing shoes to a visionary genius who transformed the mundane into the magnificent (for what were the Campbell's soup cans, Brillo boxes, Monroe screen prints, and suicidal jumpers if not the encapsulation of modern mundanity?), confirmed the wisdom of his ways, even as the comparative failure of so many of his acolytes reinforced the emphasis on quality. Not one of the self-styled superstars with whom he peopled the Silver Factory was ever to break out into anything approaching the mainstream: Baby Jane Holzer, Edie Sedgwick, and the unequivocally named Ingrid Superstar remain cult figures at best, no matter how vociferous those cults may be.

Likewise, neither Ronnie Tavel, Warhol's scriptwriter throughout the golden age of Factory films, nor Paul Morrissey, who assumed full control of the Warhol movie industry once it moved into something approaching conventional filmmaking, ever made their mark on any wider canvas. They were, and forever will be, associated with Warhol first, and their own endeavors fall a very distant second. Warhol's public reputation might well have been that of a man who produced superstars with the same deft ease as he silk-screened Brando or replicated Heinz packing cases. But in reality, there was room for only one true superstar in his firmament, and Warhol assumed that role for himself.

Lou Reed certainly understood this when he first admitted the Velvet Underground to Warhol's immediate influence; just as he came to understand, as the band's career inched forward, that the group was never going to overcome the earliest antipathy created by both their music and their associations.

It is one of the most overworked remarks in rock history, but that does not undermine its verisimilitude; Brian Eno once declared that no more than one hundred people ever saw the Velvet Underground (a deliberate understatement, of course), but everyone who did then went out and formed a band. Likewise, scarcely any more people heard the band during its four-year lifetime, but all those who did were changed forever.

David Bowie was not the first person in the United Kingdom to hear the Velvet Underground, but he was certainly among the very earliest. Even Brian Epstein was forced to wait until their debut album hit the stores, then go out and buy his own copy, while the only other musicians to publicly state their awareness of the band were the Yardbirds—those same Yardbirds that replaced the Velvet Underground in the casting of Michelangelo Antonioni's *Blow-Up*.

In November 1966, the British invaders found themselves in Detroit sharing a Michigan State Fair bill with a so-called Mod Wedding Happening ("the world's first!" screamed the handbills). The marriage of Gary, an artist, and Randy, an unemployed go-go dancer, was the climax of a contest sponsored by a local supermarket, in the days when such venues regularly organized such outlandish publicity stunts and contests—and Warhol gleefully went along with them. The happy (winning) couple not only scooped a three-day honeymoon in New York, complete with a visit to the Factory and a three-minute screen test, but their nuptials also brought Warhol to town to give away the bride, Nico to perform "Here Comes the Bride," and the Velvet Underground to play the reception. "The couple appeared out of a huge cardboard cake," Yardbird Jim McCarty recalled, but the highlight of the event was the opportunity for the group to learn a new song that would soon begin appearing in their live repertoire, "Waiting for the Man." No tape of their version seems to exist. But it was probably great.

Bowie, too, would quickly add that same song to his own set list; might even have done it (as he has claimed) before the Yardbirds pressed their version into service. But it certainly added one more layer of identity crisis to an artist who already acknowledged that he didn't know whether he wanted to be Elvis Presley or Max Miller—an English music hall performer whose often risqué performances have rendered him equally well known to posterity as "the Cheeky Chappie."

"I literally went into a band rehearsal the next day, put the album down, and said, 'We're gonna learn this song,'" Bowie said of his first ever exposure to "Waiting for the Man." "We learned [it] right then and there, and we were playing it on stage within a week." In fact, Bowie and his band the Buzz performed the song just once, as an encore at their last ever gig together. They broke up immediately after the show.

Nineteen years old, David Bowie in late 1966 was very much an artist in search of direction. A recording career that stretched back over two years had seen three separate record labels release six different singles, all to no avail, with his latest 45, "Rubber Band," for his latest label, Deram, unlikely to alter that sad scenario.

At the same time, however, music industry priorities were changing. No longer was the humble single the be-all and end-all of an artist's career. Signings were being made on a longer-term basis, with the making or breaking of an act now equally dependent upon the artist's performance across a long-playing record. Bowie was the first artist ever to be granted this privilege by either Deram or Decca, the company's parent, an indication of just how fervently the bigwigs believed in his songwriting.

His demo tape, comprising the songs "Rubber Band," the lyrically epic "London Boys," and the effects-heavy "Please Mr. Gravedigger," certainly showcased some of his most powerful compositions, while the label furthered the lad's chances of success by pairing him with Mike Vernon, one of the hottest young producers on the company's books. That Vernon was best known at that time for his work with blues artists—his first session was the Yardbirds' first demo, and his most recent hit partnership was with John Mayall's Bluesbreakers—seemed immaterial to all.

Sessions for Bowie's first album had already got under way, across two trips to London's West Hampstead Studios in late November and mid-December. There was, however, still time to tweak the record's prospective contents, and across the first months of 1967, Bowie returned to the studio to cut a handful more tracks: a new single, "The Laughing Gnome," which would add one more platter to his growing pile of flops, before being reactivated six years later for a shocking Top Ten smash; a new version of "Rubber Band"; the undeniably catchy "Love You Till Tuesday"; a sweeping ballad titled "When I Live My Dream"; and "Waiting for the Man," puffing along on a breathless harmonica, while Bowie's vocals hover uncertainly (but nevertheless endearingly) midway between his traditional mock-Cockney sparkle, and a drawl that was pure Lou Reed.

Neither was he afraid to toy with the words. Reed's lyric was defensive: "Oh pardon me, sir," his protagonist responds when asked whether he's "chasin' our women around," "I'm just lookin' for a dear, dear friend of mine." Not Bowie. He's "just looking for a good friendly behind," a none-too-subtle adjustment that absolutely rewires the song's original subtext of chasing drugs, to a celebration of rent-boy life which, in mid-1960s Britain, was possibly even more subversive. And, just in case the message didn't hit home the first time around, another amendment in the final verse confirms the song's new intention. "He's got the works, gives you sweet taste, then you've gotta *spit* because you've got no time to waste."

It would be another four years before Bowie publicly stepped out to claim he was bisexual, and he's spent a good percentage of the decades since then denying that there was an iota of truth in the statement.

But to the denizens of London's gay circuit, the good-looking boy with the odd-colored eyes was a familiar sight on the nightclub scene and, if none of the regulars ever got to take him home, that was simply because they assumed he was already taken. The Riot Squad, the band with which Bowie paired himself following the departure of the Buzz, were certainly under few misapprehensions about the predilections of their front man. "We all perceived it was about his sexuality," said drummer Derek "Del" Roll.

Bowie and the Riot Squad went out on the road in March 1967, playing the twenty or so shows that the group, a considerable power in its own right, had already booked before Bowie came into their lives. Psychedelia was rippling around them; the Beatles' "Strawberry Fields Forever" and Donovan's "Mellow Yellow" were Top 10 hits; Pink Floyd's "Arnold Layne" and the Move's "I Can Hear the Grass Grow" were bubbling under. The names of the Jefferson Airplane and the Grateful Dead were already being whispered in tones of hushed reverence.

Bowie, however, was unswayed. His repertoire largely included the songs that he intended for his album, but he used it also as a way of expressing ideas that wouldn't fit onto either his vinyl or many other people's record players, obscure underground Americana far removed from the sounds leaking out of the California scene. The Fugs' "Dirty Old Man" was a newfound favorite, while Bowie had also become enamored with Frank Zappa, whose *Freak Out!* had recently made its British appearance. "I...made them cover Mothers of Invention songs," Bowie laughed years later. "Not happily, I seem to remember, especially as my big favorite was 'It Can't Happen Here'"—an almost barbershop-like vocal number extracted from the lengthier "Help! I'm a Rock." "Frank's stuff was virtually unknown in Britain, and relistening to that song, I can see why...."

"Waiting for the Man" was another audience-unfriendly inclusion. The influence of the Velvet Underground grew more pronounced once the tour hit its stride, and the singer began experimenting with a little theatricality, Gerard Malanga style. Bowie had already insisted that the entire band don Pierrot-style face paint, and a recently acquired flashing red police lamp added to the ambience. Now he was introducing a new song to the set, "Little Toy Soldier," and, arming himself with a recently purchased whip, he proceeded to nightly flog saxophonist Bob Flag— himself secure within some equally newly purchased padding. "You couldn't help but go along with his schemes," Flag recalled. "It was powerful stuff."

"Little Toy Soldier" is the story of sexual deviance in the toy box, the misadventures of little girl Sadie after she discovers that, if she winds her little toy soldier tight enough, he will be able to administer her a very satisfying beating. Every night, Sadie would remove her clothing, wind him up, and take her medicine, which is a bizarre enough theme for any song.

Bowie, however, had his obeisances to pay, and delightfully lifted the song's refrain—which, in turn, is the little tune that the soldier sings while he flicks his whip—from "Venus in Furs." "On your knees, little Sadie . . . taste the whip, now blee-ee-eed for me." And all the while, canned laughter cackles fiendishly behind him, while Sadie grows more and more ambitious, and winds the soldier tighter and tighter, so he can beat her even harder.

Then, disaster. "One day, Sadie wound and wound . . ."; the soldier's spring snapped, "and he beat her to death!"

Bowie did not tell his bandmates of the song's ultimate derivation. "I don't know when we realized 'Little Toy Soldier' was based on the Velvets," Flag told Bowie biographer Paul Trynka. "At some point we got a tape." It made a stunning addition to the live show, however, and late at night on April 5, 1967, the crew crept into Decca studios in West Hampstead to preserve "Little Toy Soldier" on tape.

The result was what producer Gus Dudgeon described as "David having some fun. Like a lot of the songs he was recording then, there was never any serious intent of releasing it; I think he just wanted to get the idea down on tape and, because he did have a degree of free time in the studio, he went there with the band, instead of just demoing at home."

It also meant that he could keep the song far from the ears of manager Pitt, who allowed his boy a great deal of musical and creative leeway, but would never have seen the value in a recording like that. Indeed, Pitt is adamant that he wasn't even aware of the song's existence until Bowie fans started asking him about it, sometime after its appearance on bootleg in the early 1980s. For sure, "Little Toy Soldier" had nothing whatsoever in common with the music that Deram was now preparing to release as the singer's debut album in June 1967; that is, just two months after MGM's Verve subsidiary placed *The Velvet Underground & Nico* on sale, and it is highly unlikely whether listeners to one would ever have tapped their feet to the other, had they even become aware of it.

David Bowie is absolutely indicative of its creator's lack of direction, not only inasmuch as it remains utterly out of step with even the most whimsically themed fringes of the then-prevalent psychedelic underground, but also in terms of Bowie's self-presentation. Casting the singer alternately as narrator, observer, victim, and even stand-up comic, *David Bowie* is a collection of vignettes more than anything else, little stories set to music, but with their eyes set so close to vaudeville that almost every song feels as though it has stepped out of that mythical golden age that separated the two world wars, when the sun always shone, the children frolicked innocently, and a walk in the park was certain to be punctuated by the sound of a brass band oompah-ing in the pavilion.

There was, of course, a sinister undercurrent to this veneer of social innocence. You, the listener, will realize that the Little Bombardier (from the song of the same name) is simply a lonely old man who loves to befriend children because their company allows him to shed the years and travel back to his own unspoiled youth. Their parents and the police, however, have darker suspicions, the kind that have become so real in more recent years that today there are parks and open spaces in Britain which single men are all but prohibited to enter, lest they be predators searching for fresh flesh to corrupt.

Premonitory too, albeit somewhat more lightheartedly, is "She's Got Medals," the tale of a young woman so desperate to make her way in a man's world that she cuts her hair, shaves her curls, and takes her chances in the army. An update, of course, of any number of English folk standards, the song can nevertheless be seen as an early indication of Bowie's fascination with transvestism, while students of English slang will also be aware that "medals" was an only marginally obsolete term for testicles, and would certainly have been in common use during Bowie's own childhood. The fascination with so-called she-males that is so prevalent on the Internet today was scarcely a common, or even acknowledged, interest in the mid-1960s (even artist Tom Poulton's now-acclaimed studies of the breed were not publicly available until the 2000s). But again a modern point of view can imbue this wonderful little song with some exhilaratingly prophetic and perverse notions.

David Bowie sold as poorly as any of the singles that preceded it, while hopes that it might serve as a shopwindow for Bowie's songwriting talents also fell short of the mark. Both Jefferson Airplane and Janis Joplin's Big Brother & the Holding Company were offered the opportunity to record "She's Got Medals," but neither was interested. Nor, now, was his record company, which gave Bowie one final shot at a hit single, with the release of "Love You Till Tuesday" in July 1967. But its best media mention was a scathing comment from another of Bowie's musical heroes, Syd Barrett of the Pink Floyd, as guest reviewer in *Melody Maker* ("very chirpy, but I don't think my toes were tapping at all"); and while the label refrained from dropping Bowie until the following spring, it was clear that he was very unlikely to be given another chance. It would be two years before Bowie landed another record deal. Until then, all he could do was try to keep from foundering.

While Bowie watched as his own hopes fell apart, his manager continued pulling the strings that would bring the Exploding Plastic Inevitable to Europe.

There were any number of obstacles to surmount, among them British immigration's less than complimentary opinion of Nico. According to Denis Deegan, "when asked the purpose of her visit [on previous occasions], she has said such things as, 'Oh, I'm here to do a modeling job for Parkinson,' or 'I'm going to make a record.' As a result they were less than open with her." He hoped Pitt would be able to find a way through the red tape. "She is an integral part of the whole thing, and God knows unique." A notion to replace her with a local singer was certainly shot down. "That voice does not exist except in her body. Also, she is very definitely the image of the show—witness *Time* magazine and others calling her the Girl of the Year."

Elsewhere, however, all were bristling with enthusiasm, with Warhol in particular dreaming of fresh heights for the show to hit. "If we had gone [to Europe] last year, we could go as we are," he told Deegan. "Now we have to put in lots of new exciting things." He offered Pitt the use of any film footage he required, to be sent over by boat as soon as possible. Gerard Malanga and Paul Morrissey were put on standby (Mary Woronov was already in London at the time), while Deegan suggested lining up Tim Buckley ("a marvelous singer playing where Nico is now") as the opening act.

Pitt was in contact with Jennings Musical Instruments, the U.K. representatives of Vox, the band's preferred amplifier manufacturers; and he had even lined up impresario Michael White to produce the show—in later years, White would be the visionary behind such theatrical extravaganzas as *The Rocky Horror Show* and *A Chorus Line*. The Chalk Farm Roundhouse was booked for a week, beginning May 21, 1967, and by early April, Pitt was confident enough to begin booking European dates, and asked Warhol to design a suitable promotional poster. Warhol himself would be in Europe anyway, attending a showing of *Chelsea Girls* at the Cannes Film Festival; the Velvet Underground were expected to arrive in London no later than May 19.

That was on April 12. Two days later, everything began to unravel. First, the Roundhouse management backed down on an earlier agreement over the cost of the hall, and instead demanded £1,000 for the week, plus what Pitt described as "many extras." That was surmountable, but worse was to follow, as White found himself being called to New York at exactly the same time as Warhol would be in London, to oversee the launch of another play he was involved in, Joe Orton's *Loot*.

He remained willing to work with the production, but his own plans were scaled back considerably—a week in London would have to be cut down to a one-night presentation, leaving Pitt with no alternative but to either scramble for a series of one-night stands elsewhere around the country, or call the entire exercise off. He opted for the latter. "I will continue to try," Pitt wrote to his New York contact, Marian Fenn, "but hold out little hope." The Velvet Underground would never visit the U.K. during Warhol's lifetime.

4

A DENTURED OCELOT
ON A LEASH

"Everybody wanted to be the star. Of course Lou always was. But the news-papers came to me all the time. That's how I got fired—he couldn't take that anymore. He fired me."
—Nico in conversation with the author, London 1982

Andy Warhol arrived in the south of France to discover that his local agent had not set up a single screening for *Chelsea Girls*. He vacationed for a short time, then returned to the U.S. to discover that the Velvet Underground were splintering—not from one another, but from Warhol himself.

Frustrations had been mounting since the fall. The band's debut album was ready for release; had been for a couple of months now and, according to Sterling Morrison, it could have been in the stores by summer 1966 had so many feet not been dragged. "We were going crazy wondering what was going on, while things got lost and misplaced and delayed. I know what the problem was. It was Frank Zappa and his man-ager Herb Cohen. They sabotaged us in a number of ways, because they wanted to be the first with a freak release. And we were totally naïve. We didn't have a manager who would go to the record company every day and just drag the whole thing through production."

Bored with waiting, the group began shifting their live repertoire far away from the songs contained on the vinyl. "Guess I'm Falling in Love," "I'm Not a Young Man Anymore," "Walk It and Talk It," and "Booker T" weren't simply wrapped around the familiar peaks of "Run Run Run" and "Waiting for the Man"; they devoured them, and if some of the new songs seemed oddly unformed—"I'm Not a Young Man Anymore" was little more than a wired guitar riff backed into a corner by a verse that largely comprised the title; "Guess I'm Falling in Love" could have stepped out of one of Reed's song factory notebooks—there was no mistaking the band's relief at playing something different.

Besides, there were some major achievements brewing as well. Songs that today epitomize the Velvet Underground's reputation—the speed freak nightmares of "White Light White Heat" and "I Heard Her Call My Name"—were knocking on the door; the convoluted madness of "Sister Ray" was flexing its muscles. What was not changing was the number of songs that Nico was being allowed to sing.

"Lou kept telling me, 'Oh, I'll have something for you soon,' and then I'd ask again and he'd say, 'Oh, I'm working on something right now,' and I'd ask again and he'd say, 'Oh, I'm almost finished,' but then we would go to a gig and I would only have two songs to sing, and then just one and then none at all."

A handful of songs did find their way to Nico, and from there to the live arena: "Little Sister," a Lou Reed/John Cale cowrite that might easily have rivaled "Femme Fatale" in terms of subsequent impact had the band only recorded it; "Wrap Your Troubles in Dreams," that relic from the band's earliest days, which neither Reed nor Cale had ever successfully voiced; and "It Was a Pleasure Then," an elongated lament that might have found its way out of the lyrical improvisations that once haunted "The Nothing Song." Still, it was slim pickings for a performer whom many outsiders, and almost every journalist, believed was the band's true front person.

Finally, Nico snapped, and when Warhol looked back at his break with the Velvet Underground, that was the flash point he settled upon, one evening the previous September at the Balloon Farm when Reed and Nico had one more in the long line of fights that had characterized their relationship both as lovers and bandmates.

It revolved, as always, around the music, but it was certainly worse than usual, and it ended with Reed snapping, "I've had it with the dramatic bullshit. Yeah, she looks great in high-contrast black-and-white photographs, but I've *had* it." There and then he declared that she would never sing with the band again.

In fact, Nico would continue to make sporadic appearances with the Velvet Underground for a few months more, but they made just as many without her, and when Nico and Warhol turned up at a scheduled gig at the Boston Tea Party at the end of May 1967, it was to discover that she had been removed, and he had been replaced. The band had a new manager and no need for a second singer.

"Lou needed me at the beginning because he didn't have the confidence to be at the front," Nico reflected. "But he gained confidence quickly and it wasn't only me. He wanted to get John [Cale] out of the picture, he wanted Andy out of the picture. The Velvet Underground was his group, but if you listen to the records they made after I left and John [in 1968, following *White Light White Heat*] and Andy, they are not the Velvet Underground. They are Lou and a group of musicians who wouldn't fight back, who would let him do what he wanted. Plus a lot of the songs he was writing, they were so dreary. John and Andy would never have allowed them."

The band's gradual divorce from Warhol's direct sphere of influence, like the loss of Nico, was essentially a cosmetic maneuver. Although Reed did technically fire Warhol that same weekend that Nico made her final departure, Warhol essentially agreed to simply waive their contract with no argument whatsoever, and made only a vague request for Reed to honor the artist's financial stake in the band, a 25 percent royalty on the first album. Otherwise, the parting of the ways was little more than a tacit understanding that developed as the group began taking more and more responsibility for its own promotion, while Warhol's notoriously mercurial attentions were in any case shifting elsewhere.

The general public, so slow to perceive change unless it is rammed down its throat, either knew of the Velvet Underground through the Warhol connection, or they didn't know of the band at all. That was not going to change anytime soon. Warhol's name was still appearing on concert posters deep into 1968, and the band's record label was still trading on the connection as late as 1971, when a double album compilation of their music was released in the U.K. not only beneath the defiantly all-encompassing title *Andy Warhol's Velvet Underground featuring Nico*, but behind a markedly Warholian sleeve design as well, a series showing a set of lips slowly opening to grasp the straw from a soda bottle.

A clear sign of Reed's growing apathy toward Warhol can nevertheless be gauged from his response to Andy's request that he compose the theme song to *Chelsea Girls*—to be titled, of course, "Chelsea Girls." He did deliver, but not until the movie was already well into its run, and the song would instead lend its title to Nico's debut album—a record that Nico quickly learned to loathe.

Recorded during her last weeks with the Velvet Underground, *Chelsea Girls* was released in October 1967, close to a year after the movie for which it was named, and it bristled with beauty, both reflected from Nico herself, and inherent in the songs. The record was built upon the repertoire she had developed for the occasional solo shows she was now performing at the Dom (as it was once again known); her Bob Dylan number, of course, was included. Nico was swift to forget that Judy Collins had already recorded it, a year before Nico finally got it into the studio.

She was playing with whomever would back her at the time, Sterling Morrison and John Cale were her most frequent accompanists, while Reed was present in spirit at least, as excerpts from his Factory screen tests were projected onto a screen behind her. Slowly, however, they drifted away, to be replaced by an eighteen-year-old German-born army brat who was living on the Lower East Side and always seemed to be hanging around the Dom when Nico was playing. His name, he said, was Jack Browne, although he would become better known as Jack*son*.

It turned out that he was actually there for the support act, singer and guitarist Tim Buckley, but Danny Fields noticed him and engaged him in conversation, discovering first that the kid was a guitarist, and then that he was a songwriter. Working A&R for Elektra Records, Fields signed the boy to a publishing deal, then recommended him to Nico. The songs that Browne penned for her, "The Fairest of the Seasons," "Somewhere There's a Feather," and, best of all, "These Days," would come to dominate her live repertoire as comfortably as they would flavor her album.

Tim Hardin contributed one of his melancholy beauties, "Eulogy to Lenny Bruce"; John Cale provided "Winter Song"; while Lou Reed also handed over two of the songs Nico had performed with the Velvet Underground, "It Was a Pleasure Then" and "Little Sister." But the *pièce de résistance* remained "Chelsea Girls," peeping around Warhol's camera to see what was taking place in each room—Magic Markered queens posing in room 115; Brigit "all wrapped up in foil" in room 446. Ondine taking Rona Page's violent confession; Pepper, Ingrid, Mary, Susan—a panoply of Warhol superstars taking their bows in a song that could not help but be compared with Reed's next, best-known, foray into their world, 1972's international hit "Walk on the Wild Side." The colored girls might have replaced their Chelsea counterparts, but the spirit remained the same.

These were the songs that Nico took into the studio, and these were the musicians, too; Reed and Morrison on "Chelsea Girls" and "Wrap Your Troubles in Dreams," Reed and Cale on "Little Sister" and "It Was a Pleasure Then," Cale alone on his solo contribution, and Jackson Browne across everything else. Played back in the studio, it sounded sparse and barren, but beautiful in the way that a treeless plain can be beautiful, occasional flourishes of guitar looming like thunderheads in the distance. It needed drums, and Nico said so. It could have used some more guitar as well, just a little, and she said that as well.

But the sessions were fast. The entire album was given just three April days in the studio. Browne's own parts were recorded in under a day, before Reed hustled him off to the RKO Theater to catch disc jockey Murray the K's Music in the Fifth Dimension supershow. "What a day," Browne sighed, but he barely had time to process any of it before he headed out to California the following day, to begin a new career as a solo artist.

Everybody else left the studio as well; everybody, that is, apart from producer Wilson and string arranger Larry Fallon. They worked on, then called Nico back to hear what they'd done. "The first time I heard the album," she lamented, "I cried." They had destroyed it. "I still cannot listen to it, because everything I wanted for that record, they took it away. I asked for drums, they said no. I asked for more guitars, they said no. And I asked for simplicity, and they covered it in flutes! They added strings and—I didn't like them, but I could live with them. But the flute! I cried and it was all because of the flute."

Nico retreated to London, staying in Paul McCartney's house while seeking treatment for a perforated eardrum. She swept back across the Atlantic to Los Angeles and hooked up with Brian Jones, then backed up the coast to San Francisco, to consummate her friendship with the Doors' Jim Morrison—the pair almost met the previous fall, when the Velvet Underground played the Whisky a Go-Go, but watchful gossips (Warhol included) insisted that the then-habitually casual-clad Morrison was more intrigued by Gerard Malanga's whip dance and leather. They finally hooked up in New York in March, and Nico for a time was besotted.

But she was quickly off again, returning to Brian Jones in June 1967 and meeting up with Sheila Oldham, wife of the legendary Loog. He was on the organizational committee of the Monterey Pop Festival, and the cameras that caught the onstage action for the *Monterey Pop* movie would also snatch a glimpse of Nico and Jones as they passed in stately procession through the crowd. It is only a glimpse, and the cameraman appears to have recognized the Stone alone. But it is a meaningful moment as well, a split second of beauty within the madness that was both artists' lives.

That madness continued as Nico returned to the Factory, to find Warhol reveling in the unexpected success of *Chelsea Girls* (the movie) by planning more and more fresh films. Having been asked by a New York cinema owner to create a movie to rival a recent Swedish sensation, the pornographic *I, a Woman*, he intended to star Nico and Jim Morrison in *I, a Man*. But Warhol wasn't really keen on shooting porn, and Morrison wasn't interested in making a movie. *I, a Man* was completed, with Nico introducing an unknown named Tom Baker to the set, but it made few waves.

Yet it resonated regardless, for Nico and the rest of the Factory gang, after one of her costars, a radical feminist playwright named Valerie Solanis, marched into the Factory on June 3, 1968, and fired three bullets at Warhol. Just one of them missed, but when Billy Name rushed over to cradle Warhol's head in his lap while blinking away tears, Warhol's only words were, "Please don't make me laugh, it hurts too much."

Solanis continued her rampage. Mario Amaya, an art critic who happened to be visiting Warhol that day, was shot in the hip; Fred Hughes, a Factory regular, almost caught another while Solanis waited for the elevator to arrive. Had it been another moment later, Hughes later told Warhol, she would have fired. She turned herself in to the police three hours later, claiming simply, "He had too much control over my life."

Nico was living with Fred Hughes at the time, but, like many of Warhol's associates, she learned of the shooting from the television news. She did not visit Warhol in the hospital, however; her own morbid fear of such institutions kept her away. Instead she wrote a song for him, "The Falconer": "Father child, angels of the night, silver flame my candle light."

Lou Reed, too, poured his feelings for Warhol into music. The pair had not spent much time together since meeting in Boston the previous May; just once had Reed visited the Factory for any length of time, bursting in one January morning to premier a newly pressed acetate of *White Light White Heat* to his former mentor.

Of course he played it loud; it seemed as though Reed could not even hear music unless it made everybody else's ears bleed, a condition that Warhol believed could be blamed on the singer's latest apartment. He'd taken a loft on Seventh and Twenty-eighth, in the heart of the fur district, with just one neighbor in a four-block radius, a fat black junkie in the apartment above. Every night Reed and whoever he was partying with would return to the apartment, crank up the amps, and listen to music. And every night the junkie would jump up and down on his floor so hard that Reed's ceiling started to sag.

White Light White Heat had that effect on a lot of people. But listening to the songs that Reed was composing in its aftermath, it is almost as though that one final burst of noise offered more than catharsis. It also brought closure to that particular phase of Reed's musical life. The songs that would follow it were very different: the sweet and lovely "Stephanie Says," its melody looking back to the days when Nico might have sung it; "Temptation Inside Your Heart," a knockabout rocker that almost doubled as a novelty song; the undisguised folkiness of "Hey Mr. Rain," the last recording John Cale would make with the band, and the song that Reed wrote for the stricken Warhol, "Andy's Chest."

In terms of absurd appearance, "Andy's Chest" almost rivals "Temptation," a sweet melody shot through with a burlesque bestiary dedicated without notice to both Warhol and Solanas. Reed acknowledged that "it's about Andy's shooting, even though the lyrics don't sound like it." Yet his wish to be "anything in the world that flew, I would be a bat and come swooping after you" is certainly as venomous a threat as a more literal mind might make.

Reed's writing style was changing as the band itself changed. Cale was out, replaced by a young Boston kid named Doug Yule, and it was difficult not to wonder as the Velvet Underground gigged on, just how far Cale's influence had driven Reed toward sonic peaks that his own instincts might never have allowed. This was a man, remember, who was writing folk songs before he encountered Cale, and who seemed quickly to be heading back in that direction now that he'd gone.

Which is not to denigrate the post-Cale group. The same acolytes who worship the first two Velvet Underground records are just as enamored with the self-titled third album, all sinister darkened corners and a menace so understated that it might as well have been screaming, and by a fourth set titled *Loaded* because, as Reed said, it was loaded with hits.

But still, any hypothetical future that can be mapped out for the Velvet Underground necessarily perishes on the rocks of the principal songwriter's own ambitions and, occasionally, his limitations.

Like Warhol, the Velvet Underground placed themselves far from the center of mainstream attraction. Unlike Warhol, it just took people a while to find them. Today, the Velvet Underground are regarded, even by their detractors, as one of the single most influential groups in the history of rock; more than that, they are one of the most imitated, a point that John Cale might even have been belaboring when he penned "Praetorian Underground" for 1985's *Caribbean Sunset* solo album.

Cale could be dreadfully pedantic on the subject. "Anybody who said to a record company, if they wanted to be signed, that they were influenced by the Velvet Underground, would be stupid. They're the last thing you'd want a record company to feel that they're dealing with, another Velvet Underground."

He could also be petty. "Everybody's talking about this band the Velvet Underground influencing this and that," he sniffed in 1981. "They're even saying Talking Heads are reminiscent of the Velvet Underground, which has absolutely nothing to do with what we sounded like. And many of the people making these assessments never saw us live. All they've got to go by are live reissues by Lou Reed, that kind of narcissistic nepotism. He just regenerates the same material over and over again, in different form."

But sometimes he hit the nail square on the head. "All the promise we showed," he admitted in 1983, "we never delivered on it." Which is true—they didn't. Even if Cale had stayed beyond 1968's *White Light White Heat*, the six-song Dexedrine blast for which the band turned up every amp in the studio and played until the recording heads melted, it is unlikely that they could have maintained either the chemistry or the intensity that brought such savage life to their first two albums.

No, the Velvet Underground never delivered on their early promise, never followed through on the manifold possibilities mapped out by *The*

Velvet Underground & Nico and *White Light White Heat.* But perhaps they never needed to. They had already said enough. Now it was time for others to continue the conversation.

On July 3, 1969, just two days before the Rolling Stones were set to play a free concert in London's Hyde Park, their recently sacked guitarist, Brian Jones, was found drowned in the swimming pool of his home in Sussex, England.

Again, Nico was devastated; again, she determined to set her sorrow to music, and she had not even set pen to paper before she was in touch with the Rolling Stones' office, asking if she could be added to the Hyde Park bill to perform her tribute to the golden Stone.

Nico was more than an old associate of the Stones by now. Launched with a media-only party at the Factory, her second album, *The Marble Index*, had been released the previous fall, a chilling blast of harmonium and atmospherics that not only reunited her with John Cale (though few people knew enough to care about that) but which also conjured a musical miasma that was at least as stirring in its own way as anything her old band had (or would) accomplish.

Even people who had never heard *The Marble Index* had probably heard *about* it, and if not every press response to its brittle beauty was positive, at least it was opinionated. It would be no problem whatsoever to add Nico to a Hyde Park bill that was beginning to take flight beneath its own portentousness—Family, King Crimson, Battered Ornaments, and the Third Ear Band were already scheduled to perform. So long as she didn't mind not having a sound check, there would be time for her to perform two songs.

She agreed, but she did not play. "People said I had not written my song for Brian and that is why I didn't perform. I had, although it was not what it would become. I didn't perform because I was late arriving at the stage, because it is difficult for one woman to carry a harmonium across a crowded park with nobody offering to help. So I missed my turn."

She parked her harmonium safely backstage and turned her attention to the vast throng of musicians, well-wishers, and hangers-on who were congregated there, looking for either a familiar or a welcoming face. Instead she met David Bowie.

He looked, she told Richard Witts, "like a pretty fairy, but he was a bit too effeminate and skinny to be truly androgyny [sic]." She, on the other hand, was at the height of the beauty that so entranced Warhol's cameras, towering and newly non-blonde, her bangs poised strategically over her eyes, her smile rare but rewarding. If she was interested in something or somebody, one hand would raise to delicately sweep the hair from her sight line. If she was bored, another flick would lower the curtains completely.

Bowie interested her, not only with his beauty, but also his tenacity. "He was trying to sell his new record...'Ground Control to Major Tom'" ["Space Oddity"]. Almost two years after Decca lost interest in him, Bowie had found a new record deal with Philips, the company's faith in him built almost wholly upon a song he had written around what was destined to become the news event of the year—if not the decade or even the century (as the date drew closer, the superlatives simply soared)—the first man on the moon.

"Space Oddity" was not, in fact, the kind of message that any would-be astronaut would probably welcome hearing beamed into his capsule, the lonely saga of a disillusioned rocket man cutting off all contact with the Earth so that he might drift to his death in the splendid isolation of the cosmos. But the words meant nothing to the PR department, or to anybody else who would purchase the record on the strength of its awesome topicality, and even friends who had long since tired of Bowie's monotonously dashed dreams of stardom and success were admitting that this time, he might actually have got it right.

Bowie recognized Nico, she surmised, from her record sleeves or newspaper cuttings, but all he wanted to talk to her about was the Velvet Underground. It was hard work being a fan of the band in those days. The albums had made it over, but press coverage was less than minimal, and when August 1968 brought screenings for *Chelsea Girls* at the Drury Lane Arts Lab, and *Exploding Plastic Inevitable* at the National Film Theatre, it was a very big deal for anyone who cared about the band.

He was a fan, then, and he asked the questions that every fan wants to ask, about what Lou Reed meant in this song, and whether that one was drawn from a personal experience. Nico laughed, "I tried to talk to him about another band that had asked me to sing with them, Iggy and the

Stooges, but he wasn't listening. I was the first person ever to tell him about Iggy and the Stooges and he didn't care."

It was an introduction that, in later years, Bowie might have cursed himself for overlooking. "All he wanted was to come home with me because it would bring him closer to Lou," Nico smiled mischievously. But all she wanted to do was go home to Iggy Pop, "so it could never happen."

5

I LOVE YOU IN YOUR
FUCK-ME PUMPS

London, September 1977/
New York City, July 1993

It's the final night of Iggy Pop's Lust for Life *tour, a five-city British blitzkrieg, and the star is reveling in his triumph. Virtually every song he performed tonight was drawn from either the latest album or its immediate predecessor, and there wasn't a squawk of protest from the stalls.*

Even the absence of "Search and Destroy" raised no eyebrows. Instead, there was "Turn Blue," a motionless Pop crouched beneath a two-sizes-too-big Wehrmacht helmet, his bare arms streaked with makeup and his lungs bursting in confessional anguish.

"Mama! I shot myself up!"

A voice yelled back from the darkness; "[S]o did I," and Pop's lips moved in silent dismissal. "Asshole." The performance was high theater, but its motives went deeper than that. Rising above the posturing, predictions, and crazed pantomiming that was always his audience's number one preconception, Pop was a storm trooper in fishnet stockings, reaching back from the abyss to avenge himself for the way we'd screwed him up in the past.

The last time he toured, just six months before, the fans who came to wish him well were outnumbered two-to-one at least by the ghouls who hoped that he'd end the evening in bloodied pieces, spattered across David Bowie's low-key piano. This time, though, there was no safety net superstar to pull the crowds in from the corner; just the reality of the real leper messiah come to retrieve the hand he'd thrown in years before. Bowie reckoned that the kids had killed the man. Pop had returned to prove they hadn't; the rise and rise of Iggy Stardust.

Backstage afterward, everyone's rattling off questions, a line of fans, friends, and admirers who transformed themselves unbidden into a polite stream of genuflectors, each accepting that they have the time to fire just one single question at the seated, smiling Pop. One question . . . better make it count.

"If you met someone who'd never heard of you and they asked, 'Who's Iggy Pop?' what would you tell them?"

Pop looked at me hard and then cackled. "I really don't think I'm ready to answer that one. Ask me again in ten years."

Checking my watch as I headed for our rendezvous, it suddenly struck me that I was six years late. I hoped he hadn't been waiting long.

Apparently not. Or, if he had, he didn't let it show. Still seated, still smiling, he didn't even pause for breath.

"Iggy Pop is this guy who had a band called the Stooges, and he used to stick pencils in himself, throw peanut butter, puke and do crazy things, play wild music . . . I guess you'd call it punk rock, although it wasn't at the time. He took all the drugs and did some stuff with Bowie and that sounded different, but it was pretty good. He's just been around forever and ever, and every time he puts out a new album I think, 'Oh fuck, is he still going?'"

The original incarnation of Iggy Pop and the Stooges, the essential four-man core that comprised Pop, Dave Alexander, and the Asheton brothers, represents one of the great treasures of American rock 'n' roll. From the primal scream of their earliest flowering, when albums like their *Stooges* debut and the *Funhouse* follow-up sent audiences either running for cover or (less likely) staring in rapt admiration, through to the last dance of their smacked-out disintegration in 1971, the Stooges took music to extremes that the human ear could never contemplate and that the human mind could barely understand.

The Stooges were never made for the long haul, though. A full eighteen months after the young and impressionable Jimmy Osterberg caught Warhol's eye in Ann Arbor, the teenage aggregation of Pop, bassist Dave Alexander, and brothers Ron and Scott Asheton played their first major gig at the Grande Ballroom in Detroit, supporting jazz-rock architects Blood, Sweat and Tears.

Pop laughed at the recollection. "We played two songs, 'Goodbye Bozos' and 'Asthma Attack.' I used to get really fueled up on two grams of bikers' speed, five trips of acid, and as much grass as could be inhaled before the gig. I found this concoction was effective enough to [make me] completely lose my senses; then we'd gather like a football team and hype ourselves up to a point where we'd scream, 'Okay guys, whadda we gonna do? 'Kill! Kill! Kill!' Then we'd hit the stage."

Elektra signed the band after label head Jac Holzman caught them supporting the MC5 at another show in Detroit. But what to do with them? Who could possibly discipline such an undisciplined combo?

There was one name that came to mind. John Cale. A fervent admirer of Cale's work on *The Marble Index*, Holzman flew him to Detroit to run his eye over the Stooges. Cale gave them the thumbs-up, then A&R man Danny Fields flew the group to New York and set about installing them into the local firmament.

Nico encountered Pop just days after they arrived, hanging out at the Scene, a nightclub on Eighth Avenue and Forty-sixth Street. But it was Max's where the Stooges took up residence for as long as they were in New York City. Pop and Nico used to start their day by lunching there, and usually ended it there as well, with the Stooges reveling in the attention that their very presence seemed to spawn, and repaying it by throwing themselves into the lifestyle that went hand-in-hand with the venue's opening hours.

It was, the Midwesterners agreed, a world away from Ann Arbor and Detroit, where they were forced to create their own amusement themselves, amid the confines of the band's mutual home, the self-styled and so aptly named Fun House. There, sex and drugs flowed with gratuitous abandon, with even the group's music sometimes taking second place to the perpetual hunt for the next thrill.

In New York, however, the thrills came to them—even after Nico made it very plain to all onlookers that she considered the diminutive Pop her own personal property, still he was neither immune to, nor resistant to, other charms. Pop's biographer Paul Trynka recounts one episode where photographer Leee Black Childers and actor Jaime Di Carlo spotted the pair standing together, with Nico's hand thrust firmly down the front of Pop's pants. "I wonder if I could do that?" Di Carlo asked. Then he walked over to where they stood and, as Nico removed her hand, Di Carlo inserted his. Pop didn't bat an eyelid.

"For me, there were two Max's," Pop recalled. "The first Max's was the back room, behavioral New York gay intellectual performance-art

Andy Warhol credit-cards Max's. And then there was the other Max's, which was the [later] rock 'n' roll venue. The old Max's was for me. I was a kid from the Midwest who had some exposure, mainly through books and records, to both the outrageous and the arts. I was aware of John Cage, I was aware there was a concert that had been given...consisting of a woman playing nude cello while someone else beat the strings of a piano with hammers. I was aware of these things." But still, "coming into that room was kind of like [entering] a University of Dementia."

He recalled the faces he saw most regularly: "Gerard Malanga...if you could have a crush on a guy without being gay, I had a crush on Gerard. Jackie Curtis, who was basically a Warhol actor. Jackie, Leee Black Childers, and Glenn O'Brien...maybe in another era these people would have been young preppies working as interns at the White House, or maybe they would have been Senate pages. They would be doing their internships in this twisted place and wearing dresses every other day. They had a certain WASPish good sense behind it all, and a very youthful sensibility. And then there were the rock people that tended to come in less and be more musicianly." Well, some of them, anyway. "Probably in Lou and my case, a little more peaks and valleys."

Nico, Pop reflected years later, "was simply incredible. I was real interested in her. I was a kid, basically, nineteen or so, and I'd never met anyone from Europe—I was like a boy who'd gotten a toy. 'Hey, we've never had one like this before.' We started to have an affair for a few weeks and it was a full education for me." Among the lessons that he found most alluring was her love of cunnilingus. "One day we were in bed together and she said, 'Jimmy, you can do something for me....' " Nico was great, she taught me how to eat pussy, me a skinny naïve little brat. She taught me all about French wine and German champagne."

She also taught him about stagecraft. Stooges gigs at the time were essentially a riot of noise, fronted by a showman who was as much a poser as he was a performer. Pop knew that he had a great body, certainly better than anybody else's in the band, and he enjoyed flaunting it to the audience. But he was never going to go far conjuring a poor man's Mick Jagger with his self-conscious gyrations. So Nico decided to remedy the situation.

"Jimmy," she told him, "you have a problem. You are not full of poison. How can you perform if you're not full of poison? We don't want to see a person onstage, we want to see a performance, and poison is the essence of the performer."

Other times, she would catch sight of him after a few days of working out, or eating well, and would go ballistic. "Jimmy, what are you doing to yourself? You are ugly! You are only good skinny." Then, Pop continued, "Danny Fields started fussing with my hair in his usual faggy way, and he and Nico used to have these rows about it. My hair was really long and curly. He wanted it cut; Nico thought it better if it hid my face completely." One day, while they were sitting around someplace, she drew a picture of Pop, a mass of hair with "about two cubic inches of my face showing." Then she called Fields over. "This is all you want to see of Jimmy's face. This is Jimmy's face. And if you could see the rest of it, it would be a drag."

The grooming continued throughout the Stooges' stay in New York, then continued following their return to Detroit, as Nico packed a bag and flew out to join them at the Fun House. For two weeks she and Pop shacked up in the attic of the house, usually emerging only when it was time for Nico to feed her newfound family, cooking them her vegetable curry specialty, or sending out for the then-unimaginable luxury of a twenty-five-dollar bottle of wine. And when a film crew breezed into town to shoot her, she recruited the boys to play their own parts.

Art collector Francois de Menil wanted to make a short film to accompany one of the songs on her *Marble Index* album, "Evening of Light." It was shot in a cornfield behind the Fun House, barren and stubbly in the late winter chill, Nico in white and windswept, Pop in whiteface, manic and agitated, caressing and crushing the mannequin parts that littered the field, while a wooden cross is raised before them and set ablaze as night falls. It is a vivid piece of film, dense with antagonistic atmosphere and madness; scarcely surprisingly, it was rejected out of hand by Elektra Records (who had never agreed to finance the effort in the first place) and by any other media outlets that de Menil approached. Neither did Nico expect anything more. Within days of completing the shoot, she departed Ann Arbor, and the Fun House really did seem a little less fun without her.

Elektra had persuaded John Cale to take the Stooges into the studio, although the Welshman needed certain assurances first, including the band's pledge that whatever they brought into the studio with them would be completely unlike the free-form electric thrash that comprised their live set. They had no songs, they freely admitted, and in a performance setting, that was fine. It engendered spontaneity, it encouraged outrage, and Cale admitted that he was very impressed to learn that Pop liked nothing so much as sitting up all night on his own, tuning each of the strings on his lap-steel guitar to the same note, "turning it up and immersing himself in the noise. That was vision to me."

On vinyl, however, the most imaginative freak-out could only sustain so many listens before its composite deficiencies came into view, and the Stooges had an awful lot of them. They were competent musicians in a groovy garage band kind of way, but even the Velvet Underground had purposefully avoided recording too many of their early concerts, for fear of discovering that what sounded sensational while it was screaming from the stage could easily be revealed as less so in the comfort of one's own ears.

Cale demanded songs, then; two-, three-, even five-minute songs that had recognizable structure, definable hooks, and repeatable riffs, and the band delivered even faster than they expected to. Dismantling their existing repertoire, the succession of barely formed noises that culminated with the near-literal bellowing of "I'm Sick," the Stooges began rebuilding from the riff up, with guitarist Ron Asheton the architect who most frequently laid down the foundation.

"1969" was the first song they completed; "I Wanna Be Your Dog" and "No Fun" followed. A ballad of sorts, "Ann," was fashioned from an earlier piece called "The Dance of Romance," while bassist Dave Alexander brought in a mantric chant that Pop rearranged around his favorite cut on the Doors' *Waiting for the Sun* album, "My Wild Love," and titled "We Will Fall." That, the band agreed, would comprise side two of the LP. The other three songs would be side one, with the musicians convinced that any shortfall in running time could be made up with a few minutes more of improvisation.

Unfortunately neither Elektra nor Cale saw it that way, and the band scurried home to fulfill a promise that they could scarcely believe they'd just made. "That's all right, we've got plenty of other songs."

They returned to "Goodbye Bozos" and fashioned it into "Little Doll." "Real Cool Time" and "Not Right" were hammered out in barely more time than it took to play them. Twenty-four hours after assuring their paymasters that they had more than enough material for a full-length LP, the Stooges had come through and, in April 1969, the band was back in New York City, taking over the Hit Factory studio with Cale and Nico at their side, recording what would become one of *the* classic albums of the age, a record that stands alongside the Velvet Underground's debut in the annals of influence, a disc that can point to glam rock, punk, lo-fi, grunge and so many more as its ill-begotten offspring.

The Hit Factory studio was tiny, and scarcely in one of New York's most salubrious neighborhoods. Times Square was at the height of its seedy grandeur back then, with every other storefront either offering or promising some form of sexual experience; to reach the second-floor studio, poised above a peep show store, you needed to negotiate a narrow staircase with scarcely enough space for the band to manhandle their amplifiers up to the miniature room at the top.

Worse was to come, however, as the band finally got all their gear upstairs only to be told they weren't permitted to use it. "We were gonna set up to play," Pop explained, "and then they all rebelled and said you can't play with those big amps, you gotta turn down and use these little amps. I said I wouldn't do it, and John Cale said, 'But the owner of this studio is...' I can't remember his name, but he wrote 'Cry Baby,' which is a decent R&B song! And he had written some Garnet Mimms stuff, and Pretty Purdie's drums were sitting in the corner! Fair enough... [But] I took a deep breath and said, 'I don't care what the fuck he wrote, I don't care, you don't know anything about THIS!' And that was always my attitude."

Not for the last time in Pop's career, the album that would go on to wreak such aural havoc on an unsuspecting universe was a far cry from the one they originally delivered. "Ann," which served up almost eight minutes of drooling, droning tease before exploding into full Stooges rage, was hacked to less than half that length. Two minutes of astonishing guitar assault were slashed from "No Fun," the song that single-handedly ignited the punk movement of late-1970s Britain, with a riff coiled so tight that it is all but suffocating, a guitar solo that bays for blood, the almost wordless exhortations that spew forth from the yelping Pop, and, of course, a lyric that nails, for all time, the ultimate hell of crushing boredom. And that was before anybody addressed Cale's mix.

Resplendent in a newly purchased Batman cape, while Nico sat quietly knitting alongside him in the control booth, Cale fashioned an album of impenetrable density—Ron Asheton's guitar mixed no higher than his brother's drums, his solos barely audible fuzztones, and Pop's voice aching with scarcely repressed menace as Cale convinced the mixing desk to drag more and more energy from his tone. "Jim . . . was sitting there listening to his vocals get thinner and thinner," Cale confessed. "[I] went after this idea of the horror of Jim. . . . I was trying to characterize Iggy's vocal, make it a little more evil."

Too arty, was the word from on high, too thoughtful, and too bizarre. The Stooges needed immediacy, brittle tight electricity slicing through the atmosphere while Pop's vocal rolled meatily through the carnage, full-bodied and ferocious. With Pop by his side, Jac Holzman took the tapes back into the studio to remix them and try to salvage something from the wasteland.

One song that did survive unscathed was "We Will Fall"—shockingly, when one considers just how far from the remainder of the album it stood, but understandably when one recalls how few songs the band actually had at their disposal. Still, Pop understood the shock with which it was greeted, even by fans. "There's usually one song on each of my albums that has people going, 'When he fucks up, he fucks up big-time. This is absolutely unlistenable, pretentious crap, cough cough.' That was the one on my first album."

Lurking just three tracks into side one, "We Will Fall" wasn't simply out of place on *The Stooges*; it had no relatives anywhere. With Cale's ethereal viola buzzing waspishly in the distance, and Ron Asheton's guitar snuffling wah-wah weirdness into the atmosphere, the song itself was a diary, a moment-by-moment account of an evening Pop spent at the Chelsea Hotel waiting for Nico to arrive, an exercise in tension, anticipation, expectation. We never discover whether she ever turned up, and we certainly never learn what occurred if she did. But for ten minutes, the listener is thrust into Pop's soul, feeling all that he is feeling while he waits and waits.

It's a phenomenal piece of music, all the more so given the Stooges' reputation for unrepentant noise-mongering, but still, even Pop was stunned to learn, twenty-five years later, that "We Will Fall" had just been recorded by the Seattle psychedelic band Sky Cries Mary. "Of all the songs to cover," he laughed. "That's great!"

Holzman's efforts to clean the album up were in vain. *The Stooges* was in for a hard ride regardless. "Loud, boring, tasteless, unimaginative, and childish," declared *Rolling Stone*, and, though those were not necessarily bad qualities, for many years that remained the record's reputation. Even the British *New Musical Express*, which did so much during the 1970s to keep the Stooges' name alive in the wasteland of their eventual demise, was forced to fess up to its "three-chord slobbering, banal[ity]."

And that was it, really. *The Stooges* had so little in common with the music industry around it that Fate was pissing herself laughing when she decreed the record should hit the streets over the same August 1969 weekend that half a million hippies headed off to a farm in upstate New York for Woodstock, and anybody who expected *The Stooges* to sell more than a handful of copies to a handful of freaks was obviously not reading from the same hymnbook as the rest of America.

The Stooges toured in the wake of the album, creating the legend that would haunt their reputation forevermore, as audience after audience turned its back on the band in horror. Blueprinting the firestorm that, thirty years older and wiser, Pop and the Ashetons tried to revitalize for a new generation, when they reformed the band, the Stooges were violent without raising a finger, disgusting without an iota of filth, and so abusive that, when you caught the band live in the twenty-first century, and every other word out of Pop's mouth seemed to be *fucking*, you realized just how much music had changed in the intervening decades. In 1969, Pop had the vocabulary of a choirboy by comparison, and still people reeled away in disgust.

"Half the audience walked out after five minutes," sniffed the *Omaha Sentinel* of one show. "[Two hundred] years ago, people would have been locked up for acting like that. Now he's a star," growled *Record World*. And *Entertainment World* got down and dirty with the cause for all the distaste. "[Iggy] tosses himself off the stage, runs into the middle of the audience, leaps onto a table, grabs a burning candle vase and lifts it high above his head. For a moment, it looks as if he'll put it back down—dear God, make him put it back down. But no, instead he lowers it over his chest and very slowly spills all its melted wax over his naked chest."

Nico's poison had taken hold, and the Stooges became every sensitive onlooker's worst nightmare, a circus of self-mutilation and depravity that hit its public peak when the band was added to the bill for the Cincinnati

Music Festival on June 13, 1970. There, before television cameras that recorded every moment, Pop walked out onto the outstretched hands of the onlookers and, when an audience member handed him a jar of peanut butter (the late Stiv Bators, vocalist with Cleveland's Dead Boys, always maintained that he was the responsible party), Pop proceeded to smear it all over himself.

He had finally shorn away his golden locks, but Nico was wrong. He still looked good. Topless and bedenimed, with silver lamé wrist-length mitts and a studded dog collar, he bemused the show's commentary team. "Since we broke away for a [commercial], Iggy has been in and out of the audience three times.... [W]e seem to have lost him, we're trying to get a light on him now... [T]here they are... " There's one shot here, of Pop held aloft by the crowd, one arm pointing out straight in front of him, that conveys the magic of the man better than any other. And then comes another word from our television hosts, wonderingly, "That's *peanut butter*."

The Stooges had recorded and released their second album by now. *Fun House*—named, of course, for their communal hangout—was cut with producer Don Gallucci after the Stooges had already dismissed the possibility of working with Jim Peterman, the keyboard player with the Steve Miller Band, and young Jackson Browne. Other possibilities included Eddie Kramer (Danny Fields's choice) and "At the Hop" producer John Madeira (Holzman's suggestion). In truth, however, *Fun House* did not need to be produced. It simply required somebody to sit by the tape machine and watch as Armageddon unfurled.

The sessions this time were as protracted as the weeklong genesis of *The Stooges* was abrupt, as the tapes rolled through take after take of the songs that the band brought into the studio, and so frustrating did the situation become that finally, a voice in the control room snapped. Rather than hammering it all down over and over again, why didn't they simply forget all their other numbers and just release an album comprising twenty-two versions of the slow-burning "Loose," because that was how many they'd already taped. The band shrugged the suggestion off, then recorded another ten.

If *The Stooges* was tight and controlled, *Fun House* returned to the pastures that the band roamed at the beginning, before they discovered the secret of writing tunes. Pop later acknowledged that the Fun House was rocking to a lot of Coltrane and Sun Ra at the time, and if you follow the album through its programmed order, you can sense those influences building as the party progresses, from the controlled rock of "Down on the Street," to the closing denouement of "L.A. Blues," a free-form freak that closes the disc perched on the very edge of chaos. The most demanding of all Stooges' recordings, it is also the definitive snapshot of the original band as it drove toward its chaotic conclusion.

Within a year of recording the album, the band would have self-destructed, unable to cope any longer with the very lifestyle that pushed *Fun House* to such impossible extremes. Dave Alexander went missing, Zeke Zettner stepped in. Bill Cheatham, promoted from roadie to rhythm guitarist just in time for the album, departed; in came James Williamson, a savage young guitarist who'd been knocking around the same scene for years and had always been a part of Pop's private musical dream team. Now he had made it, and all the while, the music continued evolving.

"By the time we split," Pop said later, "we were more like a jazz band than a rock 'n' roll band. We'd got all these songs like 'Big Score' and 'Way Down in Egypt' which were just free-form, you know, like 'L.A. Jam' but more so." The Stooges finally split in August 1971, but not before hard rockers Humble Pie and glam heralds T.Rex had refused to sign with Elektra, because they didn't want to be on the same label as the Stooges.

6

SMOKESTACKS BELCHING,
BREASTS TURN BROWN

New York, 1996

Standing, waiting for Lou Reed to show, wide-eyed, one eye fixed on the door, and the other eye glued to a copy of Vanity Fair *on the table, open to a recent Lou Reed Q&A.*

What do you love the most in the world? it asks him.

"Laurie Anderson," he smilingly replies.

And what do you hate the most?

"Being interviewed by British journalists."

Then Lou walks in, and I let rip with "O Superman." He isn't impressed.

There again, it's always taken a lot to impress Lou Reed, and with a résumé like his, who's surprised? Founding membership of the most influential band on the planet; a run of four seventies solo albums that redefined the decade, and four more since 1989 that redefined his career. By his own admission, Lou Reed has killed off that career more times than you're able to count, but he's still out there today, and he's feeling cocky, too, because his latest album, Set the Twilight Reeling, *tears even his own recent high standards to shreds.*

So, I ask, should I put on a fake American accent?

He seats himself slowly and adjusts his spectacles.

"It'd probably be the best idea."

On August 23, 1970, Lou Reed played his last ever show with the Velvet Underground, the band he had led since its formation as psychotic anti-pop theater, five years earlier. Fittingly, the group's final shows, like their first, were in New York. The city that bred the band, informed their earliest music and, a two-year midlife estrangement notwithstanding, remained their spiritual center throughout their existence.

A lot had changed since the days when the Velvet Underground were synonymous with Andy Warhol, screaming violas and twenty-minute experiments in dissonance and noise. Warhol had gone; so had cofounder John Cale, so had Nico. Guitarist Sterling Morrison and drummer Maureen "Mo" Tucker remained, of course, but they agreed with Reed that the spirit of the "modern" band, as they launched their two-month residency at Max's Kansas City on June 24, 1970, was very different from that which had spray-painted its urban-chic reality across Warhol's Factory in 1966.

In fact, Tucker was particularly adamant on that point—heavily pregnant with daughter Kerry at the time, she'd taken a leave of absence before the Max's residency even opened, and watched the drama unfold from the sidelines.

She was replaced in the lineup by Billy Yule, a high school kid whose older brother, Doug, just happened to have replaced Cale for the Velvet Underground's eponymous third album the previous year. Indeed, by the time of their fourth, the recently issued *Loaded*, Doug Yule was as much the band's front man as Reed. When Lou fell ill during the recording sessions, Yule took over the vocals and few people could tell the difference. And, as relations worsened between Reed and the band's manager, Steve Sesnick, Yule—without seeming to even realize what was going on—was maneuvered into a position of ever-greater strength.

Considering how much of the Velvet Underground's career was lived out in obscurity—their biggest hit, their first album, reached only No. 171 on the *Billboard* chart, and their present-day renown and legend is *wholly* posthumous—it is a minor miracle that Reed's final show with the group should have been documented.

But the Factory crowd were in attendance, pouring out of Warhol's latest headquarters just across Union Square from the club itself, and Brigid Polk had brought along her little mono cassette recorder, the one upon which she recorded every aspect of her life, set it up on a table by the stage and taped both of the sets the band played that night. "I was never interested in rock 'n' roll, ever," Polk averred. "I never went to concerts. But I knew Lou. I was always taping everything and we were friends. The night I [went] to Max's, Lou was playing [so] I taped it."

It was only later in the evening that Polk learned the true significance of the show she had preserved on tape; and later still Danny Fields suggested she sell the tape to Atlantic Records, for eventual release as the Velvet Underground's final album. Impossibly lo-fi, but magnificent despite its monophonic muddiness, *The Velvet Underground Live at Max's* offers so much to thrill to, as the band veers between early classics and *Loaded*-era nuggets—an eight-minute "Pale Blue Eyes," drifting with a lyric that makes adultery seem graceful; ten minutes of "Some Kind of Love," a sweet "After Hours" and a gripping "White Light White Heat." But there are no clues to be found of Reed's apocalyptic intentions, and no suggestion that his bandmates had any idea what was about to befall them. As, indeed, most of them didn't.

Tucker insists Reed did confide his secret to her, shortly before they went onstage for what would be his final performance. "He was really, really upset and we sat there for a time. I didn't put any questions to him or argue—he had obviously made his decision." For the others, however, the news did not arrive until the band was preparing for the next night of the residency, when it came as a complete shock.

Doug Yule explained, "Apparently [Lou's departure] had been brewing between Steve [Sesnick] and Lou for some time, [but it] was a complete surprise to me. Lou didn't announce it. Sesnick just mentioned that he wouldn't be joining us for the first set of the week, shortly before showtime, and that he would continue to decline to join us from that point forward. I misunderstood, thinking he was sick, but no, Steve assured me, he had quit the band forever." In fact, Yule later discovered, "Lou was already gone at that point, having fled to Long Island to seek refuge with his parents, an indication of how upset he must have been."

That night, August 26, the Velvet Underground played their first show without Lou Reed. Sesnick, Yule continued, delivered his news "in such a way that gave us no choice but to rally our forces and play. No time to think or argue, no time to dispute, no time to do anything but figure out who would do what on at least one set of songs. I found myself singing tunes that I knew only half the lyrics to; and, on several, I did a sort of melodic mumbling that sounded like words but were nonsense."

The Max's residency ended on August 28, and the band could have chosen to break up there. But those last couple of nights had proven something to both musicians and audience that modern observers, besotted by history's insistence that Lou Reed *was* the Velvet Underground, might find hard to believe. The group could exist without him— and it would.

Yule continued, "The group was known as a collective and only later, after [Reed's] solo career was blossoming, did Lou come to be seen as the significant member. In terms of creativity, Lou certainly was the leader. But Sterling was a close second after John [Cale] left, not in songwriting but in performance and arrangement and general levelheadedness. And Maureen [was] right behind Sterl." Yule himself, he laughed, "was the young kid suffering from delusions of competence, trying to keep up." But he also knew what needed to be done.

In early September 1970, the Velvet Underground played one more New York show, at a free concert in Central Park. They then retired to review their immediate future. Yule already knew who he wanted to bring the band back up to full strength—three years earlier in his hometown of Boston, he had played alongside bassist Walter Powers in a band called Grass Menagerie—"the obligatory cannabis reference in the late sixties and early seventies," Yule pointed out. "The first band I was in was called the Nickels, another reference. So when we needed to replace Lou, I suggested [Walter], being comfortable with his style and abilities."

Morrison and Tucker agreed, and on November 19, 1970, with the drummer back on her stool, the reconfigured Velvet Underground made their live debut with a four-night residency at the Main Point, in Bryn Mawr, Pennsylvania. Six weeks later, in January 1971, the band relocated to New Hampshire, to rehearse and play a weeklong stint at the Alpine, a ski lodge in North Conway. "There's very little difference between a ski lodge and a bar," Yule chuckled. "A ski lodge is a bar in a ski country."

A local paper, the *Valley Signal*, caught them there and enthused, "The band at the Alpine this week is none other than the Velvet Underground, the group that was originally organized by Andy Warhol for his traveling show, the Exploding Plastic Inevitable. There have been a couple of changes in the four-member group over the years, but the constant has been an important one—pretty Maureen Tucker on drums. They expect to release a single for the hit market soon."

That was "Who Loves the Sun," one of Yule's own vocal spotlights from the *Loaded* album—and, today, the rarest Velvet Underground 45 of them all. It was released in April 1971, and disappeared before most people even knew it existed. Its failure, however, cannot be put down to any unwillingness to work on the band's part. The Alpine engagement was followed by two nights back in New York, at the Dom's latest incarnation, the Electric Circus. Then it was back to New Hampshire for another round of shows.

Yule continued, "We played at one place where I met my first wife; we played on a stage that was as big as a dining-room table, in the corner. It was jammed with people attempting to dance and attempting to drink themselves into oblivion; it was, in fact, one of the more popular ski bars. We played the Alpine for weeks, many weeks. We played there so long that I learned how to ski. There was no record company footing the bills and Sesnick was having trouble booking the group. So he got whatever he could."

Gigs around the Midwest kept the band going through the spring, including a handful in June that saw the lineup shift again, after Walter Powers fell down a flight of stairs in Detroit and broke his jaw. Larry Estridge took his place on the band's tour bus until the bassist was able to return. Barely was the lineup back to full strength, however, than an even greater shock arrived as Sterling Morrison quit in August 1971, following a pair of shows at the Liberty Hall in Houston, Texas.

"He abandoned us at the airport just before the flight home," Yule remembered. "I guess he was having a hard time figuring out how to break the news, so he got into the car, drove to the airport with us—he even had his suitcase. And we're standing in the lobby and he says, 'I'm not going back with you.'"

Once again the band looked to the Grass Menagerie to repair the breach. While Yule took over Morrison's lead guitar duties, pianist and vocalist Willie Alexander was recruited to gift the Velvet Underground with keyboards for the first time since Cale departed. He arrived in September, as the band undertook a string of shows around the Midwest and Canada, warm-ups for the Velvet Underground's first-ever European tour in October 1971.

Alexander recalled, "I never had a rehearsal with them, and never played the songs with them until the first gig at some festival in the Midwest. I had a sheet of paper with a few things written on it, like keys of songs and some chords. I had to learn all the Velvet Underground songs. I got most of them some of the time. It was weird." At the same time, his arrival allowed the band to undertake a thorough overhaul of the live set, dropping some of the less suitable older numbers and introducing the newcomer's own material.

"I remember showing Doug, Mo, and Walter some of my own tunes during sound checks here and there, although I don't think we started putting them in our set until we got to London." "Spare Change," "Pretty Tree Climber," and "Back on the Farm" all moved into the group's repertoire, together with covers of "Chapel of Love," "Turn Your Love Light On," and "Never Going Back to Georgia," and Yule's own "Dopey Joe." By the time the Velvet Underground arrived in London, they had a solid hour-long live set, highlighted not only by the new material, but also by some startling improvisational passages—"Some Kinda Love" and "Back on the Farm" were both capable of stretching out toward the ten-minute mark, while "Sister Ray" occasionally lurched toward twenty.

Dates for the band's British and Dutch tours had been announced back in June 1971, igniting a flurry of excitement among the handful of people who actually knew who the Velvet Underground were at that time. It would be another year before David Bowie broke through in Britain, to slap an entire nation around the head with his own love of the band, meaning the vast armies who would soon be taking the Velvet Underground to their hearts were, at this point in time, utterly oblivious to their existence. The group's twenty-two-show date list attests to their lowly status, a succession of university gigs, punctuated by the occasional nightclub. London's Speakeasy was about as high up the food chain as the itinerary took them. A short review in *Melody Maker* was the only publicity they received.

Nevertheless, there were some amazing shows—"the first gig was in a theater with Slade and Patto," recalled Alexander. Another found the metal band Budgie among the supporting cast. "The English bands were all very good," Alexander continued. "I learned a lot."

The trip itself was enjoyable. With Tucker accompanied by both her daughter and her brother, the band's rented Knightsbridge apartment quickly took on the appearance of home, and the musicians became familiar faces round town those evenings when they weren't traveling around the country. "We had a flat that was within walking distance of Harrods, and a hamburger joint that had real Heinz ketchup on the tables," Yule said. "We'd drive out on the afternoon of a gig, then drive back after the show. It was a nice easy tour, not too strenuous, not too crazed."

Neither did audiences seem to have noticed the absence of any particular band members. "Most people didn't know the band," Alexander acknowledged. "In some ways, it was like a ghost band, and I did sometimes think we should change the name of the band. But most of the audiences didn't know who was in the band in the first place. I'm sure people who [remembered past members] were disappointed, but most people didn't seem to care."

Yet the band's triumph was to be short-lived, as Alexander recalled. "As the tour came to an end, I thought we were going to go into the studio to record." Steve Sesnick had persuaded the U.K. wing of Polydor to finance a new Velvet Underground album (to be aptly titled *Squeeze*), and Alexander and Yule had already cut some demos together, booking a small studio in New York City and recording Alexander's "Pretty Tree Climber" and "Mickey Mouse Movie House." But other songs from this period, including "Pretty When" and "Burma Shave Sign," would remain unrecorded until they moved into Alexander's solo repertoire later in the 1970s. Instead, as the tour wound down, Sesnick took Yule to one side and informed him that he alone would be staying behind in London to record. Everyone else was going home. "I thought we were going to make a record together at the end of the tour," Alexander shrugged. "Oh well, ghost band, ghost record."

Yule was stunned. "There wasn't any dramatic split," he insisted, "not even a consensus to desist—it just stopped being. I suppose everyone thought it would start up again soon, but it didn't." Instead, he found himself ushered into a studio, presented with a bunch of strangers, and left to get on with it. "[Sesnick] said, 'Show up at the studio,' and I did. He said Mo would be there and she wasn't. He said go home after the sessions were over and I did. I said here are my notes for the mix and he ignored them."

An entirely new band was pieced together around a battery of session men, but when Deep Purple's Ian Paice—who replaced Tucker on drums—was asked for his recollections of the sessions, he had to admit he had none whatsoever. "I've heard the tape, but I don't think it sounds like me." "It was fun in the studio," Yule concluded. "But it's always fun in the studio."

Elsewhere, however, matters were moving fast. On the road, said Yule, "We were well received. No one yelling 'fraud' or anything. I don't remember anyone even mentioning the missing Lou." But Reed was becoming increasingly active that summer, taking his first steps into a world beyond the Velvet Underground's shadow, and he was none too pleased to see his old band taking to the road at a time when he wasn't certain he even wanted to play another live show. The past belonged in the past, not flaunting itself in his face.

Life at his parents' house was, if not idyllic, at least quiet. Reed took a job as a typist with his father's accountancy firm, while Reed senior's business expertise was put to good use unraveling the various contractual and legal arrangements that still clung from the former singer's past. Because, at first, he *was* a former singer. He had no interest in returning to rock music, or to life in a band. He had already achieved all that he believed was possible—that is, leading a band that represented everything he believed a group should. "We stood for everything that kids loved and adults hated. We were loud, you couldn't understand the lyrics, we were vulgar, we sang about dope, sex, violence, you name it."

In his mind, it was a recipe for success, and he simply couldn't understand why people backed away from the Velvet Underground, why polite ears closed when their name was mentioned, why a group that touched upon every primal preoccupation of American youth should have been so roundly rejected by that same youth. So he stepped away.

Occasionally friends would drop by to see how he was doing. They would walk on the beach together, with Reed's dog running along beside them. He might mention he'd been writing some poetry, just to stop the words from backing up in his head, but he hadn't set it to music, and no, he wouldn't be reading it aloud to anybody. He wrote it for himself, just like thousands of other poets do. He was staring his thirtieth birthday in the mouth, he was in love with Bettye Kronstadt, a stylish, sexy waitress who could not have come from a more different existence than his. It was time to start living in the real world.

Even Richard Robinson, a friend from his New York days, and now an A&R man at RCA Records, could not convince Reed that he had anything to offer the music industry of the early 1970s. Instead, they would sit around the Collective Consciousness salon that Robinson and his journalist wife, Lisa, had established as a hangout for the writers they admired, and simply talk about the old times.

Reed did agree to a poetry reading at St. Mark's Church in March 1971, combining old Velvet Underground lyrics with more recent paeans to Bettye, then topping it off with a taste of gay erotica, but as he left the podium, he was adamant. He would never sing a song again, he would never return to rock 'n' roll, and if he did, then the ghost of Delmore Schwartz should haunt him for eternity.

The Robinsons were relentless, desperate to draw Reed out of his reluctance. But even on the occasions that the guitars did come out, Reed rarely let anything new into the room.

Except sometimes, he did. He'd been talking with a production team about making a musical version of Nelson Algren's novel *Walk on the Wild Side*, growing increasingly enthusiastic as the plot came together; and, one evening in March 1971, sitting around the Robinsons' apartment, with journalist Dave Marsh looking in as well, Reed tired of playing around with the riff of "Sweet Jane," explaining how it had taken him eight months to nail it down, and toyed instead with a simple little tune that nobody had heard—it later crystallized as "New York Telephone Conversation." Then he produced another song, the merrily frolicking "Wagon Wheel." "I haven't heard that one," said Lisa excitedly. "You haven't?" Reed replied, and strummed his way through.

He dug back into the backlog of songs that the Velvet Underground had never taken past demo stage: "I Love You," a sweet song whose title said all that it needed to; "Lisa Says" and "Ride into the Sun," a plaintive, vulnerable verse that built toward the kind of crescendo that had littered *Loaded*; "Wild Child" and "Hangin' Round," semi-rockers with the sort of choruses that nobody could resist; the sweet "She's My Best Friend" and the brutal "Kid," a song that could have stepped out of one of Paul Morrissey's recent Andy Warhol Presents movies, *Flesh* or *Trash*, tales of urban decay lived out by the most squalid characters imaginable. "They've taken her children away," mourns the very first line, "because they said she was not a good mother." Years later, Nico would wonder aloud whether she was the model for the song's twisted heroine, but Reed never rose to her bait.

He had another new song to play, the title song that he'd written for the musical, a throbbing acoustic guitar line and a nonsensical tour of

New York City, "off the Broadway by the top...up into the Empire State....Take a walk on the wild side."

"This is the girl's part," Reed laughed, and his companions exploded into a chorus of "doo doo doo"s. Somebody started clapping; somebody else sang along with the chorus. "Ladies and gentlemen, Elton John," a voice joked, and Reed laughed aloud. Elton was hot property in early 1971, the first new pop star of the American decade, and the harbinger, for sure, of a whole new wave of earnest singer-songwriters.

Reed has never spoken of the moment when he realized, or perhaps was convinced, that there might be a place for him in that same upcoming firmament; that the man who wrote "Some Kind of Love," "Beginning to See the Light," "New Age," "I'll Be Your Mirror," and "Femme Fatale" might have a voice to raise alongside the James Taylors, Cat Stevenses, and Jackson Brownes—yes, *that* Jackson Browne—of the new era. There may never have been a precise moment when that happened. But somewhere between the white picket fence and the typing pool on Long Island, and an evening spent strumming to his friends in New York City, Reed realized that he hadn't given up rock 'n' roll after all. He'd just stopped dreaming about it.

They chatted around the possibility of Reed returning to action, and speculated over who could produce him. John Cale, maybe? Since *Marble Index* and *The Stooges*, Cale had continued carving an idiosyncratic path through the listening habits of the underground, with another Nico record, the just-released *Desertshore*, outstripping even those in terms of sonic brilliance. Then Marsh dropped another name into the mix. "You know David Bowie wants to record with you?" and if Reed shrugged irrelevantly, nobody could have blamed him. Who, after all, was David Bowie?

Well, he was in *Rolling Stone* a couple of weeks back, a half-page piece that pointed out that the man wore dresses ("But they're man's dresses," Bowie protested); and he'd made quite a splash in Los Angeles, linking up with local scenester and A&R guy Rodney Bingenheimer and doing the promotional rounds with him. And when that same West Coast visit took him to a San Francisco radio station, the local journalist who was accompanying him couldn't believe how excited the Englishman got when he spotted a copy of *Loaded* in the DJ booth.

In fact, it was all the writer could do—although Marsh didn't tell Reed this—to stop Bowie from insisting the disc jockey play the whole LP.

Instead, he reached back and pulled out another album entirely, the first record by a band called the Stooges. They cued up "No Fun" and Bowie was sold. Yes, he still wanted to record with Lou Reed. But Iggy Pop, he told all and sundry, was his new all-time favorite singer.

Back in England, listening to the Stooges practically became an occupational hazard for anybody who visited Bowie's home. "He listed us as his favorites in some music poll," Pop recalled. "Somebody showed it to me and I said, 'Who the fuck is that? Never heard of him!'"

Bowie, however, made sure everybody heard of Pop. Bob Grace, his publisher, recalled, "He was into kind of brainwashing or indoctrinating you into his world. At the time, he was fascinated with Iggy Pop, and he was playing me all these Stooges records."

Bowie had never stopped scheming fame, not even at the end of 1969, when the bitter wind of one-hit-wonderdom swept in in the wake of his "Space Oddity" smash with the reminder that it was the topicality of the song that had taken him to the upper echelons of the charts, not the skill with which it was written, or the beauty of the album that accompanied it. *Man of Words, Man of Music*, Bowie's second album, was released to all the fanfare that could be expected to greet the long-playing companion of a novelty hit, but only until people cracked the shrink-wrap and realized the novelty ended with the first song on side one.

Now he was about to begin recording his third album, but it was to be a very different record from its predecessor. For starters, Bowie had hooked up with a young guitarist from the northern city of Hull, Mick Ronson, who himself graduated via a string of local hard rock bands. Styling himself firmly in the mold of Jeff Beck at his bluesy best, Ronson was as impossibly inventive as his role model, as he proved when he made his live debut alongside Bowie at a BBC radio concert just two days after they met.

It was a ragged introduction. Broadcasting live from the BBC's Paris Theatre on February 5, 1970, the show opened with a solo Bowie howling through Jacques Brel's "Amsterdam" before moving onto a clutch of his own compositions: "God Knows I'm Good," from the *Man of Words* album; a cover of American songwriter Biff Rose's "Buzz the Fuzz"; and an abandoned single from a couple of years earlier, "Karma Man." Drummer John Cambridge and producer Tony Visconti, moonlighting as Bowie's bass player, joined him for "London Bye Ta Ta," another single-that-never-happened, and the album's "An Occasional Dream." So far, so folky.

Bowie had toured alone in the wake of "Space Oddity," a curly-haired youth with an acoustic guitar, and he'd had a horrible time of things. In the past, he'd gigged to people who had no idea who he was, and accepted what he offered on face value. With a hit single under his belt, he found crowds that assumed they knew all they needed to, and as he drifted through salutary rumination after cautionary epic, not one of which sounded remotely like "Space Oddity," audiences responded with brutal disdain.

He did not intend to make the same mistake again, but neither did he want to alienate the handfuls that had supported him so far. The rhythm section merely added emphasis and warmth to the songs. But a taste of the future was imminent as Ronson stepped out onto the stage and, though the guitarist later acknowledged that he didn't have a clue what he was expected to play, neither did he have any hesitation.

"The Width of a Circle" was one of Bowie's newest songs, a lengthy, wordy exploration of what Bowie later claimed to be "my experiences as a shaven-headed monk"; in common with great swathes of western youth in the last days of the 1960s, Bowie had flirted with Buddhism, although it is also easy to align the song's lyrics with the sexual identities that he would soon be bringing to the fore. Certainly the song's importance was such that, by the time they came to record it, Bowie and Ronson had expanded it to an eight-minute epic, layered with seething, screaming guitars, and prone to stretch out even longer in concert. Almost alone of the songs that would appear on the BBC broadcast, or even on the still-gestating new album, "The Width of a Circle" would remain an integral part of Bowie's concert repertoire for the next four years. Only "Waiting for the Man," which he also performed that night, could be said to rival it in Bowie's affections.

The band that came together for the BBC concert would remain intact for the next two months, a period that subsequent historians have hopefully tagged as the birth of glam rock—although Ronson, at least, was adamant that the era was scarcely the source of great joy that such an appellation would normally merit. Audiences, he said softly, hated them.

Getting it into his head that the gig-going public had had enough of the bedraggled denim- and greatcoat-clad rockers that then dominated the British (and beyond) rock scene, and keen to add his theatrical instincts to what, under Ronson's guidance, was fast becoming a furious rock show, Bowie convinced his girlfriend, Angela Barnett, and Visconti's current companion, Liz Hartley, to run the band up a set of extravagant costumes, each one representing a superhero-style cartoon character.

The group were not especially enthusiastic about the costumes, not this first night nor for some months after. Bowie laughed, "When I first heard (Mick Ronson) play I thought, 'That's my Jeff Beck! He is fantastic! This kid is great!' And so I sort of hoodwinked him into working with me. I didn't quite have to tell him in the beginning that he would have to wear makeup and all that. . . . Mick came from Hull. Very down-to-earth. 'What do you mean, makeup?' I reverted to things like, 'You looked very green tonight onstage. . . . I think if you wore makeup you'd look a little more natural looking,' and sort of lies like this, and gradually got them into areas of costume and theater. Actually, when they realized how many girls they could pull when they looked so sort of outlandish, they took to it like a fish to water."

Bowie, in blue cape and striped tights, was Rainbowman; Ronson (adapting a suit Bowie himself had sported for a short promo film he made a couple of years earlier) was Gangsterman. Cambridge, in a ten-gallon hat, became Cowboyman, and Visconti, garbed in a Superman-style outfit with a giant *H* on the chest, was Hypeman—Hype being the name of the band, after Bowie perhaps optimistically opined that onlookers would regard them as one. The problem was, a hype can only be said to function if it is noticed by enough people to either accept or reject its premise. Bowie's Hype made no impression whatsoever on its audience, and the costumes were abandoned the moment the band left the stage. All apart from Visconti's, that is. While the group were onstage, somebody entered the dressing room and helped themselves to his regular clothes. He was forced to travel home in full Hypeman regalia.

Hype lived on. The music paper *Disc and Music Echo* caught a London show on March 7 and shuddered at the intensity not of the performance, but of Ronson's guitar. "The volume . . . was so high that not only did he block out David's singing, but also completely overpowered John Cambridge's drums." A return to the Roundhouse on March 11, 1970, supporting Country Joe McDonald (while the unknown Genesis opened the evening) is recalled by a few exhilarating minutes of film footage. It seems mad, but there is more pictorial evidence of Bowie and Angela's marriage, on March 20, than there is of the Hype's live performances, and that despite the happy couple informing neither the local press nor Bowie's own mother about the event. Old Peggy Jones found out anyway, and called up a couple of newspapers, and the pop star's nuptials were preserved for all time.

Meanwhile, work toward Bowie's next album was proceeding quickly. On March 25, returning to the BBC to record a session for DJ Andy Ferris's *Sounds of the Seventies* show, Hype unleashed two of Bowie's new compositions, the still-evolving "Width of a Circle" and "The Supermen," alongside the last album's "The Wild Eyed Boy from Freecloud" and, perhaps inevitably, "Waiting for the Man," transformed now into a virtual boogie, Ronson's guitar raw edged and riding rough and riff-shod over the rhythm while Bowie's vocal is no more refined, an imploring yelp that eschews the sly innuendo of past versions, and sounds all the more desperate for it.

Hype, however, was not long for the world. Five days later, John Cambridge played his final show with the band—he bowed out after cutting Bowie's new single, a seriously electrified version of the last album's "Memory of a Free Festival." In his place, Ronson recommended a drummer he had worked with back in Hull, Mick "Woody" Woodmansey and, on April 18, the new unit headed into the studio, while Bowie got to grips with the next realignment of his career, replacing his manager of the last four years, Kenneth Pitt, with Tony Defries.

7

BEAT NARROW HEART, THE SONG
LOTS OF PEOPLE KNOW

It was Marc Bolan who set the glitter rock ball rolling. An itinerant drifter of no fixed musical abode, he was scooped up by manager Simon Napier-Bell late in 1966 and transplanted into John's Children, an anarchic four-piece whose bridging of beat and psychedelia owed more to their musical incapabilities than to any preconceived game plan.

With them, Marc learned several lessons, most notably how to harness the talent whose raw potential everybody recognized but few knew how to exploit. The band instilled in him the confidence, and more importantly, the discipline that was to be so valuable when next he struck out on his own. And while his next project would see him working once again with the acoustic whimsy which had been his delight before John's Children taught him how to play electric guitar, it was within a defiantly rock 'n' roll framework.

Having found, or at least identified, an audience, Marc spent the next three years enlarging on, and experimenting with, their limitations. His apparent plunge into electric rock on the Beard of Stars *album had already been hinted at over the course of its three predecessors, and from there it was but a small step into the full-blown rock 'n' roll of* Electric Warrior—*two decades later ranked among* Rolling Stone's *best albums of all time—and its follow-up,* The Slider.

Despite several minor chart entries—three out of Tyrannosaurus Rex's five singles made the lower reaches of the charts—it was essential to Marc's game plan that he establish himself with a hit.

"Ride a White Swan" finally catapulted him into the limelight he craved so desperately. Said Simon Napier-Bell, "It wasn't until Kit Lambert [cofounder of Marc's new label, Fly] and Tony Visconti [his producer] had spent hours working on him, trying to convince him that it was now or never as far as his electric ambitions went, that Marc finally took the plunge.

"He recorded 'Ride a White Swan' knowing that it would either make him or break him. He was so scared of it bombing out that he was going around telling everybody that he disowned the record. What he really meant was that he disowned it if it was a flop. When it was a hit, though, well, it simply wasn't worth the bother of trying to explain all that crap to people who said he'd sold out. Because now he was God, and whoever heard of God selling out?"

The success of 1970's T.Rex album (on which the new, abbreviated band name was debuted), early in the new year of 1971, added yet more urgency to Marc's striving. A U.K. tour, with specially reduced ticket prices, attracted a vast army of adolescent girls, lured by Marc's captivating television appearances. His older student hippie audience was all but obliterated, and the rumbles of discontent from Marc's old progressive stomping grounds were drowned out beneath a barrage of screams that didn't let up for another two years.

In one fell swoop, Marc's transition from underground antihero to superstar demigod had completely shattered all predictions and preoccupations for the new decade. At a time when rock was rock and fun was just for the kiddies, Marc cut through all the contradictions, flouncing onstage in sequins and satin, blasting out a joyous celebration of youth and potency.

Single-handedly, he dragged rock 'n' roll out of the grave, at the same time he screwed down the coffin lid on pretension and reserve. And with just one flick of his corkscrew curls, he ushered in the era of glam rock, and brought British pop to its most invigorating high of all time.

—from *Children of the Revolution: The Story of Glam Rock*
by Dave Thompson

The first time Bowie and wife Angela met Tony Defries, in spring 1970, they simply sat in silent awe. Born in September 1944, and barely three years Bowie's senior, Defries had not yet captured the look that would so impress Iggy Pop when he met him the following year—Pop laughingly recalled "a big cigar and a big pointed nose and a great big Afro and a smug look on his face, and an English accent and a big fur coat and a belly. It just spelled 'hot manager.'"

But he had charisma by the bucketload, and the assurance and experience of a far older man. He was somebody you could talk to and know that he was listening; and he was someone you could listen to, knowing that everything he said made sense.

A just-outside-of-Londoner, Defries grew up in the local market trade, buying and selling the relics of England's prewar past, courtesy of the country gentry who had fallen on hard times and were forced to flog the family silver.

With his older brother Nicholas, the young Defries moved through a succession of early career moves on the streets of late-1950s London—the pair owned a small chain of gas stations at one time, and also tried their hand at property speculation, before both brothers began studying law. It was a career that appealed not because Defries felt especially duty-bound to uphold it, but because he was fascinated by its sheer intractability and by the mental leaps that were required before one could find one's way through its labyrinths.

Nicholas moved into property law, and their earliest ventures seemed to point both boys in that direction. As time passed, however, the younger Defries found his attentions being drawn more and more toward litigation, an area in which he could pit his wits not against the dry and dusty statutes that governed his brother's specialty, but against other minds that might or might not be as agile and imaginative as his.

He never passed the bar exam; to this day, Defries's official status is paralegal. But day-to-day experience swiftly pushed him far beyond the standards he would have been required to attain had he pursued his studies to their academic end, and by 1963, he was a junior member of one of the most prestigious (albeit smaller) law firms in London—Martin, Boston & Associates, on Wigmore Street.

There, he was nominally among the lowest of the low, the boy—and, at the age of eighteen, that's all he was—who was thrown the occasional divorce or custody case, simply to keep him from drinking all the tea. But he was also being tutored by some of the greatest legal minds of the day, and every case he was given (and, invariably, won) was a little more important than the one before.

Defries witnessed the surreal nature of fame for the first time in 1962, when his employers were called in to represent Lord Profumo, the government minister at the center of a sex-and-espionage scandal that not only brought down his party's reign but would be named after him. The Profumo Affair remains one of the watershed moments in British political history, but beyond its political and military ramifications, Defries was most fascinated by the apparent ease with which the media and public opinion influenced powerful personalities and great events. The possibility of using that influence in other arenas intrigued him.

That opportunity arrived in 1968, when a group of leading photographers approached him to ask if he could help them circumvent the wealth of commercial disadvantages they encountered when dealing with the biggest players inside the advertising, fashion, and publishing industries. Defries led them to the promised land of the Association of Fashion and Advertising Photographers, the first ever professional photographers' guild in Britain.

Defries had already taken his first tentative steps into show business when he was brought in by record producer Mickie Most to find a way out of a dispute involving one of Most's most-storied clients, the Animals. By the end of the decade, Defries could number Donovan, the Yardbirds, Led Zeppelin, and Marianne Faithfull among the artists he had worked with, while an association with American lawyer Allen Klein added further insights to Defries' burgeoning understanding of the industry.

Already, then, it was apparent that Defries needed to make a choice between continued law practice and a career in entertainment. He chose the latter, as one of his associates, Olaf Wyper, recalls.

"I first met Defries in 1968 when he was retained as legal advisor to the group of London's then-leading advertising and fashion photographers, many of whom were my close friends. Tony worked for a firm of West End solicitors, and although he gave the impression that he was a qualified solicitor, he was in fact a solicitor's clerk, a very responsible position, but not a solicitor. I introduced him to Lawrence Myers, a showbiz accountant, who I got to know through record producer Mickie Most, and they formed the intention of starting a management company together."

Together, Defries and Myers established the Gem Music Group, an independent record label, music publishing and personal management organization set up to provide various other record labels with material from a number of different producers and songwriters. Their first release was a number one hit worldwide. "Love Grows Where My Rosemary Goes" was performed by Edison Lighthouse, written and produced by Tony Macaulay, and when Macaulay made a historic bid to wrest the control of his own songwriting publishing away from various other claimants, it was Defries who steered him to victory.

Equally significant was Defries's involvement with Stevie Wonder. For close to a decade Motown had exploited the artist, cementing him into popular mythology as the childlike "Little Stevie Wonder." By 1970, however, he was an adult, demanding artistic and creative freedom. Defries agreed to aid him, and earned the dubious honor of being offered the wrong kind of Motown contract, when a "hit" was put out on him by Godfather Berry Gordy. But Wonder got what he wanted, just as every other artist who had worked with Defries seemed to get what he wanted. Small wonder, then, that when Bowie went to Olaf Wyper, now the general manager of the Philips record label, to ask if there was anybody, anywhere, who could help lift the singer out of his rut, Wyper suggested he call Defries.

Wyper explained, "I was close to David Bowie, who asked me about changing management from Ken Pitt. I told him I had to be neutral in this and could not be seen to be taking sides or advising him in this regard. I gave him the names of three lawyers he might consider going to for advice about his contract, and the first name[s] on that list [were] Defries and Myers. He called them and the rest is history."

"I felt sorry for David," Defries said later. Bowie and Angela—who was doing most of the legwork on his behalf at this point, even liaising with promoters and booking live shows—appeared in his office looking like they'd just escaped one of Charles Dickens's bands of ragged, homeless children, and as he listened to the Bowies' tale of woe, Defries recalled, "I thought, 'Poor little chap, he's got himself in a terrible mess.'"

Was he the right person to extricate him from it, though? Defries didn't see why not, although it was only fair to warn the couple that he was comparatively new to the music business. Bowie didn't care. "I said, 'Well, you're a good lawyer,' and he said, 'Yeah, and I can sell china, too'"—which he had done, at his family's stall in the Shepherd's Bush Market. "It just went from there." Over the next two years, Gem invested over $100,000 in Bowie's career, and Myers acknowledged, "It all came back very nicely, very rapidly, and with a very nice profit."

Defries reexamined every aspect of Bowie's career so far. His old management deal was dissolved (although it would be 1975 before a financial settlement was finally arrived at with Kenneth Pitt). A new publishing deal was set up. Defries even weighed in on the fate of the Hype, pointing out from the very beginning that he had no interest in working with a group. He saw Bowie as a solo act, and a one-name solo act as well. There was Elvis, there was Dylan, and there would be Bowie.

Nothing was too good, or too much trouble for the singer. As Angela Bowie later remarked, "It didn't seem like a business arrangement. For some reason, Tony looked on us as a couple of urchins who needed a helping hand. We developed an affection for him, and he for us. Tony took care of everything."

The most powerful factor in any deal struck in Bowie's name at this time was not so much the singer's own potential, but Defries's unwavering faith in it. "David's a real star," Defries would boast. "Not in a record business style, not a Rod Stewart style or a Cat Stevens, but...a Marlon Brando– or a James Dean–type star. I see him more in that category of large-scale untouchable. It's like he doesn't quite belong here."

No matter that the biggest stars of the day, Marc Bolan notwithstanding, remained the pop-tinged Dawn, Blue Mink, and Neil Diamond on the one hand; the hard rocking Free, Black Sabbath and Deep Purple on the other. Nor that it would take more than fancy words to propel anybody up into the stratosphere beyond them. Defries had belief, and that was half the battle.

The rest, according to Myers, was that "Tony recognized David's ability to know what was good for David. That was very important."

But that was not all. Defries also sensed the singer's hunger—not only his willingness to be molded into whatever shape the moment required, but also his ability to carry that molding off. A lot of would-be performers can adopt an image, after all, but how long is it before it falls away? Bowie would not allow that to happen.

With the right approach, it is probably safe to say Defries could have ended up representing almost any star he chose, and he came close to doing so. There were certainly some nervous moments for Bowie when he realized that he could very easily lose his new manager to Stevie Wonder. Overtures for Defries's services also came from Three Dog Night, an American rock band that enjoyed a clutch of domestic hits in the very early 1970s. Defries's dream, however, did not involve repackaging an existing product. He wanted to create a new star, fastening onto Bowie's basic, and visibly malleable, desire for success, and then projecting his own, similar, fantasies onto it.

"David was not a person to be pushed around," Myers confirmed. "He's a highly intelligent man, very purposeful and resolute. He's not the sort of guy to whom you could say, 'You just stand there, sunshine, and do what you're told.' He knew exactly what he was doing." And what he was doing was listening to Defries.

Bowie's latest album was completed and scheduled for a late-1970 release. That date, however, fell away, and Defries began worrying at the record company's heels, going head-to-head with Mercury's American main office, savaging their inability to push either *Man of Words, Man of Music*, "The Prettiest Star," or "Memory of a Free Festival" into contention. At one point, he was threatening to withhold Bowie's services altogether, unless the label could guarantee more attention in the future.

A new single was agreed upon—Bowie intended "Holy Holy" to become the title track to the new album, and was furious when Mercury vetoed it as unsuitable. Reluctantly, he changed it to *The Man Who Sold the World*, but it made no difference, as both single and LP slipped into oblivion in the new year. In the studio, as the musicians worked on the album, they had joked that they were making their own *Sgt. Pepper*. But only if the Beatles were a near-penniless bar band, looking back on two years of lost opportunities.

The relationship with Mercury was clearly and irrevocably broken. No matter that Bowie's contract with the label was scheduled to run until June 1972, Defries left Mercury in no doubt whatsoever that he considered it a dead issue, and the only negotiations that were now required were those that would persuade the label to admit it was all over as well.

By the time Defries began seriously looking for a new deal for his client, in June 1971, he had negotiated the return of both Mercury albums, *Man of Words, Man of Music* and *The Man Who Sold the World* to Bowie, for inclusion in the new deal. He already believed that the $18,000 compensation that Mercury demanded would easily be recouped; so easily, in fact, that he had no hesitation in appending their acquisition to his demands from any new label.

Even more important than the financial wrangling, however, were the countless hours that Defries and Bowie spent in earnest conversation, planning out the career they intended Bowie would enjoy. Discussing the creativity that lay in Bowie's immediate future, most notably Ziggy Stardust, Defries' then-assistant Nicky Graham insisted, "The original idea was David's, but [it was] Tony who visualize[d] Ziggy as being something real," and who spotted the universe into which he could march.

All around them, as they talked, the glam rock movement that Hype had attempted to foreshadow was indeed taking shape. Marc Bolan, one of Bowie's closest friends since they met in the mid-1960s, was now leading the way, realigning the psychedelic whimsy of his Tyrannosaurus Rex duo into a full-blown electric band, T.Rex, and scoring a major British hit straight out of the box with the late-1970 "Ride a White Swan." His follow-up, "Hot Love," was topping the U.K. chart the same week that *The Man Who Sold the World* was released.

Slade, a club band that had been scratching around the circuit for almost as long as Bowie, were preparing to unleash their assault, readying a raucous, platform-booted stomp through "Get Down and Get With It" as their next 45. Pop songwriters Nicky Chinn and Mike Chapman were schooling the Sweet in the art of tarting up their bubblegum, to raise the sweetest confections to their glittering best. Nobody would have gone so far as to say a new musical movement was percolating; even fewer would have dared predict that British pop was about to reach its most intoxicating high since the heyday of the beat boom. But it was coming all the same, and Bowie could not help but pay attention.

It was Bolan who had convinced him to proceed with writing and recording "Space Oddity," even after his other friends, horrified that he could write such an exploitative novelty number, told him to can it. It was Bolan, too, who supplied the liquid lead guitar on "The Prettiest Star," Bowie's follow-up single and the first song he ever wrote for Angela. And it was Bolan whose influence lay heavy on "Black Country Rock," one of the handful of conventional rock songs that peppered the metallic prog landscapes of *The Man Who Sold the World*. The signature warble that was Bolan's to command sounded strange coming out of Bowie's mouth, but it worked.

In later years, Bowie would reflect upon his own breakthrough and admit, "We couldn't have done it without Marc Bolan. The little imp opened the door. What was so great, however, was that we knew he hadn't got it quite right. Sort of Glam 1.0. We were straining in the wings with versions 1.01 and 2.0, while Marc was still struggling with satin."

It wasn't quite that simple, of course. Bolan led the way regardless of "right" or "wrong." Stepping out at British TV's flagship pop show *Top of the Pops* to perform "Hot Love," Bolan barely paused as his publicist Chelita Secunda halted him on his way to the stage and applied a few dashes of glitter to his face. The first time the cameras zoomed in on Marc's features, Bowie was as taken aback as everybody else.

Defries encouraged Bowie to study Bolan. He laughed, perhaps, when he visited the Bowies' grandiosely named Haddon Hall home in Beckenham, south London, and found David sprawled out on the apartment floor with Bolan's latest lyrics beside him, analyzing them for any mention of his own self therein, but he had it on good authority that Bolan frequently did the same thing.

Intriguing, too, was the fact that both musicians shared the same producer. The Brooklyn-born, London-based Tony Visconti had been working with Bolan since Tyrannosaurus Rex, and Bowie since his Deram days, and both musically and stylistically, each performer's influence and interests were being communicated to the other. Intriguing, and somewhat discomforting. Without ever sitting down together to plot Visconti's removal from Bowie's orbit—they would leave those machinations to Bolan and his wife, June—Defries and Bowie agreed that future recordings should be handled by somebody else, for the sake of Bowie's own uniqueness, if nothing else.

They were still awaiting the release of *The Man Who Sold the World* when Visconti was replaced in Bowie's band by Herbie Flowers—who both produced and played bass on "Holy Holy." Visconti would not work alongside Bowie again until 1974, by which time Bolan's star was firmly in the descendant.

Bowie's, on the other hand, remained deceptive. At the end of 1970, Defries played a tape of at least four new Bowie compositions to his old ally Mickie Most. Within weeks, Most had recorded one of them, "Oh You Pretty Things," with former Herman's Hermits front man Peter Noone, and taken it into the British Top 20. "Right On Mother," with Bowie reprising the deliciously ham-fisted piano technique that distinguished "Pretty Things," was scheduled for Noone's next B-side. Two other songs, the antiwar lament of "Bombers" and the strikingly pretty "Life on Mars?" would at least be demoed by the singer, while Bowie himself continued writing and recording as fast as he was able.

"Shadow Man," "Lightning Frightening," "Tired of My Life"...so many songs were pouring out and being registered with his publishers that it sometimes seemed incredible that there was not a queue of would-be hit makers lining up outside the offices.

The artists whom Bowie was attracting, however, were the same run of friends that he had always relied upon for support. Indeed, it sometimes felt as though he was scared to step toward any wider possibilities, for fear of being turned down—it had happened in the past, after all—and, finally, Lawrence Myers could take no more. Exasperated by the amount of time and effort that Defries was pumping into Bowie, and the growing pile of unsaleable songs with which Bowie was rewarding those efforts, Myers handed the singer a clutch of Tony Macaulay compositions and snapped, "These are the songs you should be recording."

Bowie, however, was not to be distracted. He continued gigging in the wake of the album's release, both with a full band and with a stripped-down combo that might comprise just Ronson alone, strumming acoustic guitar; or expand to include pianist Rick Wakeman in the blend; or even explode to draw in a host of Bowie's other friends as well. For there, Bowie and Defries had decreed, lay the germ of a notion that was well worth pursuing.

"Tony's style is one of a family attitude," explained Myers. "He likes artists and staff all to be close. He likes them to travel together, go out together. That was one of the reasons he had more to do with managing David than I did. He'd go and sit at the Flamingo or wherever until the early hours of the morning with him, and all his staff would go along too. I work in the opposite way."

Partially the idea of creating their own musical community sprang from the arts labs that pocked the British scene at the end of the 1960s. Bowie had established his own in his hometown of Beckenham and frequently performed there either solo or with the band. Like the Film-Makers' Cinematheque in New York, the arts lab was a place where like-minded musicians and fans could congregate for evenings of personal expression, to experiment with new ideas and experience the response of their peers, away from the dangers of pressure or pain.

But that was only half of the equation because, of course, similar ventures had sprung up everywhere. The other goal was to re-create the Factory, to place Bowie as the Warholesque ringmaster around whom a host of other talents might revolve. Bowie had even written a new song to crystallize his intentions. It was called "Andy Warhol," and he'd already recorded it as well, with singer Dana Gillespie, a friend of his since their teenage years and one of the most beautiful women any of his other friends had ever seen. Defries would be handling her career, too.

Mick Ronson and drummer Woody Woodmansey, meanwhile, had already stepped out on their own under the name of Ronno, reuniting with sundry Hull friends and recording a lumberingly metallic single for the Vertigo label. Now other friends and associates were being lined up to perform. Mickey King, a startlingly handsome young man whose sexual promiscuity was legendary among his gay friends, was handed a song about Bowie's car, "Rupert the Riley." Artist George Underwood, the man whose fist, swung in a playground punch-up, was responsible for Bowie having odd-colored eyes, recorded "Hole in the Ground."

But Bowie's greatest hope was for Arnold Corns. "I've got this friend who is just beautiful," Bowie simpered. "When you meet him, you don't even question whether he's a boy or a girl. He's just a person called Freddi [Burretti], who's very nice to look at. That's what's important, to be a person, to be an individual." And Burretti was so individual, Bowie continued, that he would be the first man ever to appear on the cover of *Vogue*.

He detailed his master plan. He'd written a song for Burretti, a Mogadon plod through a bass-led freak-out titled "Moonage Daydream," gleefully laden down with random cries of "far out" and the like. Accompanied by an extraordinary young guitarist named Mark Carr-Pritchard, Bowie had built a band around the singer, the intriguingly named Arnold's Corn. He had even landed them a record deal, with the small but successful B&C label. Bowie himself would produce and sing on the record. All Freddi had to do was stand there and look ravishing.

"The Rolling Stones are finished," Bowie pronounced. "Arnold's Corn will be the next Stones." He had a high opinion of "Moonage Daydream," too. "This song is unique. There's certainly nothing to compare it with." And because he believed that "Freddi is right for now," the whole thing was put together in just six days. "There's no point in waiting."

Burretti was less immodest. "Actually, I can't just expect to bring Jagger back," he admitted. "Really, I'm just a dress designer." Indeed he was. Like Carr-Pritchard, Burretti was an art student from south London's Dulwich College, who had wandered into the Bowie camp with his girlfriend, Danielle, and promptly become immersed in the flurry of sartorial reshaping which Angela was in the process of executing. The Hype may have failed dismally in that respect, but she and Bowie remained convinced that they were on the right track, all the same.

"Every time David's band had an important gig," Angela explained, "Freddi would design new clothes for them." She also worked hard to foster the belief "that it was pointless going onstage in great clothes, if they were going to be wearing jeans offstage, so Freddi made them clothes to wear offstage as well, from mohair, cashmere, silk...anything that would make them look out of the ordinary when they were on the street."

It was this look that Burretti would now be taking into the full public glare, as though Bowie wanted to check the reaction first, before relaunching himself in equally audacious style. If Burretti was simply laughed out of sight, then Bowie would return to the drawing board. But if people accepted him in all of his finery, then the door would be open for anything else: an alligator, a space invader, a mama/papa coming for tea.

Arnold Corns, as the project would be slightly renamed, made their live debut on June 3, 1971. For the princely sum of £54, Bowie was invited to play BBC radio DJ John Peel's *Sunday Concert*, a one-hour broadcast that he immediately recast as an opportunity not only to air the best and the rest of his own repertoire, but also to give his friends some exposure as well.

Dana Gillespie was on hand to perform a breezy "Andy Warhol"; George Underwood added another of Bowie's newly composed elegies, "Song for Bob Dylan"; another school friend, Geoffrey Alexander, handled Chuck Berry's "Almost Grown," and Mark Carr-Pritchard turned up to represent Arnold Corns on "Looking for a Friend." Burretti, naturally, designed all the costumes. And there was another new face in Bowie's band, after Herbie Flowers was forced to pull out of the show with just two hours' notice. He was replaced by another of Ronson's Hull compadres, Trevor Bolder. What would become the Spiders from Mars was complete.

On June 17, Burretti, Carr-Pritchard, and Bowie commenced a week of sessions at Trident Studios. Tucked away in the darkened recesses of Queen Anne's Court, in London's Soho district, Trident was a small but implausibly intimate hangout, just beginning to establish its name on the studio circuit, and became Bowie's favored base of operations for the next year or more. There, two members of Carr-Pritchard's own group, Runk, awaited them, the impossibly magnificently named Timothy James Ralph St. Laurent Thomas Moore Broadbent on drums, and bassist Peter De Somogyi. Arnold Corns were ready for action.

They had four songs at their disposal: "Moonage Daydream," "Man in the Middle," a reprise of "Looking for a Friend," and "Hang Onto Yourself," a song Bowie had already taped once, incredibly, alongside Gene Vincent. Back during Bowie's brief U.S. visit at the beginning of 1971, the pair jammed together in a small Los Angeles studio, with the only downside of the entire exercise being that Vincent was inaudible on the finished recording—much as Burretti would be inaudible on the Arnold Corns single.

Indeed, while Bowie was insistent that a full Arnold Corns album, *Looking for Rudi*, was in the works, it was difficult to shake the impression that the whole exercise was just another way of getting some music into the marketplace without Mercury Records finding out. Which, according to Bob Grace, over at Bowie's Chrysalis Music publishers, is exactly what it was. Bowie was spending so much time making demos, Grace smiled, and getting "really slick" in the process, that "finally we decided to lease [four] of the demos to B&C, simply to try and get some money back. I think we got £300 for the masters. But because David was still contracted to Mercury, we couldn't use his name. So David came up with Arnold Corns. He never told anyone what it meant."

No matter. While veteran publicist Bill Harry was engaged to tout pictures of Burretti, who really was as lovely as Bowie reckoned, around the Fleet Street papers, B&C's own PR machinery clanked into action, flooding the music press with copies of "Moonage Daydream."

Their travails went unrewarded. Fleet Street was apathetic, and the music press was appalled. Even the best review was a stinker. Commenting upon the single's B-side in the *New Musical Express*, journalist Charles Shaar Murray dismissed "Hang Onto Yourself" as "a thinly disguised rewrite of the Velvet Underground's 'Sweet Jane,'" and the only consolation was that Bowie would not dispute that charge. The worst thing Murray's review imparted was that Bowie wasn't the only Velvet Underground fan in town.

"Moonage Daydream" flopped ignominiously. So did "Hang Onto Yourself" when it was released in its own right, backed by "Man in the Middle." And though Bowie himself still had high hopes for the projected third single, "Looking for a Friend," B&C's interest in the whole affair was waning. The existing records were deleted, and Arnold Corns's dry run of two songs that would form the bedrock of Bowie's future career were left to founder in obscurity.

Arnold Corns was never the next Rolling Stones, and Burretti was never on the cover of *Vogue*. But he did make the cover of the sexological *Curious* magazine, seductively fondling a snake, and the subsequent immortality enjoyed by at least two of his songs would at least hammer home one truth—from little A. Corns, big Ziggys grow.

Arnold Corns did not perish immediately. While Burretti returned to dress design, the remainder of the band hung fire for a little longer, teaming up with Mickey King to form the boy's eponymous All-Stars. But this project was doomed to even greater obscurity than its predecessor; and, besides, Tony Defries was demanding that Bowie return his attention to the main attraction—himself.

Just days after wrapping up the Arnold Corns sessions, Bowie, Angela, Defries, and Dana Gillespie made their way out to Glastonbury Fayre, the first of the year's summer festivals. Angela was booking the majority of her husband's live performances now, and Defries was none too pleased to discover that she'd tied him into an early-morning performance in a muddy field filled with hippies.

He wasn't even swayed when he discovered that the event was being both filmed and recorded for release. Indeed, that only added to his annoyance, as he reminded his charges on innumerable occasions. It is true, as so many past masters have mused, that there is no such thing as bad publicity. But the best publicity is that which the artist himself has total control over. Appearing in a movie that was not of Bowie's own design, or handing over a live tape when who knew what it sounded like, were not controllable. Yes, Bowie would perform—his contract demanded that much. But the sooner it was all over, the better.

It was only afterward that Defries realized that, for once, he'd got it wrong. Bowie's performance that chilly dawn was sensational. Alone with his acoustic guitar on the festival's pyramid stage, he brought the assembled masses slowly to wakefulness with one of the best sets he'd ever played. And when, as the sun rose, he swung into the chorus of "Memory of a Free Festival"—"the sun machine is coming down and we're gonna have a party"—even the cynic felt the hairs rise on the back of his neck. If Defries had ever entertained even the slightest doubts that Bowie was going to be a star—and occasionally, as the months ground wearingly on, he did—that moment dismissed them all.

He just needed the right environment in which to flourish, that was all. And that summer, they would discover where it lay. For one month at the London Roundhouse, the future was laid out for all to see in the form of *Pork. Andy Warhol's Pork.*

8

STRANGERS WERE ALL THAT WERE LEFT ALIVE

"We're going to America, the land of subways. The subways are rather like the Underground; you still get lots of people who wait for hours for the train. They all have that thing of going to the edge of the platform and looking down into a tunnel. I don't know what they expect to come out? Do they expect something other than a train to come out of it? You have to be a sadist or a masochist to take the subway in America, 'cos if you go on in a crowd, within five or ten minutes, somebody's got a good grip on you. 'Stay on three more stops and I'll give you fifty cents.' It's really quite grim and they've got a Miss Subway contest, see, and I think the only condition for entry is you have to look as though you've been hit by one, from some of the entries we saw when we was out there.

"Anyway, that's where we're going. America. Land of the living, land of the dead. Land of the dead, they've got lots of murders, as you've probably read about in the papers. That crime wave and it's kind of inbred in them to murder and kill . . . [T]hey come up with original ways of killing people; you read reports of old man battered to death, weapon believed to have been a Durex filled with ball bearings.

"That's not the only problem, you see, 'cos you've got the apartments problem as well, because you just can't get an apartment. I stayed in quite a nice one whilst I was there, all couples, no women. I took thirteen showers for excitement. One evening, somebody comes and says, 'I'm really sorry, I'm afraid I have some very bad news for you, your grandmother has died.' 'Oh that's awful, has her apartment gone yet? Did she die with central heating?'

"Anyway we're going there later."

—David Bowie, Aylesbury Friars, 1971

Andy Warhol's Pork, assistant director Leee Black Childers explained, grew out of "boxes and boxes and hours and hours of cassette tapes," comprising every single telephone conversation that Warhol and Brigid Polk had had in the past three years, and painstakingly transcribed by Warhol's long-suffering assistant Pat Hackett. "Basically, it was nothing more than a lot of pointless conversation. It was a comment on a society where nobody listens to anybody else. None of the conversations were linked, everybody just talked."

Anthony Ingrassia, the show's four-hundred-pound director, painted an even more disorganized impression. Warhol's initial vision for *Pork* comprised no fewer than twenty-nine separate acts that would have lasted around two hundred hours. Ingrassia edited this down into a fast-paced two-act play that shifted its attentions from a barely disguised Factory to a fairly recognizable Max's Kansas City and on to Brigid Polk's hotel room.

The lead character, Amanda Pork, was Polk herself in all but name. Other prominent characters included Billy Noname, a businesslike gentleman named Pall, a vicious blonde superstar called Vulva, two nude men with pastel-covered genitals named the Pepsodent Twins, and, practically immobile at the heart of the action, a pale, deadpan, laconic slice of living ennui named B. Marlowe.

And that was just about as conventional as it got.

Art dealer Ira Gale's presentation of *Pork* opened in London at the beginning of August 1971, following a single sold-out week, May 5-12, at the La MaMa Experimental Theatre Club at 74 East Fourth Street, a five-story building on New York's East Side. Distinctly and delightfully off-Broadway, the opening of *Pork* nevertheless drew the same glitterati that any other Warhol opening would attract, and much of the same confusion as well. Brigid Polk's mother, socialite Honey Berlin, was not among the audience but she did read a review in the *New York Times*, and a phone call to Warhol (which he recorded, of course) captured her response to seeing at least a few elements of her own life played out by the play's cast of apparent degenerates, weirdos, and drug addicts.

"You're nothing but a fucking faggot," she screamed into Warhol's ear. "You don't care about anyone but yourself! And your goddamn fucking fame! And your fucking Factory! And your fucking money."

Pork was notable for other reasons, however, including the fact that only one of its cast, Geri Miller, was a recognizable Warhol superstar, following her roles in the movies *Flesh*, *Heat*, and the just-released *Women in Revolt*. The remainder were an ensemble that Warhol discovered during a night out at another play, *World: The Birth of a Nation, the Castration of Man*, where they were brought together through the auspices of photographer Childers and an outrageous showman named Wayne County.

County was an Atlanta boy who'd arrived in New York City in 1968 with his best friend, Larry—they bonded, according to County, over Wayne's copy of the first Velvet Underground album. Both were gay, but there was nothing sexual going on between them. Neither would there be. Larry disappeared back to Georgia almost as soon as they arrived, and County moved into the YMCA on Thirty-fourth Street.

He took a job at a charity that put together packages to send to deserving blind people. There, according to Childers, "he used to put weird little things into the packets, little dolls and things. Then he'd sit around imagining what the blind people would make of them when they opened the package.

"We met in Greenwich Village, on Christopher Street. We were both cruising the same boy, this horrible hippie with long greasy hair. Of course, he thought he was the cat's pajamas and went waltzing off somewhere, leaving Wayne and I sitting on a stoop. So we just started talking."

A few days later, County turned up at Childers's tiny two-room apartment on Thirteenth Street. His room at the YMCA had been burgled, and he needed somewhere to stay for three days, until he got his next paycheck. The pair lived together for the next seven years.

Regular visits to the Sewer, a gay club on West Eighteenth, offered the couple their first introduction to a new world. The cast of Charles Ludlam's Ridiculous Theatrical Company was more or less based there, offstage at least, where they cavorted alongside a clutch of the city's finest drag queens. "The first time I ever saw Holly Woodlawns was at the Sewer," County recalled, "wearing a short dress and a long fall, before she became a Warhol superstar."

Jackie Curtis and Candy Darling, the doyen of Warhol's own coterie of drag queens (he fervently believed that "on a good day, you couldn't believe Candy was a man"), were equally striking. Childers met them first, scoring an invitation to Curtis's upcoming wedding, to another Factory regular, Eric Emerson. County, to his everlasting regret, decided not to attend; according to the photographs that Childers took that afternoon, he missed an absolute ball. "Eric never turned up, so Jackie married the maître d' instead. It got on the cover of the *Village Voice*, this huge wedding with all these freaks."

County and Childers naturally found their way into the world of underground theater. The first play they attended was the Ridiculous crew's *The Life of Lady Godiva*, with Jackie Curtis taking the title role so much to heart that County still admits, "I was never the same after seeing [that]. When I first came to New York, I was just a little hippie queen."

It was Curtis who showed him how to step out of that role, into the grander theater of outrage and extravagance, and Curtis who offered him his first ever stage role, too, as lesbian Georgia Harrison in Curtis's own *Femme Fatale*. County never looked back, particularly once Curtis moved into the Thirteenth Street apartment alongside Wayne and Childers—and then started moving his own friends in as well. "At one point," Childers sighed, "I had Jackie Curtis, Candy Darling, Holly Woodlawn, Rita Red, and Wayne all living there. All these drag queens and me!"

Unfortunately, it was not a happy family. They argued constantly, usually over money and whose turn it was to make sure the bills were paid. On one occasion, County recalled, it was Holly's turn. Her welfare check had just arrived; she was off to cash it, she said, and then she would pay the utilities. "So what does she do? She went off and bought a fucking feather boa. Came home and said, 'Oh darling, isn't it glamorous?' 'Yes, but our electricity's going to be cut off in two days.'"

County wrote his first play in and around such dramas. *World: The Birth of a Nation, the Castration of Man* was County and Childers's first production together. Tony Ingrassia directed; Childers was his assistant; County played Ethel, the fictional sister of Florence Nightingale; and there was one new addition to their coterie: Tony Zanetta, brought in because his college room-mate was one of Ingrassia's closest friends.

Zanetta explained, "I'd worked in a small repertory company that worked in schools, I worked in off-off-Broadway stuff, so when I saw that Ingrassia was holding an open audition, I turned up and he just said, 'Darling! You don't have to audition for my play, you can be in it!'"

In fact, Zanetta was handed two roles—Dr. Louise Pasteur and Jefferson Davis. Dr. Pasteur assisted in the birth of John Wayne's baby and ran around the stage screaming, "I don't know where I live, doctor," in a very high-pitched nasal whine ("Peter Lorre in nurse's drag," Zanetta clarified); Jefferson Davis was "a piss-elegant Southern fag who was castrated by somebody whose name I don't recall. His parts were then passed around the stage."

Ingrassia was holding auditions for some of the other roles when, according to Childers, all action stopped as "this very chic little girl walked in. Her hair had clearly been done at some Upper East Side salon, she had on these fabulous $250 lace-up boots, little designer clothes, and perfect makeup."

Childers was horrified. A brunette beauty out of Queens, a weekend DJ at Aux Puces uptown, the girl might have descended from another planet entirely. But she'd certainly landed on the wrong one. What was she doing here?

"Tony Ingrassia said, 'That's Kathy Dorritie, she's come to audition for the play.'" Childers laughed at the recollection. "Now, *World* was very weird. Very, very weird. Nearly all the lines were taken from rock 'n' roll songs, because Wayne was a real rock 'n' roll freak. There was lots of nudity, lots of simulated sex, a lot of really sick stuff. And there was this little prim thing sitting there—I was terrified! I said to Tony, 'Oh, she won't want to be in this play—just look at her!'"

The prim little thing smiled in response. "I was very shy—a little Irish Catholic strict thing—and this was my letting-go period. I had taken a lot of psychedelics, but I was [also] sophisticated because, from the time I was seventeen, I had been working on Madison Avenue in ad agencies. I wasn't as naïve as the rest of them. I was a little bit more careful. Nevertheless, I was going through the sexual revolution and wanting to be in the forefront of it, just letting it all go, not only sexually, but artistically, emotionally, intellectually, getting up and performing a song, a poem, a dance, or anything at the drop of a hat. Being an exhibitionist, as it were." *World* might have been weird, but it was also precisely what she was searching for.

Her outfit, too, deceived. Ms. Dorritie may have looked a million dollars, but she certainly never spent that much. For starters, "I always did my own hair. I was lucky to have thick, shiny, healthy hair my whole life." Likewise the boots that so bamboozled Childers. I didn't make enough money then to buy $250 boots, but I probably found a $250 pair in a thrift shop or a bargain bin for $20."

She learned makeup in a free three-Saturday charm school when she was very young, and as for the designer clothes, Dorritie had a part-time job at Bloomingdale's, Thursday nights and Saturdays, "and, in those days, they had junior clothes (I was size seven) that were very chic and not that expensive." Especially after she applied her employee discount.

The part that Dorritie was auditioning for was that of Tilli Tons, one of three nurses (the others were named Bertha Blimp and Paula Pounds) in the play, but by far the least conventional. County explained, "She had a little dead puppy dog, Spot, which she kept in a cardboard shoe box. Because she was a necrophiliac, she was always on morgue duty, and every time someone died in the play she would go and have sex with them. Then she'd take the puppy dog out of his box and have sex with him as well."

She had just two lines in the entire play, but license to repeat them as often as she liked, especially if one of the other cast had forgotten their own dialogue: "Where are you, Spot?" and, to a deceased grandparent, "I hear you, Grandfather."

"And Kathy was great!" County continued. She got the part, as it were, on the spot, while her enthusiastic approach to both on- and off-stage life quickly saw Ingrassia bestow upon her a new name. "He started calling me Party Favor because I had so much sex with two young boys in the cast."

County elaborates. "Every second there was something going on. The boys in the play all wore women's shoes, makeup, ribbons in their hair. Their pubes would be dyed. And people were dying, fucking, and killing. The police were raiding, people were cutting each others' dicks off and eating them. In the dressing room everybody would be fucking each other while they were putting their makeup on. It was really wild."

It was also an instant success. *World* . . . ran for seven months, breaking all underground theater records in the process. The Second Street New York Theater Ensemble was under permanent siege from the moment the box office opened, and Andy Warhol was a regular in the audience, jumping up and down in his seat as new depths of depravity opened up in every scene. "Warhol came to see that, and he flipped out," County recalled. "At one point I saw him standing up; he was screaming so much because some of the scenes were so over-the-top and outrageous."

Mere weeks later, he was inviting Ingrassia to oversee the production of *Pork*, and suggesting that the core of the *World*... cast be retained for the new show: County, Childers, and Zanetta were joined by Jaime Di Carlo, Geri Miller, Pati Parlamann, and more, although hopes that Ingrassia might recall Dorritie as well were dampened when it became clear that he was looking for star power for the play's title role, Amanda Pork.

"If Ingrassia had an Achilles heel," Zanetta revealed, "it was a desire to be accepted by the larger community. His genius was that he didn't take it very seriously; he could take that style of ridiculous theater and really make it work. He was great at forcing people to be who they were; he was good with personalities like Wayne and Kathy and the drag queens because he was a little Old Hollywood–ish, he was a star's director. But he had higher ambitions. He fancied himself a legitimate director."

He had already turned away two of the Factory's own suggestions for the role, the ogreish Pat Ast, who later starred in Warhol's *Heat* movie, and the then-unknown Stockard Channing, a graduate of the experimental Theatre Company of Boston. "Stockard would have been absolutely brilliant," Zanetta insists. "Pork was an East Side, Park Avenue, debutante, which is also what Stockard Channing was. But Ingrassia liked to work with people he could control."

When the open auditions turned up actress Cleve Roller, star of Rule Royce Johnson's *Recess* movie, Ingrassia had found his Amanda Pork, although Zanetta remains adamant that she was totally miscast. "But Ingrassia liked her because she was a legitimate actress with legitimate credits.... " Roller survived the New York week, but with London looming, Ingrassia took his cast's advice and recalled Kathy Dorritie—or Cherry Vanilla, as she was now calling herself.

The troupe arrived in London in June 1971, for six weeks of rehearsals and further auditions prior to the August 2 opening night—the actors' union Equity demanded that traveling productions hire local actors around their essential leads, and much of the next few weeks were devoured leading unsuspecting Englishman after unsuspecting Englishman through the catalog of depravities that constituted *Pork*. If an actor could not bear to lie naked on the bare stage with a transparent glass plate on his face while a costar took a dump on it, he was not going to get a part.

Off duty, the entire American contingent took up residence in a large flat at Langham Mansions in west London's Earls Court Square, a handy base for both rehearsals and for their chosen nocturnal haunt, the Hard Rock Café. Childers remembered, "We'd get totally blasted there. For some reason the owner liked to have us round. We used to stay there till we couldn't walk; then someone would bundle us into a taxi back to Pig Mansions" (as the *News of the World* newspaper had prosaically renamed their temporary home).

In the end, Childers simply collapsed. "I couldn't get up anymore. Then I caught clap and syphilis so I couldn't fuck, I couldn't drink. I used to just sit around and watch everything that was going on around me." Like the time Rod Stewart paid Pig Mansions a visit. He opened the door and was immediately confronted by the sight of a naked girl bending over and staring at him from between her thighs. Rod promptly turned around and left.

Pork was an instant smash, and an absolute scandal. Weeks earlier, Britain's ever-vigilant anti-obscenity squad had raided a cinema screening of Warhol's *Flesh*, and now here was Miller, one of that instantly notorious movie's stars, appearing in London in person.

Protesters, rallied by one or other of the country's watchdog fringes, descended nightly upon the Roundhouse, block-booking a row at the front of the auditorium and slow-clapping through any scene that dismayed them. Which, according to Cherry Vanilla, was most of them.

While Josie (Geri Miller) douched onstage, and Pork cavorted naked with the Pepsodent Twins, argued with her socialite mother (Suzanne Smith), masturbated with an egg whisk, and "shot something called vita-mega-vegimin" into her ass, Vulva (County) kept up a constant dialogue on the subject of shit—monkey's shit, pigeon shit, cat shit. And it was he who finally showed the protesters what *Pork* thought of them.

His pièce de résistance was a farting scene, brought on by a marathon meal of beans. Sure enough, the clapping began, "and when I farted they went crazy. I had a speech that went 'Why, it even smells better than chickenshit,' and I really spat the word *chickenshit* at them. The rest of the audience burst into applause."

Warhol was in town for the opening night, and, County continued, "One of the funniest memories of all was [that night]. We had a big party and everyone kept asking where Andy was; no one knew. I had to go to the bathroom, so I went to the bathroom and he was standing in there with his tape machine, waiting for people to come up and pee, and then running up and putting the microphone in front of their faces and asking them questions. He was just up to no good, but I thought it was very funny. I went back and said, 'Do you want to know where he is? He's in the men's room interviewing people.'"

The following morning brought the first newspaper commentaries. "We got reviews like you wouldn't believe," County laughed. "There'd be the really intelligent reviews about Andy's art and the sociopolitical side of it all, and we'd just say 'What is he going on about?' Then there'd be *The Sun* saying, 'Stop these perverts!'"

The Times described *Pork* as "a witless, invertebrate, mind-numbing farrago"; the *News of the World* complained that it made the London stage's last cultural nadir, *Oh! Calcutta!* look like a vicar's tea party. "Then there was someone who said, '*Pork* is nothing but a pigsty. *Pork* is nothing but nymphomaniacs, whores, and prostitutes running around naked onstage. The next night we were packed to the rafters!"

Tony Zanetta, as B. Marlowe, spent his time onstage in a wheelchair, being pushed to and fro by Pall (Di Carlo), either watching the action, talking on the telephone, or flicking through one or other of the magazines that accompanied him everywhere. Numbered among these was a copy of *Rolling Stone*, dated April 1, 1971, gathered up apparently because somebody thought there was a piece about the Factory therein.

There wasn't (it was the following issue that they were thinking of, with Joe Dallesandro and Paul Morrissey spread across eight fabulous pages). But another article caught everybody's attention regardless— that short, and now three-month-old interview with David Bowie, photographed glowingly in his "floral-patterned velvet midi-gown."

"It piqued our interest," Zanetta said simply. At the end of July, that piquancy came to life when Childers was reading through one of the music papers and discovered that Bowie was playing a show at the Country Club, in the northwest London suburb of Hampstead.

Childers recalled, "When we got to London, I was always looking out for David's name; 'Hey, let's go see a man who wears a dress onstage.'

One day, we saw he was playing at the Country Club, so Cherry, Wayne, and I went down there."

The trio took their seats and tried their best to be impressed. True, County spoke for all of them when he confessed he was outraged to discover that Bowie looked nothing like the Lauren Bacall he'd been led to expect, and was little more than "another fucking folkie with long stringy hair." But when Bowie introduced "Andy Warhol," Cherry leaped up and flashed a freckled breast and, backstage afterward, a fascinated friendship quickly developed.

Vanilla recalled these early days for the readership of the English teen magazine *Mirabelle*, in a weekly column called "My World," which she ghostwrote for David Bowie—it would be 1998 before Bowie publicly confessed that he'd handed the column over to the woman who was by then his publicist. "The cute thing," he laughed, "is that every now and then she'd write how I had just come from seeing this great new performer whom everyone should know about...Cherry Vanilla."

"I," Vanilla told her *Mirabelle* readers, "was playing at the Country Club just outside London. I had long blond hair then, a big felt hat with a feather and yellow patent leather 'Mary Janes.' Mick Ronson was with me and Rick Wakeman was playing the piano. Leee Childers and Cherry Vanilla walked in and the whole place just lit up. Cherry immediately introduced herself to Angela and me, and told us all about the column she was writing for a magazine entitled *Circus*, called 'Cherry Vanilla... with scoops for you.'

"After the show, we had a drink and chatted some more, whilst Cherry enticed us to come and see her show, due to open in a few days. She promised me a 'good mention' in her column, a few complimentary tickets to *Pork* and a night of dancing in a club after the show one evening. So then they left.... [T]hey had to get their sleep for an early rehearsal next morning."

They met up again a few nights later at the Roundhouse for a performance of *Pork*, and afterward, Childers, Vanilla, Bowie, Angela, Defries, and Ronson headed out for the promised late-night clubbing at the Sombrero, one of London's leading gay niteries. And it was there, because it simply couldn't have happened anyplace else, that David Bowie, Confused Folkie-Metal Drifter, was laid to rest, and David Bowie Superstar was born.

What Bowie saw in *Pork*, and what he took from it, was a mad sexuality that simply had no precedent in British society, and certainly not on the British stage. It was only three years since the country's theater had been freed from the hegemony of the Lord Chancellor's office, which had instituted a system under which every stage show intended for public consumption needed first to be submitted for inspection, vetting, and censorship. Since then, theater had been slowly becoming more liberated, but local attitudes toward sexuality and nudity remained locked in the gray straitjacket of post-Victorian formality and decorum, which were either politely echoed or else loudly rejected.

Pork did neither of these things. Hatched within an environment where none of those early neuroses existed, it approached sex (and drugs and, yes, rock 'n' roll) not as a reaction to past behavior but as a lifestyle in and of itself. It was not "liberated," because it did not believe it had anything to be liberated from. It simply existed.

Likewise, there were no raincoated old men on the *Pork* stage (although there were plenty in the audience, particularly after the *News of the World* got its teeth into the play); there were no repressed housewives or frustrated businessmen, or any of the other tried and trusted staples of British alternative theater. *Pork* was pure sex, pure exhilaration, pure magic. And that was what Bowie pounced upon.

Wayne County detailed the transformation. "We were all dressed up. You couldn't get Crazy Color in those days so Leee had done his hair with Magic Marker. And David was just fascinated with us. We were freaks. We were doing things in 1971 [that] he was still doing four years later, like painting our fingernails different colors. We all had blue and multicolored hair; we were wearing big blonde wigs and huge platform boots and purple stockings. And he was wearing those floppy hats and the long, stringy hair, and he took one look at us and you could see that this was what he wanted to do.

"Leee and Cherry looked at him and said, 'You can't keep on like you are. You've got to put on lots of makeup and freak yourself out a little.' And then Angela and Defries chimed in."

At last, everything was in place. Plans for Bowie to play a handful of shows on the continent in August, the Paradiso in Amsterdam, a festival in Belgium, and four nights in the south of France were canceled. The operation was going to target one market at a time, starting with the home crowd.

Defries had convinced Bowie not to call the band either Imagination or, worse still, Bowie's Imagination.

He had finally extracted Bowie from his Mercury contract and was now shopping around an album-length disc's worth of demos, one side Bowie songs, the other Dana Gillespie, although he had already decided that there were only two record companies worth speaking to, Columbia and RCA. Nor was he interested in dealing with the labels' London offices.

Rather, he intended approaching their U.S. headquarters in New York, the first step in a remarkable (and remarkably complicated) scheme to minimize taxable income while maximizing profits. It was a business deal that became boilerplate for any number of subsequent acts, but had rarely been engineered in the past, and never before on the behalf of a performer who was still basically unknown.

But Dennis Katz, head of RCA's A&R department, did his research, then sat back to listen to the acetate disc forwarded to him from Gem in London. Another of the label's A&R men, Bob Ringe, had already mentioned Bowie's name around the office and raved about the two Mercury LPs, but Katz admitted, "I took the vinyl for the weekend and thoroughly enjoyed the Bowie songs, but I wasn't really sold on him until I played it for my wife, Ann, who insisted that I sign him." As he told journalist Ken Sharp, "It was theatrical, musical, the songs were excellent, there was real poetry—it seemed to have everything."

Over at Columbia, Clive Davis, too, was fascinated by the singer, but he was also torn between Bowie and another act that was on offer that fall, Dr. Hook & the Medicine Show. With hindsight, it seems incredible that it was Bowie whom he let go.

"Why did we want to sign David?" asked A&R man Richard Robinson. "It's almost like asking me why I signed Lou [Reed]. It's just obvious. There are people that do it right and people that may do it right and you're not interested. It was a very strange time. There was a minor lull going on in the music business. These three people, Ray [Davies], Lou [Reed], and David [Bowie], all managed to step out in front of the curtain at that moment and be noticed. It just happened that RCA was a big record company that was trying to fill a void, and they wound up—and I don't think with any intent—with three people who actually helped them fill it and then it was over. We signed the Kinks, Lou [Reed], and David

Bowie all in a very short time, only about six months. We also signed Pure Prairie League, and they sold more records than all three of them combined."

The deal that RCA offered was generous, if not spectacular—it certainly had nothing in common with the rumors of $1 million-plus that floated around the industry grapevine, but those stories would serve their own purpose. Over the next two years, Bowie would be called upon to deliver three LPs, each eligible for a $37,500 advance. There was then an option for either one year and two albums (at $37,500 each), or two years and four albums (at $56,250 apiece), plus two greatest-hits collections. The royalty rate was 11 percent.

The formal signing of the deal was set for September 6, 1971. Mindful of economy, but intent, too, on scoring the maximum impact, Defries arranged for the party to fly to New York that same day. Taking into account the five-hour time difference, they would get to their hotel, the upmarket Warwick, with at least an hour to spare.

Defries, Bowie and Angela, Mick Ronson and Don Hunter, one of Defries's associates, checked into the suite that Defries had carefully booked for them, the same set of rooms that the Beatles occupied when they hit New York in 1965. They were still unpacking when Tony Zanetta arrived.

Throughout the *Pork* crew's time in London, it was Zanetta who had sparked the most immediate connection with the Bowies. "For whatever reason, he and Angie and I hit it off and they invited me out to Beckenham one Sunday afternoon." Zanetta was bewildered by the invitation to the small town perched on the very edge of southeast London, and far from any tourist guide's index. "I didn't know what Beckenham even was. But they sent a mini cab to collect me, and it was so cute—there was this little middle-aged woman driver in uniform, and she drove me to Beckenham.

"I spent the day with them, we had dinner, we talked about theater and music and New York and London, and they pretty much sucked me in. I thought they were fabulous. Then they came along to the closing night of *Pork*, and they said they'd be in New York in a week or two to sign the record deal. And sure enough, I'd only been back in New York for two weeks, they called me up, and I spent most of that week hanging out with them." He recalled David reintroducing him to Defries with the words "Here's the actor who played Warhol in *Pork*," and promptly being appointed the party's New York connection to Warhol himself.

Typically, the scheduled meeting at RCA was only one of several pieces of business that Defries intended concluding during his time in New York. Others included setting up agency representation for Bowie, in readiness for his first American tour, and the launch of Andy Warhol into the world of mainstream cinema. Which, he suggested, was where Zanetta could maybe help him. Zanetta did not bat an eyelid. No problem. Although he barely knew Warhol at the time, he picked up the phone, called the Factory, and fixed up a meeting for the following afternoon.

Then it was time to hustle, out of the hotel, into a cab, and across to the RCA building, where the A&R hierarchy of Dennis Katz, Richard Robinson, and Bob Ringe awaited them.

Bowie looked spectacular. His shoulder-length hair was cut Veronica Lake style, colored bright red, and topped with a black bolero hat with the balls hanging down. Eye shadow and mascara enhanced his natural beauty. A long black cape shrouded his body in mystery and elegance. But he said little during the brief meeting, just signing his name where he was asked to, and preferring simply to watch Defries winkle the company's marketing plans into the daylight.

Bowie was not going to be an easy sell for America, after all, and if RCA had ever had cause to doubt that in the past, the singer's appearance swiftly put them right. He wasn't wearing a dress, but he'd done so in the past, and Katz had the *Rolling Stone* clipping to prove it. How, Defries wanted to know, was an act that looked like that ever going to be sold to Middle America?

It was a fascinating conversation, and an illuminating one. Katz had ideas aplenty, and his colleagues were eager to chime in. Yes, there were a few people passing through the offices who looked askance at the company's latest acquisition and wrote him off as another of Katz's eccentric playthings. But the overall mood was more positive than anything Bowie had ever heard from a record label in his life. He was already feeling good when Katz dropped the bombshell that would make his day. They'd concluded all the business they needed to. How about if they met up later that evening for a celebration dinner at the Ginger Man restaurant on East Thirty-sixth Street? "I know how much you love Lou Reed," Katz told Bowie as they said their goodbyes. "I'll invite him as well."

Chalk and cheese, oil and water. Reed and Bowie were never going to become instant fast friends. Rather, they would circle one another, Bowie silently weighing up the tautly wrought, sarcastic New Yorker whom he'd idolized for almost five years, Reed sharp and sharklike, taking the measure of the new kid in town. Conversation ran in short, sharp bursts, Reed machine-gunning a question or a comment, Bowie batting the answer back with as few soft words as he could muster.

It was like a clumsy courtship, Reed the brusque butch suitor, Bowie the demure Southern belle, and when they parted at the end of the evening, Bowie almost simpered as he shook Reed's hand. The party was moving onto Max's Kansas City now, but Reed was not in the mood to tag along. So they said goodbye. "This has been such a thrill for me," Bowie said gently. "I do hope we see each other again."

There was just one ragged edge to the evening. Somewhere along the line, the name of Iggy Pop came up in conversation. "Don't talk to him," Reed warned. "He's a junkie," But Bowie wasn't listening. He'd never seen a ghost before.

Part

INSERTS

9

IF I HAVE TO DIE HERE, FIRST I'M GONNA MAKE SOME NOISE

New York, September 1971

Iggy Pop was watching Mr. Smith Goes to Washington *when the telephone rang. He considered just letting it ring, but the bell was ultimately more annoying than the interruption.* "Yeah?"

It was Danny Fields, owner of the telephone, the television, and the apartment itself.

"*He says, 'You remember that guy David Bowie?'*" *Pop grunted. The limey who'd listed him as his all-time favorite singer.* "Yeah. What about him?"

"'*Grab a cab down to Max's; he wants to meet you.' So I said okay . . .*" *and then went back to the movie.*

A few minutes passed. The phone rang again.

"Hey man, where are you?"

"I'm on my way." *And then back to the movie.*

A few minutes more. Another call, another promise. "I couldn't tear myself away from the movie, 'cos Jimmy Stewart was so sincere." *But the insistent ringing of those endless phone calls so disrupted the flow of the film that Pop had no choice but to throw on some clothes and call a cab. This Bowie character had better be good.*

Iggy did not know what to expect when he got to Max's, but he didn't particularly care, either. He was well aware that the music industry—or at least that corner of the industry that was aware of him—had long since written him off, but it was not a thought that kept him awake at night.

It was true that he was effectively without a band—the Stooges had shattered in disarray earlier in 1971, and he'd been not sung a word in anger since then. It was true, too, that he didn't have a record deal. Elektra still held his contract and had made occasional noises about a solo album. But nobody took them seriously. According to the company bean counters, the Stooges albums were $80,000 in the hole. An Iggy Pop record wasn't going to change that.

Iggy knew all of this, but he didn't care. "I didn't have a...sense of operatic doom! I felt different, different weeks. One week we'd be, 'I've done this horrible dope deal, I'm in a big mess, I'd better straighten it up.' Another week, we'd be, 'I've got this bank check, it's about to bounce, but nobody knows that, maybe I can...,' you know, and so on and so forth, and you're not really looking in a big picture. But always I was writing." Always, he believed, he remained a contender, and just a few minutes in the company of Bowie and Defries convinced him he was correct.

They hit it off immediately, Pop because he knew that these two Brits, these two "nutters...could be good for me right off"; Bowie because everything that he'd imagined he heard in the two Stooges albums was bound up for real in Pop's wiry frame and lightning-fast brain; and Defries, because Pop instinctively understood that the man knew how to get things done, and he played him accordingly. "I thought he was a character," Pop said. "I thought, 'People will go for this guy.'"

Pop that late night was at his most outrageously loquacious, and mesmerizingly magical. He was among friends, after all. Max's was a happy hunting ground for him, its nocturnal denizens a nonstop parade of color and crazies for him to flirt and toy with.

While his audience sat at their table, Pop danced around it, rapping out the life that filled in the gaps around the two albums that Bowie assured him he loved. Born in a trailer park, schooled in garage rock, hooked on smack, coming down on methadone. "Heroin was my main man," Pop celebrated. "But now I'm getting my shit together. I'm on my way to being clean."

The conversation turned to music. "When I first met David in New York, he was saying how great I was, how much he loved my singing, but I thought his work stunk and I told him so." Pop had checked out his admirer's output sometime after Bowie started dropping his name in the music press, and he wasn't impressed. Still, Bowie was exuberant. Pop had no band, no plans, nothing whatsoever to keep him in the U.S. Why didn't he come to London with David? And all the while Defries was nodding silent approval as Bowie rattled out his plans.

"We'll bring you to England," he chattered, "hook you up with a band...." He knew which band as well, Third World War, a hard-hitting blues-rock trio fronted by Terry Stamp's lethal guitar, held together by the rhythm section of Paul Olsen and Jim Avery. They'd had a story in the same February 1971 issue of *Rolling Stone* that carried a review of *The Man Who Sold the World*...a small world indeed. He hadn't asked them if they needed a new singer, because he didn't know them. But he knew Defries well enough to believe that all Tony had to do was snap his fingers, and whatever Bowie wished for would come true.

Pop was less trusting, but he was intrigued. He murmured assent. England sounded great, and they could talk about musicians later. For all his admiration for his newfound friends, Pop had the personal sense that he could twist them around his finger. He arranged to meet them the following morning at the Warwick Hotel, where Bowie and Defries were staying. "I'll come on by on the way to the methadone clinic," he promised, and devoured six full breakfasts while the "deal" was made. Defries would become Pop's manager, Bowie would be his producer. As for a record company, Defries would sort that out as well.

Pop's reputation did not faze Defries. To the contrary, it astonished him, excited him. He didn't see Pop as the agent of destruction that so many other industry heads imagined; and when cautious whispers reached his ears concerning the antics to which Pop was prone, Defries's only concern was that people were still talking about them, weeks, even months after they happened.

One night back in May 1971, the Stooges had played the Electric Circus in New York City. Slick with baby oil and showered in glitter, while his bandmates pumped out a repertoire of all new songs, Pop had been dancing across the stage when a voice rose out of the audience: "Hey Iggy!" He glanced down, recognized actress Geri Miller standing real close. "Let's see you puke," she cried. So he did. All over her.

Sometimes it felt as though every time somebody came over to their table at Max's, they brought with them their own tale of the trail of carnage Pop wrought—the peanut butter and the broken glass, the molten wax and the bleeding flesh, and Defries filed them all away. He was already aware that a picture is worth a thousand words—one of the first items on the agenda when they returned to London was to assign Bowie his own full-time photographer. Now he realized that a legend can sometimes be worth a thousand pictures; and, although it was difficult sometimes to look over at Pop, ragged and shambolic, all crooked, elfish features and Alfred E. Neuman ears, and see him through the eyes of the never-ending parade of horrified witnesses, that only added to the boy's appeal.

The only drawback he could see was Pop's infamous appetite for drugs, although Pop quickly reassured him on that point. He was undergoing methadone treatment and had almost made it through. A few more weeks and he'd be clean; which was great, Defries told him, because a few more weeks, and he'd have a new record deal.

Everything Defries had seen of Pop convinced him that he was in the presence of a genuine star. There were moments, in fact, when he foresaw an even brighter future for Pop than he did for Bowie. Pop was self-assured but, more than that, he was self-contained, a raconteur in true carnival barker style.

Bowie, for all his willingness to be molded, and the intelligence with which he adapted to that molding, had so many personal insecurities. Left to his own devices, he was far more likely to curl back up in the nest of his closest friends' admiration and never stir again than push himself to the forefront of everyone else's attention.

Pop, on the other hand, was ebullient, a mad puppy dog who could disarm the world with a smile and then keep it hanging on his every word, no matter what he talked about. Because he could talk about anything, off the top of his head, without even knowing what the subject was. Bowie followed conversations; Pop directed them. The question was, could he be trusted to stay off the dope? Pop swore that he could. He was heading back to Ann Arbor in a few days to complete the cure. As they parted, Defries promised again that he'd be in touch.

Bowie, Angela, and Defries continued their tour of New York's high spots, beginning with that much-anticipated visit to the Factory, and Bowie was in fits of nervousness as they made their way to the former Consolidated Edison substation on Thirty-third Street and Madison Avenue. Defries was less overwhelmed. To him, the meeting was as much about business as it was networking Bowie, and the party had no sooner been ushered into the great man's presence than Defries and Paul

Morrissey were discussing ways of maximizing Warhol's visibility outside of the underground movie scene.

Floppy-hatted and baggy-trousered, Bowie, meanwhile, was undergoing the tortures of the damned. He had so much he wanted to ask Warhol, or say to him, and he'd lost every single word. Even Angela seemed awed by the diminutive blonde man who stood surveying them without, apparently, even the slightest intention of breaking the silence. Instead he just looked David up and down, turned his attention to Angela for a few moments, and then looked back to David. And all the while, the silence grew more and more painful. The presence of Michael Netter, one of Warhol's assistants, documenting the meeting on a hand-held camera only added to the tension.

Bowie small-talked of his love of Syd Barrett and his shock at the cost of LP records in New York City. Warhol nodded in response. Bowie performed a little mime, expressing his admiration for Warhol by dragging his beating heart out of his chest. Warhol smiled wanly. Occasionally he would whisper something to one of his companions. But finally, he spoke.

"What pretty shoes."

Bowie was staggered. "It was my shoes that got him. That's where we found something to talk about. They were these little yellow things with a strap across them, like girls' shoes. He absolutely adored them."

"Thank you. I got them . . . " Mortified, Bowie found himself standing before the man he believed to be the most significant artist of the century, prattling on about how he'd bought a pair of shoes. And Warhol was just lapping it up. He produced a Polaroid camera and began photographing the shoes, while Bowie died another thousand deaths. He had to break the spell cast by his footwear.

"I've written a song about you . . . for you," he said softly. "It's called 'Andy Warhol.' Would you like to hear it?" In his hand he clutched an acetate of the song, pressed for this very opportunity and, without waiting for Warhol to reply, he cast around for a record player, only to discover that the agonies he'd suffered while they all stood in silence were nothing to the pains he felt as his ode to Andy spun on the turntable, and every eye in the room now lit onto his.

The track finished. There was silence. According to Tony Zanetta, "Warhol didn't know what to say, so he said nothing." In fact, Warhol was feeling hurt. He had forever been conscious of his looks, had battled eternally to keep Andrew Warhola, the shy, shortsighted, thin-haired albino from Pittsburgh as far from the public gaze as he could. Now here was this Englishman telling the world that Andy Warhol looks a scream. A scream?

Bowie looked on in horror. If the ground could have opened up and swallowed him, he'd have welcomed it. "He hated it. Loathed it. He went, 'Oh, uh-huh, okay...,' then just walked away. I was left there. Somebody came over and said, 'Gee, Andy hated it.'"

"Sorry, it was meant to be a compliment."

"Yeah, but you said things about him looking weird. Don't you know that Andy has such a thing about how he looks? He's got a skin disease and he really thinks that people kind of see that."

Mortification piled onto Bowie's embarrassment. "I was like, 'Oh, no.' It didn't go down very well."

Silence reigned again, punctuated only by the whispered conversation that Defries and Morrissey were now winding down. It was time to leave. Warhol's final words to Bowie as they departed were, "Goodbye. You have such nice shoes," and it was only once he returned to England and related the story to various friends that Bowie understood precisely what Warhol had been telling him.

Bowie's former mime teacher, Lindsay Kemp, speaks up. His mother, in her youth, attended a lot of theatrical performances, "and it used to worry her that [the actors] only ever had one pair of shoes. When she took me to the local rep, she'd point out that whether they were playing police inspectors or archbishops, they were wearing the same shoes as they had in the street.

"To this day," Kemp concluded, "she numbers my success by the pairs of shoes I have lined up under my bed."

Back in the U.K., Bowie and the band played what amounted to a show-case gig for their new label at the Aylesbury Friars on September 25. The album for which they'd been recording for so long was on the release schedule—RCA would be issuing *Hunky Dory* in December, and a single, "Changes," in the early new year. But such glories were far from view this particular evening. Bowie remained long-haired and floppy-hatted, initially taking the stage with Ronson alone and admitting to the crowd, "We didn't know what kind of songs to do tonight, so we just decided to endeavor to sing the kind of songs that we'll hope you'll enjoy. It's what we call entertainment—we want to entertain you. 'Entertain you.' It's an old word, we want to make you happy 'cos we want to be happy doing them."

Two Biff Rose songs, the old favorite "Buzz the Fuzz" and the recently adopted "Fill Your Heart," opened the evening; "Space Oddity" ("this is one of my own that we get over with as soon as possible") and "Amsterdam" followed. Finally the rest of the band took the stage, while Bowie chattered happily about their plans to return to the United States as soon as possible—there was talk of a tour taking place as early as the new year, and he could scarcely control his excitement.

They ran through the set, "The Supermen," "Oh You Pretty Things," "Changes," "Song for Bob Dylan," "Andy Warhol." The crowd, as they say, was going wild.

Bowie hushed them for a moment. "This next one is about a friend of mine in America called Lou Reed, who's the singer with a band out there called Velvet Underground who aren't that well known...." He paused while a roar from the audience drowned out his next words. "Yes they are, sorry, sorry. A very well-known band over here called the Velvet Underground...they don't know about them in Beckenham, I tell you. Anyway, Lou is very funny, outrageously funny, and this is a song for Lou."

They kicked into "Queen Bitch," a song Bowie originally wrote for what would have been the Ronno band's debut album earlier in the year, but which never attempted to disguise its inspiration. How could it? It sounded more like the Velvet Underground than the Velvet Underground themselves had, as if Bowie had sat down and isolated every last nuance of what made an old Lou Reed song tick, and then cemented them together in the most blatant manner he could, a tribute that bordered upon body-snatching. Even on vinyl, an accompanying sleeve note bore the simple notation "Some VU white light returned, with thanks."

Years later, in 1978, Bowie would insist, "There are very, very few parallels between me and Lou Reed. I think I've only ever written one song like his, and that was 'Queen Bitch,' and it was only recognized as a Lou Reed song—and I know this for a fact—because I wrote next to it 'For Lou.'"

But Reed was not fooled. "He played me *Hunky Dory*," he once reflected, "and I thought, 'Aha, how about that?' And I knew there was somebody else moving in the same areas I was. I especially loved 'Queen Bitch.' David's always been so up-front about these things."

Reed himself arrived in London in late December, with wife Bettye and the Robinsons in tow, to record his self-titled debut solo album at Morgan Studios. "We [wanted] a change of pace. We thought it would be interesting to get out of the New York thing." Plus, he admitted, "all the good-sounding records were coming out of England; it was amazing, the sound was more powerful, punchier, brighter. Who knows why?"

Reed had a new manager now. Dennis Katz's brother, Steve, was a guitarist with the jazz-rock band Blood, Sweat and Tears, and recommended that Lou link up with their manager, Fred Heller. It was an awkward match. Heller packed enthusiasm by the bucketload, but he was also, observed a few of Reed's friends, very square—a geometry made plain by his best-remembered public pronouncement following Reed's arrival on his books: "Lewis is going to be very big in the business."

Neither did he especially shine as he pieced together the clutch of top backing musicians that would contribute to the proceedings. All were stellar players...pianist Rick Wakeman, fresh from Bowie's *Hunky Dory* sessions; guitarists Caleb Quaye, from Elton John's band, and Steve Howe of Yes; Humble Pie's Clem Cattini. But they were also very straightforward, a far cry from the breed with whom Reed might have been expected to surround himself.

There again, so were the songs that Reed had selected to record. All the talk about who might produce the record, meanwhile, fizzled out when Reed finally decided that he and Richard Robinson would do the job themselves.

Installed in a hotel suite overlooking Hyde Park, Reed happily entertained fans, friends, and reporters. Publicly, the singer insisted that *Lou Reed* was "the closest realization to what I hear in my head that I've ever done. It's a real rock 'n' roll album. I don't think anybody who has been following my stuff is going to be surprised...[but] I think the general audience will find it more accessible."

But it was a laissez-faire operation all the same. The new songs that Reed had so proudly premiered to Richard and Lisa Robinson just nine months before remained, for the most part, untouched. In their stead,

Lou Reed revisited the last months of the Velvet Underground and the vast corpus of songs that band had recorded but never released; in years to come, as the Velvet Underground's archive was plundered and replundered for a host of well-meaning posthumous compilations, prototypical versions of so many of the songs emerged that Reed could have released much the same record without even leaving his New York apartment.

Recording and mixing were swift. Reed arrived in London on December 28, 1971, and on January 29, 1972, RCA staged a listening party at the Portobello Hotel, unveiling the finished album to the world's press, and astonishing even his old-time admirers. "The album is beautiful," New York journalist Lillian Roxon proclaimed. "You can dance to it and fall in love to it, and you will certainly want to buy it for someone you are crazy about."

Maybe you could. But nobody did. The record's sales, critical response, and even Reed's opinion of it would leave history to judge *Lou Reed* as a barely formed irrelevance, a stepping stone between the brittle beauty of the Velvet Underground and the never less than thought-provoking majesty of his subsequent solo career. That night at the Portobello Hotel, however, with the raucous fuzz of "I Can't Stand It" and "Wild Child" blaring out of the speakers, with "Lisa Says" and "Berlin" taking the mood down to introspective beauty, and "Ocean" crashing finales like a chamber orchestra, *Lou Reed* was an absolute triumph, and the only person missing from the party was Lou himself.

While the media lapped up *Lou Reed*, its maker was at the Bataclan in Paris, playing his first live concert since his last night with the Velvet Underground, and his first with John Cale and Nico in five years.

While Cale and Nico had remained close since their successive departures from the band, Reed was a comparative stranger to both now. According to Nico, he was only persuaded to appear at the concert (which was being filmed and broadcast by French television) at the next-to-last minute, after the show's producer grew "very overexcited" at the prospect of already having two former Velvet Undergrounders onstage together.

"I kept hearing that Lou was going to do it, then that he wasn't, and then John didn't want to do it with him so it would be Lou and I, or that Lou didn't want to do it with me so it would be John and Lou."

Every permutation seems to have been put forward before the three finally came together and launched into three days of rehearsals. "Then, when it was over, Lou wanted to do it all again, and it was John and I who said no." But Cale contributed stately piano to Reed's cigarette smoke–wreathed opener "Berlin" and a gentle "Waiting for the Man," then broke out his viola for "Heroin" and "Black Angel's Death Song." Their acoustic guitars meshed perfectly for Cale's "Ghost Story," a song from his now year-old debut album, *Vintage Violence.*

Nico swung sweetly through "Femme Fatale," and sonorously through "Abscheid" and "Frozen Warnings," the viola a chilling counterpoint to her droning harmonium. She brought out her now completed tribute to Brian Jones, "Janitor of Lunacy," then returned to the Velvet Underground for "I'll Be Your Mirror"; and then it was into the closing salvo, as Cale unveiled a couple of new songs, "Empty Bottles" (which he later gave to singer Jennifer Warnes) and "The Biggest, Loudest, Hairiest Group of All," the salutary tale of the incredible rise and precipitous fall of the greatest rock band ever.

It was not even vaguely autobiographical, he insisted, but you did get the feeling that he wished it was.... "Just a week ago we were in Texas, tomorrow night we play the Albert Hall, sorry there's no time to talk to you right now."

10

YOU'RE STILL DOING THINGS
I GAVE UP YEARS AGO

"The success was very overnight. It was like waking up one morning and finding that we were superstars, with no preparation for it at all. And suddenly we could have anything we wanted. If you needed a car, you could hire one, if you needed a guitar, go get one. I always remember the dinners...."

Growing up in a working-class family in a working-class city, going out for a dinner was a rare treat. Mick Ronson remembered "saving up for a month or something, and going out to Bernie's Steak House for a 7/6d steak, and that only happened once every three months. You didn't have a drink with it, just the steak. That, to me, was dinner." Now the band dined out every night ... sometimes twice a night ... they could have as many drinks (or steaks) as they liked, and the bill certainly came to a lot more than 7/6d. "Huge giant shrimps and spareribs! I couldn't believe it!"
—Mick Ronson, in conversation with the author, 1986

Among the handful of newspaper articles that surrounded the release of *The Man Who Sold the World*, the greatest attention by far was paid to Bowie appearing on the LP cover resplendent in a dress. Now, with *Hunky Dory* on the streets, the burning question was, what had happened to it? Or so *Melody Maker* journalist Michael Watts assumed. Why, he asked, was Bowie not wearing a woman's dress for the interview?

"Oh dear," Bowie sighed. "You must understand that it's not a woman's—it's a man's dress."

So why wasn't he wearing a man's dress? Because he didn't feel like it. If the interview had taken place on another day, maybe he would have. He'd been wearing them for two years, after all, and he saw no reason to stop now; especially with society finally waking up to the fact that not everybody's sexuality could be neatly filed away in the traditional man-and-wife-shaped boxes. There were homosexuals in the world, Bowie smiled, and people were finally recognizing that fact. Bisexuals as well. And did he consider himself to be one of them? Yes, he did. It was only afterward, as Bowie sat awaiting that particular interview's publication in the paper's January 15, 1972, edition, that he became aware that "all fucking hell is going to be let loose in a lot of areas."

"I first realized I was gay when I was about twelve," he told the adult magazine *Club International*. "Of course I was much more secretive about it then. I was always a pretty lonely sort of guy. It took me till I was about eighteen to sort me head out enough about it. [But] I'm not totally gay, I'm just a bisexual. Whether that means I'm a boy who comes over very gay, or what, I really don't know. I get very lost in that."

So did the commentators who rushed to either praise or, the deeper you moved into "straight" society, condemn his words. With a wife and a newborn child, Zowie, at home, Bowie scarcely conformed to any of the stereotypes that his "confession" would normally spark. Although homosexuality was illegal in the United Kingdom until as recently as 1967, and even now was merely "decriminalized," as opposed to being wholly legal, few people were in any doubt as to how the typical homosexual might disport himself. The mannerisms and speech were a favorite subject among comedians of all persuasions, and the grapevine hissed insistently about the predilections of this or that public figure.

But Bowie wasn't gay, and he wasn't even bisexual. He talked a good game, that's all, and he has been insisting that much ever since. Bisexuality was simply one more calculated step in his drive for fame—and we know this because if it wasn't, if he really had been enjoying affairs with a string of male lovers, one of them would have sold his story to the press by now.

"Truthfully, I never believed David was gay or bisexual in those years," *Pork* star Cherry Vanilla admitted. "I always thought of English boys as fooling around with each other in school years and such, but I didn't think that made them bisexual, just curious. Even after Angela said she found Bowie and Mick Jagger in bed together, I thought, 'So it was drug time and they could have passed out together.' Did she actually ever see them going at it together?"

At the same time, however, friends, associates, and musicians dating back years before the *Melody Maker* story hit the newsstands acknowledge not only that they had their own opinions on the subject, but that Bowie never made any secret of his fascinations, either. For them, the fear was not that Bowie was indeed bisexual, but that somebody else might take the story to the papers and expose him.

That fear remained, and only grew more pronounced as Bowie's name began to pick up currency in the wake of *Hunky Dory*. Saleswise, the record was scarcely any more successful than its predecessors. But the reviews were good, and the album's first single, "Changes," was even elected "Record of the Week" by BBC radio disc jockey Tony Blackburn, host of the corporation's weekday morning show. People were beginning to pay attention to David Bowie. The need now was to make sure that they paid the right sort of attention, and the possibility that somebody might try to "out" the rising star grew more pronounced every day.

With and without entourage, Bowie was a frequent visitor to both the Sombrero, London's premier gay club at that time, and the handful of other well-known hangouts that peppered the city's West End. His associations with mime artist Lindsay Kemp and fashion designer Freddi Burretti were common knowledge; his penchant for unusual clothing was, of course, already out in the open. As far back as 1969, he had been interviewed by *Jeremy* magazine, at that time Britain's leading gay publication; while the intelligent reader could take songs as far apart as "The Width of a Circle" and "Queen Bitch" and read into their lyrics a subtext that at least confessed to certain sexual conflicts.

With all that in mind, and the pile seemingly growing all the time, Defries and Bowie were in full agreement. They knew it wouldn't be very long before somebody blew the whistle. So they decided to make their own announcement, and get the shock value for themselves. It was one of the central tenets of Defries' entire operation. By keeping control of the announcement, they kept control of how it could be promoted, and it would remain the only reference people would have until they chose to say anything else on the subject.

"We all took the stand that he was bisexual," Vanilla continued, "because we thought it was something that added to his mystique at the time. Personally, I thought he was straight, but the confusion about the issue kept it going and kept it interesting."

In later years, Bowie would be adamant that "it...wasn't a premeditated thing. I've never understood why I said that." But he did, and, of all the masterstrokes that he and Defries were to foist onto the British public during the first half of 1972—that is, through the months preceding Bowie's now-seemingly imminent commercial breakthrough—the issue of his sexuality was the greatest.

Without it, he would have been just another rock star with a penchant for dressing up, a role that Marc Bolan, Slade, the Sweet, Alice Cooper, and so many more had already grabbed for themselves. But that was all they did. They dressed up and nobody believed Alice wore mascara and a boa constrictor when he went out on the golf links. Bowie had an image, for sure. But he also professed a lifestyle that could not be hung up and left in the metaphorical closet when he was off duty. As Lou Reed so caustically put it, "You just can't fake being gay. You're going to have to suck cock or get fucked."

"I am a photostat machine," Bowie paraphrased Christopher Isherwood's "I am a camera." "I haven't got a new concept; I simply juggle with everybody else's. What I'm saying has been said a million times before." He described himself as a reflective surface. If he was degenerate, then the world around him must be degenerate too. Conversely, if he was wonderful, then the world must be pretty damn good as well. To praise Bowie was to praise yourself, to knock him was to knock yourself. It was, quite simply, brilliant.

Behind the scenes, Defries plotted on. It was time to up the ante a little further, by putting into motion the plan that he and Bowie had developed the previous year around Arnold Corns. With Bowie, of course, the figurehead of the empire, Defries intended to surround himself with musical and artistic talent, each new star working with, and separate from, the main man. It was to be a vast musical cooperative, an updating of the Beatles' Apple Corps pipe dream. The difference was, this time the dream would come true. As Allen Klein's London eyes, Defries had seen for himself where Apple went rotten. He would not make the same mistakes.

The first step was to break away from Lawrence Myers and Gem. The two men frequently disagreed over the Gem office's function. Myers saw it as a place of work, Defries regarded it as a venue where artists could hang out together. Those disagreements were now coming even more regularly.

"The thing which brought about the split," recalled Myers, "was the decision that Bowie had a better chance of making it if he moved to America. Tony was prepared to set up there with him, and that's where we broke up. He set up MainMan and we went our separate ways quite amicably."

Taking its name from a phrase that Iggy Pop had used during their breakfast together in New York, when Pop suggested that Defries replace heroin as his "main man," (and which Marc Bolan had already hung two songs on: "Telegram Sam" and "Main Man"), MainMan offices were promptly opened at Defries's home in Gunter Grove, Chelsea, a leafy side street off the Kings Road, and soon to become a magnet for an army of teenage fans. Daily, for the next three years, the street would bubble with juvenile fantasies; across town, in the even leafier suburbs of Beckenham, Haddon Hall was under almost permanent siege as fans congregated in the garden outside, desperate for a glimpse not only of Bowie, but of Angela and baby Zowie as well.

It was a massive intrusion upon both the Bowies' and their neighbors' privacy, but Defries remained adamant that they accept it. Defries's girlfriend, a stunning American beauty named Melanie MacDonald, happily drifted in and out of the offices to say hello to the fans and distribute cups of tea. When Angela was in town, she, too, would chip in, even though she'd probably spent half the day doing the same thing back at Haddon Hall.

At precisely the same time as the nation's music press grumbled into its typewriters that access to the rising star was growing harder and harder to obtain, the fans faced no such prohibitions—and besides, if anybody did overstep the unspoken bounds of propriety, Bowie's bodyguards were seldom far from view.

And what a stroke of genius that was. Elvis Presley had bodyguards, Frank Sinatra had bodyguards, the president of the United States of America had bodyguards. But David Bowie? What did he need them for?

To make people ask that question, that's what. Officially, and particularly in the United States, Defries let it be known that Bowie's sexual stance was so extreme, and his fame so enormous, that the bodyguards were required simply to allow him to go about his life without interruption. But the reality was far more prosaic. At the time the two minders were first engaged, there were precious few people who would even recognize Bowie on the street, let alone pursue him fanatically down the road. It was publicity, and it paid off the day *Rolling Stone* flagged the question so prominently at the front of the magazine. "Why does this person need two bodyguards?" Because Tony Defries hired them.

An incredible amount of money was being spent, long before Bowie began earning any, and most of it was being lavished on Bowie himself. He and the Spiders had been touring solidly since the end of January 1972, hitting colleges and clubs for the most part, but branching into bigger venues, town halls and civic centers, as word got around about the sensational live show. Yet though their earnings were rising, the tour was certainly not bringing in a fortune.

An average £100 to £150 per night when the band set out had risen to £250 per night by the end of February, and £300 to £400 by April—the vast majority of it paid out in cash. Gigging alone earned the band close to £5,000 during the first six months of the year. But still much more was being poured back into the show, going for everything from new guitar strings and cymbals to a growing wardrobe of clothing and accessories.

The £300-per-month contract that Bowie so gratefully signed with MainMan on March 31, 1972, has since been dismissed by many observers as a wholly disproportionate 50-50 split of all profits between Bowie and his management company. But how many artists can ever say they earn 50 percent of their profits while maintaining unprecedented control not only over their music but how that music is marketed?

Such figures were unimaginable properties in a music industry that had hitherto been controlled by record companies and agents, who considered an artist fortunate (if not downright greedy) if he could lay his hands on even 10 percent of his proceeds. Likewise, Defries's understanding of the prevailing international tax laws and investment havens ensured that those bills were substantially less than they might have been, while Bowie's overall income was further boosted, not (as so many other chroniclers have implied) reduced, by the fact that his earnings were based on net income, not gross, with MainMan effectively paying half of his expenses before the profits were ever divided.

Anything at all that could be deemed a career-related expense was covered, from clothing to transport to food, and if there was any wastage involved, a lot of it was by Bowie's own volition, for he, too, understood just how important it was to make a loud impression upon all who looked at him—and money talks loudest of all.

But the rewards were already being felt. Interest was rising. In March, filmmaker Adrian Hughes approached Bowie to appear in and score a

Nico with the Velvet Underground. "If there exists beauty so universal as to be unquestionable, Nico possesses it," said Gerard Malanga. (Adam Ritchie/ Redferns)

Warhol and Edie Sedgwick, Lou Reed's original "Femme Fatale." (Maron Films/Photofest)

Cherry Vanilla and the *Pork* crew at the Roundhouse in London, 1971. (Amnon Bar-Tur)

A made-up Lou Reed and Sterling Morrison backstage at the Café Bizarre, December 1965. (Photofest)

The Stooges in the fields behind the Fun House in 1969. (Robert Matheu Collection)

The Spiders from Mars, 1972. *Left to right*: Trevor Bolder, Woody Woodmansey, David Bowie, and Mick Ronson. (Photofest)

Bill Wyman, Elton John, and Iggy getting cozy. (Michael Ochs Archives/Getty Images)

Open up and bleed. (Michael Ochs Archives/Getty Images)

That night in Oxford in spring 1972, Bowie simply told photographer Mick Rock
to be on the lookout for something special occurring on stage. Rock turned it into
one of Glam's most iconic images. (Photo copyright Mick Rock 1972, 2009)

Right: Iggy shaking up the hippies at the grand ballroom, 1970. (Robert Matheu)

Below: "I Wanna Be Your Dog," 1969. (Robert Matheu)

Bowie strips for action. (Photofest)

Lou Reed, a "bubblegum Kenneth Anger," according to Lester Bangs. (Photofest)

semifictional documentary about writer Jan Cremer, as he sought out fresh material for a new novel in London. He was turned away, just as so many others were. Bowie was hot, and his next single, "Starman," was still weeks away from release.

Not everything went according to plan. In February, a dispute with the William Morris Agency, which had only taken over Bowie's concert arrangements in December, threatened to derail the tour before it started, while the return to New York that Bowie talked about from the Aylesbury stage, a high-profile one-nighter at Carnegie Hall on February 25, was abandoned when it proved impossible to set up so quickly.

That same month, a show in Glasgow was canceled at the last minute, when the venue manager realized the nature of the evening's entertainment—he hated rock 'n' roll and was not going to permit it to besmirch his hall. What he missed, and what a near-sold-out audience of disappointed ticket holders missed, was a wild performance, a blur of movement and activity, shot through with some seemingly wholly unscripted, but nevertheless indelible moments—Ronson passing his gold Les Paul out into the crowd so that the kids could add their own noise to the feedback-drenched solos that punctuated "Moonage Daydream"; Bowie himself jumping into the crowd on at least one occasion, at Kingston Polytechnic in May, to join Angela as she whooped and screamed through "Suffragette City." Kingston Poly was her old alma mater; this was an important show for her.

By the beginning of May, with Bowie's third album in fifteen months, *The Rise and Fall of Ziggy Stardust and the Spiders from Mars*, now imminent, it was clear that the momentum was approaching fever pitch. By the end of June, crowds of hundreds—and on one occasion, over a thousand— were routinely being turned away from the sold-out shows. "Starman" was on the charts now, and the moment on *Top of the Pops* where Bowie draped one arm around Mick Ronson's shoulders was already enshrined in adolescent folklore—men did not embrace on television in those days, and they certainly didn't embrace on a family show.

A gesture that would not even be noticed today not only polarized the country, it jumpstarted teenage hormones the length and breadth of the land. *Pork* for the underage crowd, "Starman" and all the speculation and suspicions that bubbled around its maker took hold of the joy of sex, the love of sex and, most of all, the *need* for sex, all the things that generation after generation of British teens had struggled to even comprehend, let alone examine, and dropped them firmly on the kitchen table for all to see.

"Starman" was Top 10 bound, and suddenly the two-year tease that Marc Bolan had been dancing was breaking out everywhere. No sooner had his "Metal Guru" left the top of the U.K. chart than Slade's "Take Me Bak 'Ome" was there to replace it. The Sweet's "Little Willie" was chasing its tail, a stomping little bubble-bopper whose appeal in no way ended with the childish innuendo of its title. Gary Glitter, an unfashionably portly, but nevertheless captivating, vision in spangles and platforms, was chanting the joys of "Rock and Roll," and Alice Cooper was slashing his own tart brand of glam-drenched horror across the playgrounds of the nation. Glam rock was a fact of life, and all it needed now was a cock of the walk. Bowie intended to be that cock.

The tour ended with a Save the Whales benefit at the Royal Festival Hall in London. It sold out within hours of tickets going on sale and, once it was over, *Melody Maker* would splash Bowie across its cover beneath the headline "A Star Is Born." But really, that was apparent long before the doors even opened for the show.

Mott the Hoople, a Hertfordshire band that had been kicking around the U.K. circuit since the end of the 1960s without ever elevating themselves above the status of a well-heeled cult, were originally booked to open the gig. At their best, they were capable of selling out the Royal Albert Hall, and turning in such a riotous performance that the venue actually banned rock 'n' roll from its doors in the aftermath. But four albums had done little, and in March 1972, with the group on its final legs, the quintet announced their intention to break up once their last run of scheduled gigs was complete.

It was Bowie who pulled them back from the brink.

Many bands caught Bowie's eye. Appearing on television's *Lift Off with Ayshea* to perform "Starman," Bowie espied a young band named Hello, preparing to make their debut TV appearance. Smiling, he sat down and talked them through their first-night nerves. Or dropping by the RCA offices, he found himself regularly bumping into labelmates Jook, a raucous pop act whose drummer, Chris Townson, was in John's

Children with Marc Bolan. "Bowie was a chum to Jook," bassist Ian Hampton recalled. "We met often—although perhaps we were more chums to him."

Mott, however, intrigued him far beyond mere friendship and advice.

On the surface, Mott had very little in common with Bowie; a hard-rocking rabble with an avowedly working-class following, they were bricklayers to Bowie's Christmas fairy. But in 1971, enamored by the dense metallics of Mott's second album, *Mad Shadows*, Bowie sent them a demo of his newly written "Suffragette City" and suggested they record it. Mott declined. Bassist Overend Watts explained, "We played it and thought, 'Dunno, really.' It was a good song, but we didn't know if it was right for us."

Now it seemed as though nothing was right for them. Their last album, *Brain Capers*, by their own admission was the sound of a band tearing itself apart, and, sitting around his apartment wondering what to do now that the last rites had been read, Watts picked up the tape that Bowie had sent him and dialed the phone number. He wondered if Bowie knew of any bands that were in need of a bass player.

"We got talking for an hour, an hour and a half, and I was telling him about the group," Watts recalled. "He said, 'Look, I've got a song I've half written; let me ring you back in an hour or two, I have to speak to my manager.' He rang back and asked if I'd like to go and listen to the song. I said I didn't know how the rest of the group would feel, but I'd come over. He came and picked me up in a beaten-up old Jag; we went round to his manager's place and he played part of 'All the Young Dudes' on acoustic guitar. You could tell it was a great song. He'd got all the chorus written, but he hadn't got some of the verse words."

At dinner, Watts had the distinct impression that Tony Defries was simply along for the ride. "But then he started talking. He was saying things like, 'What are we going to do with my new group?' and 'We'll get you off Island [the band's current label] for a start.'

"I got home and phoned the rest of the band. They thought it was amazing. We still had some gigs to fulfill, so David came to see us at Guildford, met everyone, fixed up a recording date." On May 14, while Defries was still extracting the band from their current deal, Bowie and Mott went into Olympic Studios to record "All the Young Dudes." It was, Watts understated, "a whole new lease on life."

Defries went into his meeting with Island supremo Chris Blackwell intending to appeal to the man's sense of fair play and kindness. It was obvious that Island had little idea of what to do with Mott; no matter how much support the company appeared to offer, the group remained fish out of water in Island's arms.

"Let them go," Defries reasoned. "Let me take them somewhere else, give them the hits they deserve, and the chance they deserve." Island could keep the group's publishing and back catalog; Mott would be given their freedom. Unspoken, but present in the room regardless, was the threat that, without a deal, Bowie and Defries would walk out of the group's life as precipitously as they'd entered it; that Bowie would release "All the Young Dudes" as his own next single, and Mott could just get on with disintegrating. Blackwell agreed and, seemingly days later, Defries was able to call the band together to inform them that they were now CBS recording artists. Contracts were exchanged on June 1.

Lining Mott the Hoople up for the Royal Festival Hall show made sense when the posters were printed. But the closer the show loomed, the less certain Mott were. Their own headlining tour was scheduled to kick off less than two weeks later, and they would be indebted enough to Bowie once the single came out and, assuming all the prophecies were correct, became one of the biggest hits of the year. He was producing their next album as well. Opening his concerts was simply one subservient step too far, especially as the bulk of the audience wouldn't even be paying any attention to them. There would be scarcely a soul in the venue who wasn't waiting for Bowie and Bowie alone.

So Mott pulled out and they were right to do so. They were not missed. Sets by the JSD Band and Marmalade passed off with little more than a polite ripple from the impatient audience. Not until the air filled with the opening strains of Beethoven's "Ode to Joy," the Spiders' intro tape since the beginning of the year, did the crowd finally turn its undivided attention to the stage.

Musically, the Spiders' set had solidified long ago, a mix of *Ziggy* newies, *Hunky* oldies, a clutch of covers ("Amsterdam" and Cream's "I Feel Free," thrown into the mix at Ronson's insistence). Visually, however, it was still developing—costume changes were the exception, not the rule they would later become, and if Bowie was beginning to reintroduce his sixties love of mime into his presentation, he was also searching for new tricks as well. There would be the night in Oxford, for example, where he mimed fellatio on Mick Ronson's guitar for the very first time, while photographer Mick Rock fired away with his camera, having already been primed to expect to see something different that evening. Rock processed the photos that same night; the following day, Defries shipped the best of the batch to the *Melody Maker* offices as the heart of a full-page advertisement, set to run in the very next issue.

For audiences who had never seen Bowie before, the move never failed to shock and surprise; for kids who'd never seen such an act before, it added further fission to the sheer sexuality that Bowie represented, the sense of liberation and freedom that made every past self-appointed spokesman for juvenile libido sound pale and anemic. By the time Bowie and Ronson severed their partnership the following fall, the blow job was getting as much applause as many of the songs.

Not tonight, though. If Mott the Hoople were unwilling to step into Bowie's limelight, for fear of what it might do to their subsequent reputation, Lou Reed had few such qualms. It was a closely guarded secret, even within Bowie's own entourage, that the New Yorker would be making his U.K. concert debut at the Royal Festival Hall, stepping onstage toward the end of Bowie's set, in the aftermath of a devastating "Moonage Daydream," black clad to counter Bowie's bright white, and in absolutely no doubt as to whose stage he was stepping out upon. It was his own.

Bowie knew it as well. Meeting Mott the Hoople for the first time, in Guildford in May, he'd apparently been trembling with nerves when he first shook hands. Meeting Warhol back in September, he'd been shy and embarrassed into small talk. He was beyond those emotions with Reed. They had been friends for nine months, and were soon to become collaborators as well. But still, there was something more than simple pride in Bowie's voice as he stepped up to the microphone and made his introductions.

While Ronson retuned, Bowie mumbled, an indistinct handful of words that clarified only when he mentioned "an American band called the Velvet Underground"—cue a roar from the crowd, and the expectation among those in the know that it was time for "Waiting for the Man." But Bowie wasn't finished yet.

Back during Lou Reed's last visit to London, in December, he and Bowie had spent a lot of time together, easing past the caution that haunted their first meeting, and planting the seeds of genuine friendship—of a working partnership, too. Even after Reed returned to New York, Defries was moving to put into place the agreement that would see Bowie produce Lou's next record—and, Defries fervently hoped, might also add Reed to his managerial roster.

In later years, it was suggested that the main reason Reed agreed to let Bowie produce him was because RCA insisted upon it, even threatened to drop Lou unless the marriage went ahead. And it is true that a few mutual friends around the office—Robinson, Katz, Ringe—did believe the partnership might work. But they didn't know whether Bowie was even capable of the job—he'd never produced a record before; and though Bowie certainly had a lot of self-confidence, he didn't know the answer, either. For him, working with Reed was simply the opportunity to get close to one of his idols; and for Reed, it was a chance to grab back some of the attention that Bowie was now getting—grab *back*, because Reed had no doubt whatsoever where a lot of Bowie's ideas originated. They were friends, of course, but Reed had lots of friends. This was a business decision.

Bowie positively glowed as he stepped up to the microphone. "The man who wrote this number is still playing, and this is his very, very first appearance on any stage. . . . Ladies and gentlemen, Lou Reed!"

In fact, it wasn't his first—two months before, Reed had played a single show at the Millard Fillmore Room at the University of Buffalo. But it was scarcely noticed and barely remembered, just a nervous-looking Lou with a bored-sounding band, plodding through a clutch of songs and never so happy as when they went home afterward. Tonight, however, was the real thing. This was where Lou Reed's life resumed. And while the entire hall exploded, out he swaggered, in an outfit that Angela Bowie had pushed upon him, rhinestones and leather and a deathly white–powdered face.

The entire venue was on its feet, handclapping along with the building rhythm—"White Light" exploded around Reed's bellowed count-in, Bowie condemned to backing vocalist at his own coming-out party, Ronson scything the riff around Reed's insistent rhythm guitar before looping into a solo that seemed as integral a part of the song as any of Lou's lyrics. It was a spellbinding performance, and it had only just begun.

"Waiting for the Man" was next, building gently out of another barely audible Bowie intro, pacing itself around the riff that Ronson had perfected so many gigs before, but crackling with excitement regardless as Reed raised his voice and upped the tempo, spitting out the familiar lines and then glancing over to where Defries stood by the stage.... "I'm waiting for my man, my Main Man!"

"Sweet Jane" closed the spot, and Reed was in his element now. Bowie and the Spiders had never played the song together before, had scarcely rehearsed it beyond its rudiments prior to the show. Lou took over completely, relegating his hosts to the role of mere accompanists, even after Ronson picked up the riff alongside him. Reed had to leave the stage after that, because who knows whose gig it might have turned into? As it was, Bowie's own set finished one encore later, with an urgent thrash through "Suffragette City," and Reed's parting thank-yous still ringing in the ears. Yes, a star was born that night. But another one was reborn.

11

THINGS SEEM GOOD, SOMEONE CARES ABOUT YOU

"Tony Defries received, for my services, $100,000 from CBS Records, payable to MainMan as a production company. I had an employee contract, so I had no right to touch a penny of it, and that was huge money in 1972. Defries would play each of us off against the other. Bowie would ask him, 'Well, where's my money?' and Defries would say, 'Well, Iggy needed some dental work'. And Bowie gets flipped out. Meanwhile I'd be wondering, 'Where's my money?' and I'd see five or six employees at the MainMan office and I'd think, 'There's my money.' Things were at an impasse."

—Iggy Pop

Defries did not let Iggy Pop down. Returning to New York in October 1971, he hauled the singer back from Ann Arbor for a fresh round of meetings, installed him in a suite at the Warwick Hotel, and called up Tony Zanetta to take him shopping and generally act as a babysitter. Passing the North Beach Leather chain store a day or two before, Defries spotted a pair of magnificent silver-colored leather trousers. They could have been made for Pop. He handed Zanetta five hundred dollars. Go and get them. "The way Defries acted," Zanetta said, "we thought he had millions and millions of dollars. We spent the five hundred dollars—that was a lot of money to both of us. But we didn't know each other so well, so we were both pretending that it wasn't."

Defries already knew which label he wanted Pop to be signed to; but first, of course, he had to extricate him from his old deal. He made an appointment to meet with Elektra's Jac Holzman, and hit him with the simplest pitch imaginable, the same pitch he would use with Chris Blackwell. What is best for the performer? Not for "Iggy Pop," the madman; not for "Jimmy Osterberg," the boy behind the mask. For the performer himself.

He formalized his client's given name almost beyond recognition. "James," he told Holzman slowly, "James is not doing well. He's gone back to drugs, he's not writing, he needs a change. And if I can take him on, I can give him the change. I can get him back to writing, get him off drugs. We can make a great album, hopefully, and you'll benefit because you'll have the back catalog and some publishing."

Holzman agreed, and that was that. Pop was released from his Elektra contract, and Defries moved on, up to Clive Davis's office at Columbia. They nailed down the rudiments of a deal. Now all they needed was for Pop and Davis to meet, face-to-face. Which was when, according to Pop, he fell into one of the most memorable exchanges he had ever been party to.

They were talking about the kind of music Pop intended delivering to the label.

"Will you do Simon and Garfunkel?" asked Davis.

"No, I won't," Pop replied.

"Will you be more melodic?"

"No, I won't."

"Will you do what anybody asks you to?"

"No, I won't. But I can sing. Wanna hear?" Then he lay across Davis's desk and belted out "The Shadow of Your Smile," while Defries and Tony Zanetta looked on in wry amusement. If there'd been any doubt about the deal beforehand, there certainly wasn't now. It would take a few months more before all the contractual *t*'s were crossed and the *i*'s were dotted, but Iggy Pop was now a Columbia artist. Contracts were finally exchanged on March 1, 1972. Now it was time to form a band.

The union between Pop and Third World War that Bowie was musing upon when they first met was never going to happen. Nobody had thought to approach the band before deciding that Pop should link with them and, when a tentative inquiry was sent in the War's direction, it was quickly shot down. "I heard about that," guitarist Terry Stamp admitted, "but the truth of it all was, when they got a taste of Third World War, 'those two lightweight bitches backed off'—that's what I heard from our manager, John Fenton."

Not that Pop was at all perturbed. He'd never been convinced that he could simply slip into an already existing band, and besides, he had convinced his new mentors to spring for a second air ticket, for Stooges guitarist James Williamson, "the only man who understands me."

"You mean there's two of you?" Defries asked uncertainly.

"Yes, there's two of me," Pop hit back.

Neither musician, however, could have predicted what awaited them as they stepped off the British Airways jet, straight into the arms of the authorities. "We were immediately detained on suspicion of vagrancy," Pop recollected. "They built a little cell for us in Heathrow out of movable walls." It was hours, it seemed, before Defries finally arrived to spring the hapless pair and transport them to what he thought would be a suitably bohemian hotel, the Portobello, in Notting Hill.

It was a short-lived sojourn, said Pop. "We couldn't work the showers and I didn't like the English hippies and the cramped quarters. I didn't much like James, either...."

The pair were moved on, to find themselves happily if somewhat bemusedly ensconced in the Kensington Gardens Hotel, a small, and relatively inexpensive Victorian pile just off the Queensway shopping district. Whoever took the booking apparently thought Iggy was a girl's name, and planted the pair in the bridal suite. They shared a bed that first night, but the following morning Pop went out and picked up a Murphy bed.

The Americans spent most of their downtime either writing songs or watching television, marveling at a country that could get by with just three channels to choose from. Nights were spent touring the clubs, and getting to know their adopted city and its scenic highlights.

On March 18, they caught Marc Bolan and T.Rex at the Empire Pool, Wembley, the peak of what the press was calling T.Rexstacy, and the source of the year's biggest rock movie, *Born to Boogie*. Pop's opinion of the bopping elf Bolan? "Kinda chipmunky." But impressive as hell. "James and I went to his show and it was just great, great live." In later years, looking back on the songs that he and Williamson would write and record during their London stay, Pop was quick to pinpoint Bolan's impact. "I think he was a great influence. If you listen to some of those songs, you can hear some T.Rex in there."

Word of their arrival spread. Journalists drifted past, captivated by the legend they had already heard, and knowing that Pop would only amplify it every time he opened his mouth to speak. "Things do sometimes get a little out of hand around me," he would agree. "I remember this one show when..."

One night, he related, "I was grabbed and held down, while one chick was trying to pull my pants down. Some others were trying to French kiss me, and another used her mouth on me. All the while, I'd be kicking one, hitting another. I like to fight chicks. It turns me on."

There was no shortage of future contenders. For a time, Pop was seeing a girl named Johanna, a smackhead whom he met who knows where, but who became a remarkable muse for the short time she was around. A song bearing her name would become part of Iggy's repertoire the following year, while another, "Your Pretty Face Is Going to Hell," was inspired not only by Johanna, but also every other woman he'd ever met who flaunted her beauty like a weapon in her youth, but certainly wouldn't be looking so good ten years down the road. "Not gonna be whistling such a smart-ass tune then, are ya?"

Another girlfriend set MainMan hearts in their mouths when it was revealed that she was seriously underage, although Pop pleaded absolute innocence. "I never met her." She was a phone friend, "must have called me a hundred times on the phone since I've been here. Two or three times a week. Any time of the day or night. Might be four or eight in the morning. She won't give up, just keeps on ringing and ringing till you answer the phone."

But she was "okay," he insisted. "Just wants to talk. About what I do and what I like. Never anything special. Finally I asked her over. We were all dying of curiosity, but she never showed!"

Other girls did. Singer Michael Des Barres, touring the clubs with his band Silverhead, recalled, "Williamson was like a character, an unbelievable guitar player. And also a huge cock, by the way, the Stooges had the biggest cocks. That's why the girls...I saw James Williamson fucking this girl at a party—it was the bedroom where the coats [were], a pile of coats and Williamson fucking this girl. And I said, 'Yeah, raw power!'"

Bowie came around to visit when he could—one afternoon they lunched together in the hotel restaurant. Bowie ordered a bowl of sugar lumps; Pop asked for a jar of honey. Or else Bowie would invite the pair down to Haddon Hall for the day, but his time was growing increasingly precious as the release of *The Rise and Fall of Ziggy Stardust and the Spiders from Mars* approached.

"I thought he was very canny, very self-possessed, and a not unkind person," Pop mused. "Which you don't usually see in people so self-aware, who also knew his way. I listened to his stuff and I realized, 'Oh, he knows how to do things A, B, and C,' and he can, he can make a chair, and he can do an inlaid tabletop, if we're talking about songcraft in terms of, you know. It was not anything to do with what I was trying to do. But I watched him, pretty interesting, watched him changing clothes, changing hair, and acquiring new friends in the new world. And I never had a problem with him. Never had a problem with him."

"It was bizarre," James Williamson puzzled. "We were trying to find chicks. Bowie was high style and Defries and everybody was driving round in Jags and really playing up the part. It was very difficult to relate to this, but who's to complain—we're hanging out in Kensington Gardens and we had cash, but eventually we had to do something, so first we started rehearsing like crazy."

Bowie suggested that the duo try playing with Twink, onetime drummer with the Pretty Things, a founder member of the Pink Fairies, and a permanent presence on the underground scene of the day. But when the drummer called Pop to arrange an audition, he was told, "No, thanks, we're going back to America and don't need a rhythm section."

Other names were floated and promptly forgotten, filing through the doors of ACM Rehearsals, the cheap underground studio that Defries had block-booked. There, beneath the damp, paint-peeling walls and the tatty posters left behind by past denizens of the darkness, Pop and Williamson patiently ran the visitors through their paces, but the magic was never quite there.

Michael Des Barres caught one rehearsal. "It was exactly how you want it to be, dingy damp carpet curling, underneath was yellowish felt whatever. I remember these dreadful remnants of hippie bands, an aura, a stale smell of incense, posters of the Pretty Things and Hawkwind, and a shirtless imp. He was in front of three pedestrian musicians and it didn't matter. A pickup band. I don't know what he was doing there."

"Anonymous musos," James Williamson called them, and it was clear that nothing at all was happening. "Here's a couple of guys from Michigan and we show up and England was quite a different environment for us at that time. England was really Rod Stewart, big hair, that style of music, and so that's the way we played. When we tried to audition people, they always came from Defries and Bowie's contacts, and we weren't interested in how they played and what they did."

The hotel bill mounted and Defries moved the duo on, this time to Lawrence Myers' house in Little Venice, overlooking Regent's Canal. That lasted for as long as it took for Myers to drop by one day and clock the damage that they had caused to his home. Defries was still working to find them new accommodation when Pop announced they would need somewhere bigger. It simply wasn't working out trying to lace him up with a British rhythm section. "Who we need," James Williamson had announced, "are Ron and Scott." Defries breathed a sigh of relief. At last, they'd made a decision.

Defries had been trying to get Iggy on the road almost since they met. As early as the previous November, he was offering a Pop show to the Rainbow Theatre in London, only to be thwarted by the absence of any backing musicians. Months later, he contacted the Stooges' former agency, Michigan-based DMA, and was gratified to learn that they remained devoted fans of the band. But still there was no band. Finally, he decided to force their hand. He didn't care whether they were ready or not. They would be playing the King's Cross Theatre in London on June 15. And that did the trick.

The Asheton brothers were flown to London on June 6, 1972, and the quartet was installed in what became known far and wide as Stooge House, the mews apartment home of novelist Frederic Raphael, at 19 Seymour Road in Fulham.

It was an idyllic arrangement. A macrobiotic cook was ordered in, and a warm English summer kept a cheerful sheen over life. But Pop did not make the move. He'd recently taken up with another girlfriend, and preferred to stay in a nearby hotel where they could be alone when they wanted to, rather than vie for privacy in a flat full of musicians. Nightly or so, Williamson would cart his guitar the few blocks to the basement rooms where Pop was installed, and show him the latest riffs he'd come up with. "And we'd work up the tunes."

There was little time for the newcomers to find their bearings in the new city. Rather, they were thrown straight into rehearsals, with instructions to get to immediate grips with the new songs that Pop and Stevenson were crafting. There was not even enough time for Ron Asheton to come to terms with the conditions under which he was brought onboard, as a bassist instead of the lead guitarist that he once was. It was a source of some resentment, he freely admitted. "It was Chump City for me and my brother—we were reduced to being sidemen in our own band." But he accepted the role, and threw himself into it, savaging his bass guitar as though it alone were to blame for his musical demotion.

A new rehearsal space was booked. Bowie and the Spiders were already spending time at Underhill Studios in Greenwich; so was Lou Reed, as he got to know his new band, the Tots—the four piece he'd formed for the University show back in April, and had now flown over to London.

The names of guitarists Vinny Laporta and Eddie Reynolds, bassist Bobby Resigno, and drummer Scottie Clark rose and fell in rock history without leaving a trace; they were tight but unimaginative, but that was what Reed needed at that time, a group that would do what they were told and allow him, for the first time, to depict his songs as he saw them. Leaking out of the rehearsal studio as the band got to grips with Reed's repertoire was, for the first time, what the Velvet Underground might have sounded like if Lou had been left to his own devices all along.

The Stooges, on the other hand, delivered nothing but noise, fitting themselves into the studio around their compatriots' schedules to both work up new material and remind themselves of their older songs. Their concert debut was scheduled for the day after Reed and the Tots played their first show, at the same venue, and the Stooges needed to be sharp— especially once they caught an earful of what Lou Reed had in store.

There was just one small mercy to be grateful for. If they should screw up, at least there wouldn't be many people to see it. Bowie was playing his own showcase that same evening, around thirty miles away in Aylesbury, and he'd be taking half of the London music press with him.

Aylesbury Friars would be Bowie's final show for a month, before he headed into the studios first with Reed and then Mott the Hoople. It was also designed to be Bowie's introduction to an American press that Main-Man had flown in for the occasion, writers and tastemakers who had read so much about the new British superstar in the imported papers, but were still waiting to be convinced themselves. The Spiders' U.S. tour was now scheduled for September 1972, and if all went according to MainMan's plan, reviews and reports from the Aylesbury show would see the excitement reaching fever pitch right around the time of the first concert.

Wined and dined at the height of luxury, lodged in the finest hotels, and shepherded every place they needed to go, the American journalists felt like royalty as they were driven into the leafy confines of Aylesbury, ushered into the Friars club—and confronted with an audience that was even more rabid than the British press reports had ever warned them. Boisterous though they may have been, and determined to remain aloof, that first rush of adrenalined shrieking caught them off guard, sending their ears reeling before they'd even found a place to stand. Then their eyes took over, bombarding their senses with the sight of a thousand wide-eyed Bowie clones, Angela doubles, Ronson doppelgangers.

"Ode to Joy" piped through the PA, loud enough to shake coherent thought from their heads, but not so deafening as to be painful, and then the band appeared, ripping straight into "Hang Onto Yourself," and all reservations fell away. The show was stunning, the performance seamless, and when Bowie started throwing his silk scarves into the crowd, the writers were as desperate to catch them as the kids.

Then it was back to London and another live show—Iggy and the Stooges.

The Lou Reed show the previous evening had been a revelation. Taking the stage shortly after midnight and kicking right into a deliciously clunky "White Light White Heat," Reed was at his best, a spectral ringleader, not quite ad-libbing his lyrics but certainly having a wonderful time teasing the Tots with his timing, and if he was the only person in the room who didn't cringe a little when the band unleashed their backing vocals, that didn't detract from the sheer thrill of seeing him up there.

"Waiting for the Man," layered with flourishes that the song had never before carried; a resonant "Ride into the Sun"; a fragile "New Age," Reed singing instead of mumbling as expected; on and on through the best of *Lou Reed* and the finest of the Velvet Underground, Reed may have been leading the crowd into uncharted territory for much of the set, but the roar that greeted "Sweet Jane" was as heartfelt as the smile with which Reed repaid the recognition. "I Can't Stand It" was punchy, "Going Down" was gentle, "Wild Child" was brittle, "Berlin" was beautiful, and if "Rock 'n' Roll" picked up more applause than the eerie, closing "Heroin," that just proved how much easier it was to find *Loaded* in a British record store than any of the records that preceded it.

The Stooges would really need to be on form to top that.

Again the show started after midnight, allowing the handful of Bowie fans who'd also hit Aylesbury to race back in time for the Stooges, together with all the journalists who accepted MainMan's offer of a bus back into London. A few of them might even have thought they knew what to expect, nursing memories of the shows the band had played back in New York a couple of years before. But they left their expectations on the dance floor. Mick Jones, four years away from forming the Clash at the birth of the British punk movement, was there, astonished by the incandescence of the show. "The full-on quality of the Stooges was great, like flamethrowers!"

Pop was everywhere, trailing a mic cord the length of the building as he wandered out into the audience, alternately grabbing and caressing whoever lay in his path. One girl discovered him sitting in her lap, staring into her eyes as he serenaded her; one boy found himself being shaken like a rat as Pop grabbed hold of his head and used it to catch the rhythm of the song.

"We did a bunch of things that were new and we started wearing lots of makeup for one thing, so that was different," Williamson recalled. "I think we had rehearsed pretty much by that point. It didn't seem unique to me. We did a lot of stuff in the crowd at that show, which was bizarre for the Londoners, but it was typical for us. That's what we were used to doing."

They took Pop's activities in stride. "It was part of the show, but we had to really cover a lot for him because he was very improvisational, as was the whole band. We knew, but if you weren't used to it, you didn't know when he was going to start a song or when it was going to stop or what to do in the middle because it wasn't exactly the way you'd recorded it. He was very unpredictable."

There was a problem with the sound. Pop stood for a moment, stock-still and scowling, then howled with rage and hurled his mic to the ground. It shattered on impact, so he walked to another one, and treated the silent crowd to "The Shadow of Your Smile," a suave a cappella croon that kept everyone entranced while the problems were solved. Then it was back into the programmed set, loud, lewd, and brutal, and bristling with so many new songs that even the handful of veteran fans present didn't know what they were listening to.

Neither did photographer Mick Rock know precisely what he was preserving. When MainMan called him down to the show, he was told only that the night needed to be captured in all its flaming glory. It would be another year before one of the shots he took that evening was blown up for the cover of the Stooges' third album, a close up of the singer's torso, leaning on his mic stand, his face set and beautiful, staring into space. Pop later claimed that he hated it.

Pop, Rock said, "was already in my mind more mythological than human. His appeal was omnisexual; he was physically very beautiful, [and] the silver hair and silver trousers only added to the sense of the mythological. He seemed to have emerged from some bizarre primal hinterland, so much bigger than life, emoting and projecting a tingling menace. He was . . . a cultural revolutionary, operating well ahead of his time." The question that nobody dared ask was, was anybody truly ready to take that burden on?

The following day, Pop and Reed joined Bowie at the Dorchester Hotel, to meet the American media. To his eternal fury, Bowie missed the King's Cross show, and it was only later that he took solace from a videotape somebody showed him, of the Stooges' Cincinnati Festival performance, and he discovered, "I didn't like it very much, because . . . I saw the violence, and that's not what I heard from the lyrics."

Today, though, he was still steaming, asking everyone he spoke to what they thought of the show; what he had missed; how amazing it had been. Only when the journalists started to arrive did he put all thought of the previous night out of his head, and transform himself into the superstar they'd all come to meet.

Bowie, Angela, Defries, and Melanie MacDonald had stayed at the Dorchester the night before, adding to the visitors' perception that Bowie's stardom was already assured—who else, after all, could have afforded to stay in such swish surroundings on a whim? Angela and Melanie greeted everyone at the door, offering drinks, handing out food—by the end of the afternoon, so many trays of food had been delivered to the reception that they started stuffing them into a closet, just to get them out of the way.

Everybody was on form. Bowie himself offered Pop to the masses, telling the gathering, "Iggy has natural theater. It's very interesting because it doesn't conform to any standards or rules or structures of theater. It's his own, and it's just a Detroit theater that he's brought with him. It's straight from the street."

Omnipresent shades perched above a rugby-style shirt, Reed passed through the crowd, maybe a little disdainful, or perhaps that was how he always looked when faced with a roomful of journalists—he had a long memory when it came to the press, and he'd taken a lot of the shit that they wrote to heart. But he could smile with the best of them and, when the flashbulbs started popping, there they all were, Bowie wrapped in a paisley nightmare, Pop in a T.Rex tee, and Lou all smiling for the photographs, even when they didn't know the cameras were actually pointing toward them.

The following day, the Stooges went into Olympic Studios with engineer Keith Harwood. Soon to become one of the hottest names on the London studio circuit, "a slammin' dashing young dude about town," said Pop, "making Stones records [he engineered 1974's *It's Only Rock 'n' Roll* and 1976's *Black and Blue*, alongside many others], in his Ferrari, etc., etc.," Harwood was only beginning his mercurial rise at the time. But "it was good working with him."

The sessions were hard work, for the listener if not the performer. Oft-recycled on so many compilations in the years since they were laid down, songs like "Gimme Some Skin," "Tight Pants," a brutally obscene revision of "Louie Louie," and the tight, spiraling miasma of "I'm Sick of You" were never guaranteed to appeal to anybody outside the band's own tightly knit nihilistic fan club. But they weren't especially intended to. It had been more than two years since the Stooges last made a record, and they weren't sure whether they were yet ready to start again.

Some of the material was intact. Written during the months that separated the end of the Stooges from Pop's meeting with Bowie, "I Got a Right" shone especially brightly, a racing rocker built around a heart attack drum line and a Mach 3 James Williamson guitar, a frantic, frenetic number that didn't simply predate the speed-crazed punks of the post-Ramones 1970s, it made them look like positive slouches.

Other songs, however, were transitional at best, as Pop has since explained. "My particular insanity bar was raised so high at that point, and nothing sounded bent enough. Ever. I liked the songs. We recorded things like 'Fresh Rag,' 'Scene of the Crime,' and 'Search and Destroy,'" Pop remembers. "And Defries freaked. 'I would never allow you to put out anything like this. This is not music! Aaaarrrgghh!'"

Perhaps it is true that "I'm Sick of You," written by Pop for the same girl who inspired the Stooges' "Dog Food" ("my girlfriend Betsy… she's just thirteen"), was dropped because it sounded too much like the

Yardbirds' "Happening Ten Years Time Ago"; bearing in mind what Bowie was about to do with the same band's "I'm a Man" riff, as he twisted it into "The Jean Genie," that is not too great an imaginative stretch.

For the most part, however, Pop was correct. Defries hated what he heard. "It was far too violent to be associated with David. He let us keep 'Search and Destroy' and the riff to 'Tight Pants' [which became 'Shake Appeal'], then sent us back into the studio. Defries didn't know what to do with us. To his ears, it sounded even worse than the Stooges!"

Defries's plans for the band were going awry. Pop reflected, "Bowie was producing Mott the Hoople [at the time], which was probably how [we] would have gone, I'm sure. He would have written a big hit song for us, then we could have done our other songs and it would've had a certain sound, and that would have been fine." But Pop had already rejected Bowie's offer to produce the Stooges and, looking back, he admits, "I have a feeling Defries said, 'What should I do with this guy?' to which David probably told him, 'Listen, the best thing to do is let him do what the fuck he wants to and get it over with.'"

"We rehearsed and rehearsed and rehearsed," Pop said. "Every morning the Stooges would troop dutifully to this filthy basement to practice. After about two months, they said, 'Iggy, what are we practicing for?' It was *The Bridge on the River Kwai*. I felt like Alec Guinness. Why are we building this bridge? To blow it up! But Defries didn't want us to gig, because Bowie was hot, then. If I'd been on the road, I would have been hot too."

Trident Studios, home to Bowie's most recent recordings, hosted the sessions for Mott the Hoople's album. The "All the Young Dudes" single was still awaiting release—CBS had a July 28 date on it, allowing Bowie's current hit, "Starman," to run its course, but all concerned were convinced that it would take a miracle to prevent it from becoming a hit, and that was the mood that accompanied the band and their producer into the studio.

Demos for what would have been Mott's next Island album were pawed through and, for the most part, rejected. The last few months had seen the band's own writers, front man Ian Hunter and guitarist Mick

Ralphs in the main, but also organist Verden Allen, strike a rich new vein of songwriting inspiration, not only writing but also rehearsing a complete album's worth of material before even Bowie arrived at the studio. Hunter recalls the band played him just one song, "Sucker," and even the vague notion of Bowie bringing a few more of his own songs to the party was abandoned. "I don't see why I should have to write anything," he smiled. "You sound like you're doing great."

"All the Young Dudes" aside, there would be room for just one non-Mott song on the set. Playing around in the studio during the original "Dudes" recording session, Bowie began strumming a riff on a nearby guitar. Assuming they were in at the birth of another classic, and instantly responding to the riff, the band jammed along with him, and then were astonished when he told them what it was—"Sweet Jane," by the Velvet Underground. "Maybe we ought to add it to the album?" Bowie suggested. Maybe we should, the band agreed, but they were even more amazed, a few days into the album sessions, when Bowie walked into the studio with the song's composer, who had agreed to shepherd Hunter through the lyrics.

It was not, from all accounts, a happy encounter. Mott drummer Dale Griffin laughed as he recalled Reed "turning white" when he heard how fast the band had recorded the backing track, but Hunter reflected only on how he and Reed took an instant dislike to one another. "This slob comes in and goes 'eeaugh' all over the microphone," Hunter sniffed—although Reed's fans might argue that the vocal performance on the resultant demo is among the most instantly discernable that Reed has ever sung, and that it's the tape he sings along to that is at fault, a lightweight and characterless romp that still stands among the most disappointing performances in Mott's entire canon—particularly when compared to what else Reed had up his sleeve that summer.

Reed was living in Wimbledon for the duration, far from the madness of central London. "When I first got there I had a hash cookie and it took me about a month to recover," he deadpanned later. The suburban idyll helped him keep grounded, not only from further cookie-induced weirdness, but also from the nonstop partygoers who circulated the city looking for the next pad to crash.

Still, the Trident Studios staff grew quite accustomed to sitting around reception, watching as Reed traipsed back and forth between the studio and the control room, unsteady in his platform boots and looking just vague enough that when somebody whispered the single word *Valium*, everybody else nodded in knowledgeable agreement.

Nights were when Reed was at his best. Trident Studios was set in the heart of London's Soho, the nest of streets that make up the city's red light district, and all of them at that time conveyed a seedy charm that the tourist guides had yet to make a plastic mockery of. Reed loved it, particularly in comparison to New York—according to Bowie, his favorite word for Soho was *quaint*, but it wasn't a put-down. There, in the twilight world of tramps and drunks, hookers and junkies, strip clubs and revue bars, he could wander the sewers of local society without ever having to watch his own back, for fear of being jumped or mugged or worse.

London's crime rate was less than any single street in New York, and Reed had never felt so free to simply walk and observe. Warhol and the denizens of the Factory might have been the overt influence on the songs that he would be recording there, and Reed acknowledged, "I used to keep a notebook...to put down good lines, funny things people used to say." Even the back cover photo, of Reed's road manager Ernie with a banana down his pants, echoed back five years, to the apartment the Velvet Underground had shared above the firehouse on West Third Street, and the Halloween parade who floated through it. Rotten Rita, the Duchess, the Turtle, Silver George—they all sashayed through the twilight at the back of every song. But it was New York seen through the scuzzy neon light of a rainy night in Soho, Times Square wrapped in a long brown raincoat.

Even as he gathered his own team around him—Mick Ronson and engineer Ken Scott would both accompany him into the sessions—Bowie was uncertain precisely what Reed expected of him as producer. "I felt so intimidated by my knowledge of the work he had already done. It seemed like Lou had this great legacy of work, which indeed he did have." Bowie, by comparison, was very much the new kid on the block, five years Reed's junior and still trying to attain the same artistic peaks as he envisaged his hero as having scaled from the outset.

He was right as well, as Reed acknowledged two decades later. "Glam rock. Androgyny. Polymorphic sex. I was right in the middle of it. Some say I could have been at the head of the class."

Bowie shut his ears to such whisperings, but still, "I was petrified that he said yes to working with me in a producer's capacity [alone]. I had so many ideas," and not until they actually got into the studio would he discover whether Reed was going to prove receptive to them. He quickly learned, however, that Reed was no more certain of how this new record would, or even could, sound than he had been six months earlier, recording *Lou Reed* with Richard Robinson. He had the songs—he knew that. What he did not necessarily have was the vision to realize them, the vision that past collaborators—the rest of the Velvet Underground—layered on simply through their interpretations of what he gave them. It was a handicap that he would eventually shrug away, but for now, he accepted it wherever it fell.

Once again, Reed had raided the Velvet Underground's unused songbook for at least some of the material—"Andy's Chest," a song written back in 1968, following Warhol's shooting, was dusted off; so was "Satellite of Love," a song he'd written in much the same spirit of moonwalking adventure as Bowie had called upon when he penned "Space Oddity," and at much the same time.

But the majority of the songs came from the fevered burst of writing that accompanied his retirement to his parents' house, and the tapes he recorded in Richard and Lisa Robinson's apartment—the acerbic putdown of "Hangin' Round," the irresistible levity of "Wagon Wheel," the pouting camp of "Make Up," with its "we're coming out" rallying call the most explicit statement of gay intent that British rock had ever heard . . . and "Walk on the Wild Side."

Plans for that song to theme a projected musical had faded from view now, scuttled when Reed's would-be partners moved onto another project, *Mahogany*, "so I had a song called 'Walk on the Wild Side' and I rewrote it, and I put in everybody from the Factory." Indeed, the song was torn so far from his original, vaguely worded prototype that now it stood as a virtual casting call for some as yet unknown Warhol movie; or even an update of the five-year-old "Chelsea Girls." There was Holly Woodlawn hitchhiking from Florida to New York City—Woodlawn was astonished the first time he heard the song; he'd never even met Reed more than once. "How does *he* know I shaved my legs?" he demanded to know.

Candy Darling circulating the back room at Max's on his hands and knees. Little Joe Dallesandro—the star of Warhol's *Flesh*, *Trash*, and

Heat—on the hustle, Jackie Curtis speeding away, and a drug dealer friend of Warhol's ("or somebody," shrugged Reed) named the Sugar Plum Fairy, who got into the song because how could anybody resist immortalizing a name like that?

"I thought they were going to claw my eyes out when I got back to New York City," Reed chuckled the following year. "But Candy Darling came up to me and said she'd memorized all the songs and that she wanted to make a *Candy Darling Sings Lou Reed* album. That would be great, but it probably wouldn't sell more than a hundred copies."

Reed introduced every song the same way, either playing back a demo he'd recorded, just his voice and an acoustic guitar; or sitting down and performing it "live," singing and strumming while Mick Ronson settled alongside him, learning the chords, figuring out the arrangement, translating Reed's musical intentions into the wide-screen marvel that each song would eventually be transformed into. "*Transformer* is easily my best-produced album," Reed acknowledged later. "That has a lot to do with Mick Ronson. His influence was stronger than David's."

It was Ronson who replaced the acoustic guitar base of Reed's fragile "Perfect Day" with the so sweet and sensitive piano that now drew the song along; and played it, too, to the astonishment of everybody who had him pegged as a guitar picker alone. It was Ronson's guitars that sashayed and soared through the rockers, and his string arrangements and recorders that gave the album its ultimate lushness. "He was a talented guy," Reed mused following Ronno's death in April 1993. "Which was amazing, because you could not understand a word when he was talking." Ronson's accent was so thick, Reed swore, that "he'd have to repeat things five times."

Bowie was by no means idle, of course. The lyrics Reed wrote for "New York Telephone Conversation" may have been little more than ninety seconds of Warholian ennui and gossip, set to a pretty little tune that Reed had been carrying around since those days in the Robinsons' apartment. But Bowie's vocal follows his with catty spite and catlike precision, a duet between two socialites who have so little to say that they simply echo one another.

It was Bowie, too, who came up with the so-simple but effective backing vocals that "bum-bum-bum" through "Satellite of Love." "It's not the kind of part that I could ever have come up with," Reed admitted.

"But David hears those parts, plus he's got a freaky voice and can go that high and do that."

Only Bowie, too, could ever have envisaged a backing chorus of "spoke spoke" for a song with the already unconventional title of "Wagon Wheel" (as in, "won't you be my..."), and it was the little flourishes like that, allied with Ronson's more thunderous flashes of genius, that conspired with some of Reed's career-best lyricism to create the masterpiece that *Transformer* became.

"With Ronno and David there was a real simpatico, which is what we had in the Velvets, and was miles above what we had on the first *Lou Reed*, where there was nothing simpatico," Reed reflected. "I just ran over the songs, the chord structure, and the melody..." and they did the rest. Add engineer Ken Scott, already accustomed to Bowie after they worked together on *Hunky Dory* and *Ziggy Stardust*, and Reed had an unbeatable team at his back.

But still, everybody took a back seat behind Herbie Flowers. The bassist was at home when Bowie called up and asked, "Have you ever heard of a group called the Velvet Underground? I said, 'I think so,' and he said, 'Lou Reed's making a solo album, it's at Trident Studios, do you want to do it, it's three days' work.'"

Flowers agreed and, having already established himself as the star of the show for the inspired bass lines that he laid down behind "Walk on the Wild Side," he now took hold of the supremely forlorn "Goodnight Ladies" and relocated it so deep inside a 1930s jazz club that it could have stepped out of the sound track to *Cabaret*, if Weimar Berlin was removed to Max's Kansas City. "I don't know whose idea it was to bring in an oompah band," Reed puzzled. "But they went and got one."

The remainder of *Transformer* epitomized the glam rock mood of the day, but it was "Goodnight Ladies," the last song on the album and the last song recorded for the album, that reminded listeners just how universal and timeless that mood really was, and with the *Cabaret* movie itself having just launched in London (and drawn a frenzied audience that was quick to draw the historical parallels), it was a well-designed move. "Goodnight Ladies" rings down the curtain on the rest of *Transformer*'s freak show with a finality that no other song in sight could ever have mustered.

12

MY VOODOO MASTER,
MY MACHINE

"There's an awful lot of assholes in the music business, and the idea of having to hire these people, to work with them, was nauseating. The most sensible thing to do was to hire actors to act the parts. Tony Zanetta became Tony [Defries]'s assistant, and within three years he was president of MainMan. That was great! He did it fantastically. He wears suits, he can nod, he's a brilliant actor, a brilliant set designer, and a brilliant director. He would set the situation and he would direct the situation, and all the time he'd be acting out the role of president.

"Leee Black Childers had done a lot of press. For Leee to deal with the press, it was a fucking piece of cake. The same for Cherry, who was a writer. That is why MainMan was so successful, because those people did the things the way they had to be done, not the way they'd been done before, not because of twenty years in the music business."
—Angela Bowie in conversation with the author, 1986

With a month to go before their U.S. concert debut in Cleveland on September 22, 1972, Bowie and the Spiders kicked off another few weeks of U.K. touring in August, with the first shows over two nights at the London Rainbow. With success joining MainMan in encouraging Bowie to pull out all the stops, the London gigs were to be nothing short of a spectacle.

Bowie assembled a team of backing singers. The Astronettes, David proudly announced, comprised his old friend Geoff MacCormack; a former cocktail waitress whom he'd met at a Stevie Wonder backstage party, Ava Cherry; and Jason Guess, a designer who made leather clothing. MainMan insiders asked one another how on earth Bowie had unearthed "the only black people in Britain without a sense of rhythm," but there was no denying that they looked good.

With just seven days' advance notice, Bowie's old mime teacher, Lindsay Kemp, was recruited to choreograph a dance troupe—Angela traveled up to Edinburgh to collect him, and was entertained all the way back to London by Kemp's memories of his earlier collaborations with her husband, including the dancer's affectionate rebuke, "Bowie got it all from me. His dresses, his hair, and his makeup."

Two weeks of rehearsals were booked, eschewing the traditional route of renting a simple warehouse or hall and taking over the Theatre Royal in Stratford, east London. It was an almost unprecedented expense, but Bowie was determined that everything would go according to plan, and his plans were ambitious indeed. Kemp's dancers alone saw to that, and so extravagant was their costuming and choreography that they became the undisputed focal point of the promo film that Mick Rock was shooting to accompany Bowie's next single, "John, I'm Only Dancing."

At the same time, however, plans for Kemp and company to accompany Bowie to the U.S. were abandoned, partially because Bowie and Kemp could not help but fall into the same argumentative ways that had helped break them apart in the past, but also because it simply wasn't cost effective. At home, it made sense to keep upping the ante and offering the fans something more spectacular every time. America, however, was virgin territory. Even the blow-job guitar solo was going to give audiences a heart attack.

"I thought I'd come with the complete theater performance that I have been doing in England," Bowie would muse. "Then I realized that would be a mistake. I should come over with minimal gimmicks and props and theatrics the first time and present the songs the way I like to present songs. Then I can give myself a platform later on, next year, for different styles and other things to keep me happy."

Even before the doors opened, the Rainbow shows promised to be an event. Bowie, after all, was not the only newly crowned superstar on display. The support band was Roxy Music, a defiantly art school–inflected rock band whose own costuming and imagery had dropped them firmly alongside Bowie at the top of the glam rock tree. "I love them," Bowie enthused. "They are the nearest thing to being decadent at the moment."

It was not the first time the two had played together. Weeks before, Roxy warmed up the audience at Bowie's Croydon show. Back then, however, they were an unknown quantity, still awaiting the release of their debut single, "Virginia Plain." Now they had a major hit behind them, and a follow-up on the way. Their debut album had fallen with at least as resounding an impact as *Ziggy Stardust*; dissenting voices in the Rainbow audience might well have wondered which of the two acts really deserved to be headlining.

Backstage, Bowie's people left Roxy in no doubt as to who the star was, prompting guitarist Phil Manzanera to remark, "His management were rather disagreeable... but Bowie and the Spiders were very nice people."

Significant, too, was the presence of two people in the support band's ranks who would go on to have their own impact upon Bowie—model Amanda Lear, who introduced Roxy Music onstage, then spent their set, as singer Bryan Ferry recalls, "gyrating in the background with a couple of other... rather slaggy girls," and Brian Eno, the band's onstage sound engineer-*cum*-manipulator. His experimental approach to sound and music was already drawing attention from across the spectrum; he and Bowie became friends first, and within three years of meeting for the first time, they were blueprinting the complete reinvention of pop.

Bowie's set was as dramatic as it needed to be, a nest of surprises that began unveiling the moment the group hit the stage, not with the expected punch of "Hang Onto Yourself," but with the slow piano-led melody of "Lady Stardust," a song that was so patently written about Marc Bolan (when he first emerged on the mainstream stage, people really did stare "at the makeup on his face") that nobody was surprised when his portrait lit up the screen behind the Spiders.

A multitiered stage allowed the dancers all the scope that Kemp demanded. Bowie and the Spiders, for their part, turned in a show that stepped so far beyond the traditional realms of rock concerts that afterward, Bowie seriously talked of taking over a theater for a few weeks, and restaging the event every night. By the time the show ended, with "Moonage Daydream" the first evening, "Waiting for the Man" the second, scarcely a single witness could deny that they had experienced something magical—including Bowie, who even ad-libbed a lyric to what was still his best-known number: "there's a starman over the rainbow." Bowie was well aware of the melodic similarities between the two songs,

"Starman" and the signature theme from *The Wizard of Oz*, and he didn't care who else recognized them.

The Stooges and Lou Reed were both guests of honor the first night, not only sitting in on the afternoon rehearsals, but also being given front-row seats for the show; afterward, Reed, at least, was effusive in his praise. The concert, he insisted, was "amazing, incredible, stupendous... the greatest thing I've ever seen." What he did not tell anybody was that was the view from the bar. Three songs into the set, Scott and Ron Asheton rose from their seats and made their own way out to the bar, assuming they'd already seen all they needed to. There they discovered Lou sitting comfortably. He hadn't even made it into the auditorium.

Bowie and Angela had had a fight. It was the night of the Aylesbury Friars showcase, in July. The couple hadn't had a holiday in what seemed like forever. With at least a few days yawning free of work ahead of them, Angela wanted to get away to Cyprus, the Mediterranean island where her U.S. military father had been stationed at the time of her birth.

Her husband, on the other hand, had no interest in the vacation whatsoever, and the more Angela pressed, the more vehement his refusals became, and the more desperate his denials. Finally he uttered the words that would change the course of at least a part of his career for the next year: "I can't go. I'm scared of flying."

It was a newfound phobia, to be sure. Less than a year before, after all, he had happily jetted to New York to meet Warhol and sign with RCA. Now, however, he was adamant. "If it flies, it's instant death," he insisted. But when word of that terror reached Defries, nobody could have predicted his reaction. Problems, he insisted, could either become so significant that they tripped you up, or they could become another way of propelling you forward. Defries always looked toward the latter first.

He called RCA, told them the grim news, and announced that henceforth Bowie could travel only by the most luxurious and earth-based means possible—beginning with the best available berth on the *Queen Elizabeth II* ocean liner to take him to America. Once on dry land, he would alternate between limos, trains, and buses to get him where he needed to be, and the more coverage the situation was given by a gobsmacked U.K. media, the more entrenched in the legend the story became. Soon, Bowie's pteromerhanophobia was as much a part of the star's persona as any other aspect of his career.

Over in New York, meanwhile, the American friends he'd made among the cast of *Pork* eagerly awaited his arrival, all bristling with news of their own recent lives.

County was now house DJ at Max's Kansas City, with owner Mickey Ruskin's blessing to play whatever he wanted, provided he kept it underground. "I was playing the Velvets, the first Mott the Hoople album, the first Alice Cooper album, which had some really freaky stuff on it..."

Childers was a photographer at *16* magazine, standing the day's top pop stars "up against the wall, making sure their cigarettes didn't show, and if the bulge in their pants was too big, I'd have to rearrange their cock so they didn't look too threatening to the eight-year-olds."

And Vanilla was working for a friend's advertising agency, handling PR for Jimi Hendrix's *Rainbow Bridge* movie, among others, and generally having a good time.

There was another assault on theaterland in the form of *Island*, written and directed by Tony Ingrassia, stage-managed by Childers and, essentially, a large-scale reunion for the *Pork* crew—Miller, Vanilla, Zanetta, County, and Di Carlo were all involved, together with a still-obscure New York poetess named Patti Smith. She'd worked with a few of them back in 1969, in another Ingrassia production, *Femme Fatale*, and they still remembered the first time she turned up at Max's—Mickey Ruskin refused her entry, she looked so drab and dirty. But she was in good company. He once barred Janis Joplin for much the same reasons.

Described by Zanetta as "probably Ingrassia's best play," *Island* told the story of a bunch of freaks having a picnic on the deck of a Fire Island beach house, at the same time as a U.S. army invasion was making its way across the island to arrest all the weirdos besmirching the socialite paradise. County played a transvestite revolutionary; Smith was a speed freak whose lines basically revolved around the fact that Brian Jones was dead; Vanilla was a sex-crazed hippie who fucked everyone in sight. "I think I was just called 'the groupie,'" Vanilla recalled. "I always loved being with those people, onstage and off. There was an eating scene at a big table that was chaotic and brilliant!" Tony Defries came by to see it during another of his whistle-stop visits to New York, and thoroughly enjoyed himself.

"Tony was coming to New York quite often now," Zanetta relates. "Every couple of months he'd call me up, and I would run because he'd always give me $100 or $200." When *Hunky Dory* was released, it was Zanetta whom Defries entrusted with making sure that copies of the record reached the "right" people, as opposed to those whom RCA's publicity department sent them to. "He had me and Cherry go up to RCA and get records and press kits to give to all our friends, so we were becoming this unofficial promo team."

A couple of months later, in June, another call sent Zanetta—or Zee, as Defries now insisted on calling him, to obviate the confusion of having two Tonys in the room—to visit Defries's New York lawyer, Norman Kurtz. "He told me Norman had a $5,000 or $10,000 fund that I could tap into, so I could get an apartment and furnish it. Basically, I was preparing MainMan for his arrival." The duplex apartment that he secured at 240 East Fiftieth Street would remain the heart of MainMan's American operations for the next eighteen months.

August brought Zanetta to London, just ahead of the Rainbow shows, sleeping on the floor at the Gunter Grove offices, and just doing whatever was required of him—or that he sensed was required of him—to ensure the wheels kept turning. On the road for the handful of shows around England, for example, Zanetta noticed that whenever the band rolled into a new city, nobody seemed to know what to do.

"We arrive, and it's mass confusion—everyone would get into the hotel and sit there in the lobby because nobody checked us in, nobody did anything. So [I], being American and a little impatient wanting to get to my room, just began to take charge. I began to organize a little bit on tour, and then back in London making plans for the American tour, they had the most grandiose plans. Defries is saying we have to charter a train and I was saying, 'Charter a *what*?' So I began organizing that as well, and bringing some of the plans back to reality, and it just picked up from there."

Still, the news that Defries delivered once Zanetta returned to New York came as a shock. Defries did indeed intend opening a MainMan office in New York City, and he wanted the freaks to staff it. But not because they were freaks. He did it because he wanted to get the job done properly.

It was a principle Defries had already put into practice at the London office, hiring a musician, Hugh Attwooll, to act as agent for the MainMan stable. Attwooll happily admitted that he had "absolutely no idea what I was doing, which suited Defries because he liked to have people who didn't know what they were doing, so they could do things the way he liked. He knew he could beat the system and he did it."

This first visit to the United States was a case in point. "It was a big organization," Attwooll continued. "There were sound men, security men, and when he took Bowie to America, that's how he did it. He conned the world. He took a huge entourage and booked them all into the Plaza Hotel in New York and told them all to use room service. When the time came to pay the bill, he just sent it to RCA, who got so deep in that they just had to make it work. It was a masterstroke, really." Staffing MainMan New York was to be Defries's most defiant gesture yet.

Wages were not spellbinding. "In New York, Cherry, Leee, and I worked for a subsistence of about $100 per week," Zanetta recalled. "However, anything else that we needed, like shoes, dental work, winter coats, etc., [was] paid for out of MainMan petty cash. This was the system used for most of 1972, into the spring of 1973, when we all went on salary." MainMan would also cover the trio's rent.

In return, they were expected to work their asses off. They were not simply launching a new pop star. They were marketing a product, instigating a brand, and Defries made it clear not only that he would not accept failure, but that he did not even acknowledge the possibility of it existing.

No matter that America had seldom been more than tolerant of British imports, or that Rod Stewart and Elton John alone could claim to have achieved more than one- or two-hit wonderdom in recent years, as the country continued its love affair with earnest singer-songwriters, faceless stadium rock bands, and soulless balladeers.

No matter, either, that Bowie's distinctly English glamour and mystique simply had nothing in common with mainstream American tastes. Three Dog Night, the band that Defries turned down so that he could devote more time to Bowie, had the No. 1 single in America the week that Bowie landed; the week before, the chart was ruled by the Looking Glass's grisly "Brandy"; the week after, it would be Mac Davis's "Baby Don't Get Hooked on Me." The competition wasn't simply strong, it was ghastly, but Defries shrugged when somebody asked him how any unknown star could ever get past the behemoths that stood in their way.

If he knew that, he wouldn't have hired them. They would simply have to use their imagination.

And that was one quality that all three possessed in abundance.

"We decided to travel by bus," Zanetta recalls, "and I'll never forget leaving New York. We're sitting in front of the Plaza, everyone's on the bus waiting for someone—Woody Woodmansey, I think—and there's this bag lady outside the hotel. She takes down her pants and takes a big crap in front of the bus. That was our farewell to New York. And then Tony tells me I'm to be the road manager, so I asked him what does a road manager do, and he says, 'Oh Zee, just make sure you all get to Cleveland.' And we were off."

Traveling a few days ahead of the tour, Leee Black Childers and his assistant Dai Davies were the advance team, charged with finding their way around each city in turn, so that the main party would know where to go, who to meet, and what to do in and around the shows—it was a leisurely voyage, after all. A tour that would devour most of the remainder of the year was scheduled to touch down in no more than two dozen cities, although at least a handful of those had yet to be finalized. "It was kinda chaotic," Zanetta laughed, "and sprawling. We only did seventeen dates and took three months to do it, and we spent $400,000 to make around $100,000."

For his first ever concert appearance in the United States, in Cleveland on September 22, 1972, Bowie earned a princely $2,641—$1,500 up-front, and the remainder in cash following the show. Memphis, two nights later, brought in $9,000; but that long-awaited, long-delayed Carnegie Hall showcase struggled to clear $3,380. St. Louis came in at a grand less than that; while an appearance at Seattle's Paramount Theatre on November 1 attracted fewer than eight hundred curious onlookers, and prompted local reviewer Carole Beeres to sniff, "His reputation precedes him and nearly overshadows the man himself. He is small, slight... [and] gentle enough, not the outrageous and pushy rocker one might expect from the advance flack. He sings about astronauts, lasers, death, and other current topics...."

"But what do Seattle reviewers know?" promoters Concert West asked wearily.

Absent from the road was Cherry Vanilla, "the only one of us," explained Zanetta, "that had ever had a real job." With the MainMan office now open for business, one of the earliest requirements was somebody to answer the telephones. Actress Cyrinda Foxe, one of several glamorous women drawn into the organization's orbit very early on, was their first choice, but she swiftly proved unsuitable. "So Cherry came in to answer phones for a couple of days. Meanwhile, Defries, if you're sitting in front of him, will ask, 'Can you do this, can you do that,' and Cherry being a very capable person, she could do these things, and suddenly she began organizing the place and turning the chaos into a real office. She was superefficient and superorganized, and she just took over the office. She became secretary, administrator, everything. And that's the way it was for the first American tour."

Vanilla was also in charge of one of the most audacious of Defries's ideas—namely, making sure that Bowie's face was seen in every city in the United States, regardless of whether he was there or not. Few people knew exactly what David and Angela looked like; a shock of carrot and a flash of blonde was enough for most people to assume they'd seen the real thing, so Vanilla began rounding up potential look-alikes wherever she could find them, then dispatching them out to the most visible places—clubs, gigs, bars and so on, and then circulating the news that the Bowies were in town.

Rarely was the subterfuge discovered. Indeed, some nights, sightings might be reported from three or four venues (in three or four cities!) more or less simultaneously. Anything to push Bowie's name and image deeper into the local subconscious. It was all in good fun, Defries and Vanilla believed, but there was one evening when a similar deception looked like it might become a necessity as well.

As Bowie and the Spiders crisscrossed the country, Mott the Hoople, too, were enjoying their first headlining American jaunt, an outing set to climax at the end of November with two nights at the Tower Theatre in Philadelphia's Upper Darby satellite, immediately before Bowie's own two-night stand at the same venue. The entire MainMan crew had already arrived; so had the band and the equipment. The only person missing, in fact, was Bowie, who was probably the most important one of all. Not only was he meant to join Mott onstage for the inevitable "All the Young Dudes," he was also supposed to be introducing them onto the stage.

But Bowie was missing in the wilds of Pennsylvania, somewhere between Pittsburgh, where he'd played the previous evening, and Philadelphia.

The support band, Brownsville Station, had done its duty. Now, as show-time approached, nerves were tingling. "Bowie was meant to have been there hours earlier," recalled Brownsville frontman Cub Koda. "I didn't know who any of the people with Mott were, apart from the fact they were management, but they were all pacing back and forth looking at their watches, and just going crazy, wondering where he was—had he had an accident? Had he met up with somebody and just disappeared back to their place? There were rumors flying all over the place."

Finally, Defries made an executive decision. Looked at in a certain light, Melanie MacDonald had a similar build to Bowie, and certainly a similar hairstyle. Bowie's wardrobe had already arrived at the venue; clothing was procured, Melanie was dressed. She was all ready to take the stage and at least look like she was introducing the band—it wouldn't be her fault if her mic was faulty and the noise of the crowd drowned out her words—when finally word came through that Bowie had arrived.

Mott were held back another few minutes, and Bowie was hustled onto the stage.... "Good evening. Uh ... I've never introduced anybody before, but it's quite exciting and this is a great band to introduce. When I was in England about six months ago, I saw this band for the first time and I thought they were a really great rock 'n' roll band ..." and then the intro tape, Gustav Holst's mighty "Jupiter," started rolling, and Mott exploded onto the stage at last.

While Bowie and Mott toured a foreign land, Lou Reed found himself in bizarre competition with a part of his own musical heritage. He was not enamored by it.

A sporadic handful of British gigs through July presaged a full-blown British tour in September, both leading up to and in the wake of the release of *Transformer*. Reviews alone had assured that the album was going to absolutely outperform its predecessor, and the Bowie connection ensured that an audience who'd not even heard of *Lou Reed* would be queuing up to enter Reed's blow-by-blow-job tour of the New York underbelly. But any intention Reed might have had of pushing the new album hard through his live shows was trashed by the arrival, in his hour of greatest triumph, of a ghost he thought he'd disposed of more than two years earlier. The Velvet Underground were back once more, and touring around the exact same circuit he was.

Atlantic Records, the Velvet Underground's last label, had already hauled out Brigid Polk's long-mothballed Max's tapes, released them as a budget-priced live album, and watched as *Live at Max's* outsold *Lou Reed*. But Steve Sesnick, still managing Doug Yule's career, wanted more than that. He wanted the Velvet Underground back on the road in their own right, especially now that they had an album in the can and a reputation that couldn't be beat. A British tour was lined up to prepare the way.

Yule shuddered, "When Sesnick set up the tour, I was on my way to Denver in a Dodge van with a baby girl and a new wife, intending to work as a carpenter. Instead I went to Europe and pretended to be the Velvet Underground."

Although there were hopes that Mo Tucker and Sterling Morrison might be prevailed upon to throw their lot in with the renewed group, neither showed any interest. Instead, Yule wound up making the journey with an entirely new lineup, comprising drummer Mark Nauseef and two members of brother Billy's new band, the Red Rockets—guitarist Rob Norris and bassist George Kay.

It was, affirmed Yule, "an eye-opening visit. Sesnick abandoned us in London with no money, no amps, and no hotel. We slept in a cold-water flat for a few nights before I found a room in Camden, where my sister lived...no heat, a loo under the stairs, bathtub in the backyard. We convinced the promoter to put up some money for a deposit on the equipment. We traveled in an old Jaguar saloon that had no windshield washer, and the roadie would squirt water from a dishwashing liquid bottle to clear the schmutz from the road, while driving at 3 A.M. People were friendly, and we saved our pennies and enjoyed the adventure of it. But it was easier to do that in retrospect than it was while it was happening."

The Velvet Underground played nine shows around the U.K. that winter, and again, Yule found the reconfigured lineup to be of little concern to onlookers. Although the grapevine informed him that Reed, predictably, was not at all happy with the situation, crowds were enthusiastic, and when *Melody Maker* covered one show, writer Meredith Noel readily affirmed that the Velvet Underground were "every inch a rock 'n' roll band. A lot of material was old stuff—necessary, as the band pointed out, because British fans have yet to hear the new material [*Squeeze* was still awaiting release, a year after it was recorded]. Old faithfuls like 'Waiting for [the] Man' and 'Sweet Jane' harked back to the days when Lou Reed was in the band.

"Half the audience were there to see a group which must be legend now. The other half was there to rave, so everybody was happy. The Velvet Underground had been jamming in the dressing room for two hours before they came on stage—they obviously like playing. People were listening, people were dancing, and everyone had a good time and an encore—'Heroin.'"

Some nights, fully half the Velvet Underground set had been aired by Reed just a few nights before (or would be a few nights later)—"White Light White Heat," "Waiting for the Man," "Some Kinda Love," "Sweet Jane," "Rock and Roll," "Heroin." Yule's band even got it into their heads to attempt "Sister Ray," and didn't do a bad job of it either, merging it into a surprising "Train Round the Bend" and winding up with a fourteen-minute marathon that positively dwarfed the eight or nine that Reed and the Tots devoted to the same violent encore.

Once more, however, any successes that the tour might have stacked up were never to be repeated. "I don't think the group played together again once we got home," mourned Yule. While Lou Reed continued to enjoy the biggest hit of his career, *Squeeze* was released in February 1973, to be greeted by what Yule described as "a collective yawn."

Wrapped in a *Loaded*-look-alike sleeve, and critically devoid of any lineup information, the album was harshly reviewed and scarcely promoted. It knocked around the remainder racks of the U.K. for a while, drawing in a few curious Lou Reed fans, but ultimately it vanished completely. A few months later, at the inevitable ski lodge in Vermont, the Velvet Underground—Doug Yule reunited with brother Billy, plus a couple of friends—finally breathed their last.

They would not be mourned, but Yule would be forgiven. In 1975, he turned up aboard Lou Reed's latest band and, one night in New Zealand, even depped for the main man when illness left Lou unable to perform. "Anyone who wanted their money back could have their money back," Yule explained. "Then we went out and played, and I sang." It really was just like old times.

13

FOR SCREECHING AND YELLING AND VARIOUS OFFENSES

Any garage, any town, 1977

The Stooges are a legend. More than that, they are Year Zero for the new-born punk community, and everybody is racing to stake their allegiance to the band. The Damned included "1970 (I Feel Alright)" on their Damned Damned Damned *debut album. Richard Hell was covering "I Wanna Be Your Dog," and the Dictators recorded "Search and Destroy." And the Sex Pistols cut their own take of "No Fun" and basked in Pop's reaction.*

"That band walk tall," he proclaimed. Listening to their "No Fun," he said, was akin to "looking at a pile of rubbish and knowing that you made it rubbish. I really like the Sex Pistols. They're doing something in their own right, carrying on in their own direction from something I sense they respected in what I was doing."

Years later, he elaborated further, albeit a little less enthusiastically. "I saw a superficial correlation between punk and what the Stooges had been doing, and I knew exactly what was happening; that accidentally, the superficial aspects of noise, energy, aggression, irresponsible negative preening, and emotional exhibitionism were finally being adopted by the mob and their various frustrated mentors, who couldn't create anything themselves."

The little Iggys clambering out of the woodwork, he swore, "used to irritate the shit out of me. And when some of them started making lots of money, it really flipped me out for a while. But then it came full circle, and I'm glad it happened because . . . otherwise, it would be like I'd crawled out on a limb and someone had sawn the tree off. Instead, the tree grew in that direction, and because of that, those people who play bubble-gum cards with music—see who's done what, who's better than who, who's richer than who—think, 'Oh, he started a movement.'"

On September 10, 1972, the same day that the Bowies boarded the *QE2* to begin David's first American tour, the Stooges entered the CBS Studios on Whitfield Street, London, to begin recording their MainMan debut album. The timing, they congratulated one another, was perfect. Defries, too, would be heading out to New York in a few days time. Unsupervised and unwatched, the Stooges could make the album the way *they* wanted to.

From the outset, Pop had turned down Bowie's offer to produce him, insisting that he and Williamson were more than capable of doing the job themselves. They were clean, they were enthusiastic, they were bristling with ideas. Unfortunately, they were also wrong. Although the dynamic duo was certainly proficient enough to get their noise down on tape, the niceties of mixing, overdubbing, adjusting levels, and seeking out atmospheres, the tiny tricks of the trade that separate a great producer from a mere sound recorder, left them foundering. They knew they had enough songs for an album—more than enough, in fact. But the songs did not make an album, even after they took on board the one piece of constructive advice that Defries did offer, which was to make sure they alternated the harder songs with the gentler ones.

By the first weekend of October, the band had done all they could—and created, essentially, a chaotic mess. Revisionist opinions of the various early mixes that have leaked out onto the collectors circuit notwithstanding, the songs that became *Raw Power* were little more than so many slabs of tinny garage guitar, slammed onto tape with little regard for the rudiments of balance or even stereo separation. The first time Bowie heard the tapes, he was horrified to discover that, faced with the technological majesty of a twenty-four-track studio, the Stooges had employed just three tracks—one for the vocals, one for guitar, and one for the bass and drums. Then, for what they considered to be the final mix, they crammed all the instrumentation into one channel, while Pop alone clung thinly to the other. It was horrible, and it wasn't as if the band did not seem to care. They did not even seem to have noticed!

On October 6, Pop flew out to Detroit to visit his parents and hook up with Bowie when he played the local Fisher Theatre two days later. They remained in Motor City for a few days more. Bowie's next show was almost two weeks away, in Los Angeles, and only slowly did the party move on, a sprawling entourage of thirty-odd people block-booking into the bungalows of the Beverly Hills Hotel. Back in London, however, Pop's bandmates were climbing the walls.

Pop had left them with instructions only to keep rehearsing, although why, they couldn't begin to imagine. Still, they followed orders for a few days before finally deciding that it was easier to stay at home—which is where Angela Bowie, back in London, came across them, slobbed out in the remains of Stooge House, itself a sea of cigarette burns, unwashed dishes, and unpalatable stains.

"I don't think much disaster went on," said Hugh Attwooll. "When I had to go and meet Frederic Raphael and smooth some slightly ruffled feathers because [his house] wasn't in pristine condition, it wasn't a disaster [so much as] a matter of saying, 'Don't worry, the cigarette burns will be paid for.' It was the juxtaposition between Frederic Raphael and Iggy Pop. I always think if I had been Frederic Raphael, I probably wouldn't have rented my house to Iggy and the Stooges."

Nevertheless, Angela could not stand the thought of the trio spending the rest of their lives cooped up in the rubble. So she scooped them up and flew them home to Ann Arbor; then they, too, made their way down to L.A., to discover that Pop was now admitting that the *Raw Power* tapes possibly weren't up to scratch.

"There was not a sensible mix of it because basically, I just seemed to want more treble than existed in the world at the time," Pop later conceded. When Defries suggested that Bowie fill some of his spare time by taking the tapes into Western Sound studios in Hollywood, for a remix, Pop had little choice but to agree. Handing the tape over to Bowie, he simply shrugged, "See what you can do with this." Bowie listened once and then turned in amazement. "Jim, there's nothing here to mix."

Which did not mean that Pop was happy with what happened next. Bowie did what he could to salvage the murk, rerecording backing vocals and playing around with a Time Tube, a delay effect that at least brought a hint of intrigue to the band's full-frontal attack. The end result, however, left nobody content—Pop once snarled, "That fucking carrot-top sabotaged my album," while the carrot-top itself bemoaned the impossible rush and implausible materials that stood between him and a job he could be proud of.

Which in turn determined that nobody was more surprised than Bowie and Pop when, three years later, *Raw Power* was adjudged one of *the* primal components in the DNA of what became British punk rock—"a hallmark roots sound," as Bowie rather more precociously put it. TV Smith of the Adverts was eighteen when Iggy and the Stooges' third album was released, in May 1973, and he could not even begin a new day without first listening to *Raw Power*.

"'Search and Destroy' was certainly *the* song, so blistering, and it's totally unlike any other record has ever sounded. Dirty guitars mixed right up, jagged and raw. The Stooges were probably the one band that you have to pull out and say they made a difference. There were bands like the Velvet Underground that impressed me and were interesting, but what Pop brought was this incredible violence and aggression and energy, violence against a society that wasn't working for me as a teenager.

"I didn't like what I was seeing in the world, and here was someone else who didn't like it and who was roaring against it. To get up every morning and put on *Raw Power* filled me with energy—there was this great scream of aggression, and somehow it gave me a very positive feeling that you can say something about what's going on, despite everything. Fight back and kick back."

So what if Iggy and the Stooges lost few opportunities to damn the few days that Bowie spent remixing the record? Whether by accident or design, what he created was an album that was further ahead of its time than any of his own music; further ahead than anything anybody else was even dreaming of at that time. When people said they hated *Raw Power*, what they meant was they hated the future . . . a future that would soon be bearing down fast on all of them. And even Pop grew to love it in the end. "I'm very proud of the odd, eccentric little record that came out."

The Stooges remained at the Beverly Hills Hotel for the next few days, even after Bowie and his party had departed, with RCA unknowingly footing the bill for their stay. Only when the company bean counters finally worked out what was happening did Defries decide to move them along, instructing Childers to seek out suitable accommodation for himself and the band, at what became the nerve center for MainMan's West Coast operation.

At the end of November 1972, Childers settled upon a five-bedroom house at 7755 Torreyson Drive, off Mulholland, for $900 a month. A few days later, Defries arranged for Pop and Williamson to each receive $100 a week wage—paid in its entirety into Williamson's bank account, while they waited for Pop to either get his ID card sorted out or open an account of his own. A month later, the Ashetons were placed on $50 a week each, with another $75 a week dispensed to Eric Haddix, a longtime friend and former roadie, who was now back on the scene in much the same role. Except there was not so much roadieing required.

With the house commanding views of Burbank in one direction and Los Angeles in the other, and a heart-shaped swimming pool installed by a previous owner, actress Carole Lombard, to become the center of activity, the Stooges were living high, but life itself remained a relentless grind. Every morning, Childers would shepherd them out of bed, through a quick breakfast, and then out to the car for the fifteen-minute cruise down to Studio Instrument Rentals (SIR) studios on Sunset Boulevard, where the MainMan cache had landed them a hefty discount off the usual rates. There, they picked up basically where they'd left off in England, a daily routine of aimless rehearsals while they waited for something, anything, to happen.

It never did. Working to break Bowie in the U.K., Defries was happy to allow the Spiders to work the circuit, building up from the smallest venues to the largest as word of mouth spread. But the United States was too vast for that to ever be an option, unless he was willing to simply send the Stooges out on the kind of tour that every other band in the land was stuck with, scratching around at the bottom of somebody else's bill, and inching their way up the pecking order year by glacial year. The Stooges, he decreed, when they were finally let off the leash, were going to be bill-toppers from the outset, just like Bowie, and it was MainMan's job to make sure that happened.

Unfortunately, with both Bowie and Mott the Hoople on the road, MainMan simply didn't have the time to devote to anybody else. And so the Stooges sat there, lazing by the swimming pool with just Leee Black Childers, his secretary Suzi HaHa, and a wall caked with fans' graffiti for company.

History cannot help but sympathize with the Stooges, lifted up on such high expectations, and then left to rot by their management. Even Childers felt sorry for them. Pop was a performer, but for months he couldn't perform. Nobody knew what the group were rehearsing for, they simply rehearsed, and when Leee asked Defries why they weren't working, the reply was that the band wasn't ready for it.

It was Childers's responsibility to keep the band away from drugs, a monumental task as he recalled it, and one that was going to receive little encouragement from the Stooges. Indeed, he swiftly discovered that the best he could hope for was to regulate their intake and pray that when he packed them off every morning, they would return in the evening. Otherwise, his night would be spent scouring Los Angeles, hunting through the bars and alleyways to locate whichever hole it was that the band had chosen to collapse into that night.

"They had a lot of unauthorized parties," Childers recalled. "A lot of broken glass in the pool. A lot of fights with me. They brought in a bunch of junkie groupies and they were shooting up around the pool. All I ever said to Iggy was, 'Be discreet, just be discreet.' Therefore, the one thing he couldn't do was be discreet."

Bowie rounded off 1972 with his biggest U.K. hit yet, "The Jean Genie." One of several songs written on the road in the United States (and recorded in New York just weeks before its release), "The Jean Genie" was also one of two songs intended for his next album that took their inspiration directly from Iggy Pop—no matter what Marc Bolan thought.

The Bopping Elf confided to several friends that he knew for a fact that the song was about him, even as Bowie was telling concert audiences that it was about "a friend of ours, Iggy Pop." In fact, it was a straightforward rocker that he wrote for Cyrinda Foxe while they were hanging out in her apartment one day, and she challenged him to write a song. So he did, a pounding riff-rider dedicated to "a white-trash kind of trailer park kid...the closet intellectual who wouldn't want the world to know that he reads."

Was that a fair description of Pop? (Or Marc Bolan, come to that?) Probably not. Pop's presence hangs only loosely over "The Jean Genie," subverted among other things by the title's punning reference to French playwright Jean Genet, and the lyrics' own dash into a multitude of alternate realities.

The other new song, "Panic in Detroit," on the other hand, was pure Pop. One night after a show, Pop and Bowie burned the after-midnight oil, with Pop rapid-firing his memories of the five days of rioting that shook Detroit in July 1967, and the neighborhood revolutionaries who looked so chic and radical on the streets of hometown America. Pop was living, he said, in a burned-out ghetto squat at the time, loosely redecorated but so close to the front lines that it was scarcely worth chipping the black charring away from the woodwork.

That imagery alone was worth a verse or two and, though "Panic in Detroit" certainly took on a temperament all of its own before it was finally recorded (back in London in January 1973), its inspiration is pure urban Americana, refracted through whatever distortions a mere four years of history can layer upon events. With its guitars screaming like sirens, and backing vocalist Juanita Franklin shrieking murder behind them, "Panic in Detroit" captures all the fear and violence of that nightmare week, before feeding it through the cracked prism of the song's closest relation, the Rolling Stones' "Gimme Shelter."

Aladdin Sane, as Bowie's new album was to be titled, was completed by the end of January 1973. A harder, harsher, record than its predecessor, it also packed a more thought-provoking sleeve, as Bowie's made-up face was slashed by a bolt of lightning—suggestive, mused the critics, of the schizophrenia of stardom, or even of madness itself. The first glimmerings of Bowie's personal background were beginning to become public, the half-brother Terry who had spent much of his life in and out of asylums. Was Bowie fearing a similar fate, asked those people who spend their lives analyzing such things? And was this new "character" (for it was automatically assumed that Aladdin Sane *was* a new character, a new role for Bowie to play on stage) a way in which he might work out those fears?

Of course it was all so much psycho-babble, just as it is needlessly complicated (and impossibly stupid) to assume that every time Bowie changed his shirt for a photo session, he was assuming a whole new persona. But of course Bowie played along with the thought train. If something kept people talking, then it kept his career moving.

Aladdin Sane was scheduled for release in April, at the tail end of another U.S. tour, kicking off in New York City on Valentine's Day.

Compared to the pre-Christmas jaunt, this outing was a far more coherent affair, and if Bowie's continued refusal to fly ensured that the gaps between shows were just as large as before, that only gave the Main-Man team more time in which to prepare the way.

Plus, reasoned Zanetta, "we only did ten cities, the ten cities that we had done the best in on the last tour, which was very well thought out on our part. RCA was a big help in terms of the logistics of it, and at the same time, our roles within MainMan began to get a little more structured."

The biggest shake-up came in terms of Bowie's tour publicity. "We'd had an outside press agency working for us in the past, who were basically worthless, so we decided to do it ourselves. Meanwhile, Cherry didn't want to be sitting in the office all day, and she certainly didn't want to be Defries's secretary, so she decided she should be doing the press." And so the legend began.

Wayne County explained, "Tony Defries would send Cherry ahead to cities to make a scandal. And it worked." She had a gift for controversy, for turning the most innocent remark into headline news; she could do the same with a not so innocent remark. "David never knew what she was up to," County continued. "But Tony Defries did. He knew what sort of girl Cherry was. They sent her to Nashville, and big articles appeared in the newspapers saying, 'Don't let this Communist faggot play here!'"

The February 23 return to Nashville was still a few weeks away when Vanilla breezed into town, to talk up Bowie's brilliance and, if the questioners demanded (as they so often did), to give a little of her own colorful background as well. It was a routine she had submitted to on many past occasions, so she happily did so now.

Back around the time of *Island*, Vanilla had become involved with poet John Giorno and militant Abbie Hoffman's Radio Hanoi, an anti–Vietnam War exercise that intended to go head-to-head with Armed Forces Radio—*not* necessarily for political reasons but because, as Giorno said, "AFR . . . wouldn't even play the Rolling Stones or the Beatles."

Of course, there was a lot of political content, much of it aimed at persuading American troops to throw down their weapons and stop the war, but there was a great deal else going on as well; "one program was a rock 'n' roll program. We had our feminist half hour and then Jim Fouratt and the various gays had another half hour. And then country western. Anybody who wanted to do a program, we just put it together, in half-hour segments, and we'd have various people emcee."

Cherry's contribution, recorded at Radio Hanoi's WPAX studios in New York, was utterly apolitical, "playing songs by rock stars I'd either fucked or just knew, and telling stories about them." But Hoffman had long ago made it clear that "the whole point of doing this is to be busted for treason. We'll be the first persons busted for that since Aaron Burr." While he was to be disappointed in that regard, still Radio Hanoi inflamed a lot of sentiments across the country. In Nashville, a local right-wing newspaper seized upon Vanilla's involvement and drew the obvious conclusions. She was a Commie and so was the ship she sailed on. With an anti-Bowie campaign suddenly in full swing, there was no alternative but to cancel the upcoming show.

Vanilla was shattered by the news, but undaunted. Interviewed on air in Los Angeles a few days later, she detailed the entire sorry saga and in the process created such a wave of interest that not only was the show reinstated, but the publicity resulted in one of the first sold-out concerts of the entire outing. And the handful of pickets who turned out to protest what they perceived as Bowie's Communist connections were completely overwhelmed by the kids who just wanted to see the show. Justification, once again, for Defries's belief that even the disasters could be made to work to his advantage, if only everyone kept their head.

Childers, meanwhile, was also in Los Angeles, continuing to outfit MainMan's West Coast office, and now out shopping for a car, a big green Cadillac. "Now, I'd talked to the dealer and told him I worked for David Bowie and all that stuff, and on the radio was Cherry. She was doing this interview and the subject got round to the sexual question. The guy doing the interview asked if it was true that David was bisexual, and Cherry said it was. So he said, 'Well, how do you know?' and Cherry replied, 'Well, everybody who's worked for him has fucked him.' And I was there next to this very straight Hollywood car dealer and I just went, 'Oh dear!' One of my more embarrassing moments!"

"I'm not sure I remember it quite that way, but I like it," Vanilla counters. "I believe I used to defend David as straight by saying how good he was in bed with me. When people said he was bisexual, I usually said things like, 'You can't prove that by me.' I often said I helped recruit girls from the audience for him, and that I only saw him take girls to his room, never boys. But I like Leee's description, and who knows? It might be true. I often said things just for their effect, not caring if they were true or not. I thought that was what PR was! Ha ha, actually it is."

One thing she didn't make, however, was the oft-repeated claim that "we pedaled David's ass like Nathan's sells hot dogs."

"Someone asked me if David was indeed considered 'product,' like Tony Defries called him, and if we marketed him as such? I replied with a line I said many times in my life, because it was something my dad always said when asked such kinds of things.... It was more like, 'Well, as my daddy always says, 'Does Nathan's peddle hot dogs?' The writer just tried to make it more sensational. So many papers picked it up and repeated it... but it was never accurate."

Equally inflated were the much-recycled claims that she spent the next year of her life screwing DJs across the country, simply to ensure they played Bowie's records. Rather, she made a point of calling up a handful of ex-boyfriends who were working in the DJ trade, and persuading them to give Bowie a spin for old time's sake, if nothing else. But when journalists asked her if there was any truth to the rumors, of course she told them what they wanted to hear. "We saw all of this as theater, don't forget, so we often made up lines for effect. We didn't sit and think them out, we just improvised. Everything was happening so fast, that's all we had time for. We went for sensationalism."

The American tour was the first leg of what the MainMan machine was now calling a full world tour, although in truth, the global reach of the outing was considerably less than the headlines suggested. From the States, the Spiders moved on to Japan in early April 1973, and then it was back to the U.K. again for a British tour that would run from May 12 to July 3. But with Bowie's fear of flying still firing news stories into the stratosphere, simply placing the singer on the Trans-Siberian Express to commence his journey home was a genius idea.

The band's live set shifted as the *Aladdin Sane* material fell into place; shifted, and shed a lot of its early naïve charm. "Amsterdam" had slipped away to be replaced by another Brel chestbeater, "My Death"—an infinitely more appropriate song, of course, given the downward spiral that both Ziggy Stardust and his schizophrenic successor, Aladdin Sane, seemed destined to take.

But "Waiting for the Man" and "White Light White Heat" had also fallen from view, shunted out of the repertoire, perhaps not coincidentally, around the same time as it finally became apparent that Lou Reed was not going to pledge his managerial troth to MainMan. Bowie would not revive "Waiting for the Man" until 1976, and his first tour outside of the MainMan empire. "White Light White Heat" would be forced to wait even longer.

Defries, whose admiration for Reed was almost as powerful as Bowie's, made no secret of the fact that, of all David's playthings, Lou was the one he most desperately wanted to add to the roster. But Reed was evasive at first, and contrary later. He knew all the advantages of having MainMan in his camp at that time.

But he also knew the disadvantages as well, and as *Transformer* translated its critical reception into solid sales, and "Walk on the Wild Side" spiraled off the long-player to become his first hit single, it also became clear that Lou Reed was a saleable item in his own right, without any need for superstar endorsements. "I never thought of having a hit," he puzzled. "'Wild Side' be a hit? You're kidding. I never thought of anything being a hit." But there it was in black and white, and all across two continents, knowing ears smirked at the naïveté of the disc jockeys who allowed Candy Darling to work her magic upon a world of unsuspecting listeners.

On January 27, 1973, Reed played his first New York gig since the end of the Velvet Underground, headlining the Alice Tully Hall. "Walk on the Wild Side" was still to chart at the time. It would be another three weeks before hell froze over, pigs began flying, and Lou Reed became a pop star—which, in turn, meant this was one of the last shows where he would be playing to the converted alone, before the chart-hopping masses stopped grooving to Grand Funk and got into "Heroin" instead.

A partisan New York audience made him feel at home, though, and if the Tots were still a little too fussy, the nifty little guitar licks and drum fills that flickered and flashed through every song gave the performance a cheerful buoyancy that Reed rarely permitted in later years. "Walk and Talk It" was pure pop, of course. But so was the opening "White Light White Heat," and when "Waiting for the Man" threatened to descend into dissonance, an unknown onstage voice demanded, "Cut down on the feedback!" Cut down on the feedback at a Lou Reed gig? Yeah, right.

The *Transformer* tour kept Reed occupied through to the end of May 1973, and the legend grew as he traveled. In Detroit in April, *NME* writer Nick Kent watched as the men's' room filled with kids "barter[ing] for reds, Quaaludes, and cocaine; a review of the show appears two days later in a local Detroit paper titled 'Obscene Rock Star Performs in Vulgar Show.'" But Kent's most lasting memory was reserved for the après-show bash, when Reed, "looking even more wasted" than usual, turned to the handful of reporters who were milling around and snapped,

"I know why you're all here. You just want to get a headline story, 'Lou Reed ODs in Holiday Inn,' don't you?"

So Reed was doing very nicely on his own, and the more he thought about Defries's offers, the less he wanted to accept them, even after he and manager Heller broke up. Dennis Katz was on the verge of leaving RCA at the time, and making noises about moving into management himself. Reed agreed to become his first client and, watching how the New Yorker's career continued to flourish, how he seemed to be enjoying the best of both worlds, a Bowie-produced hit and a manager of his own, Mott the Hoople could not help but feel a little envious.

Those long-ago plans for a swift follow-up to "All the Young Dudes" had first been delayed, and then plunged into seemingly eternal abeyance as Bowie reclaimed "Drive-In Saturday" for his own next single and the band realized they needed look inward for the all-important next release. It would be spring 1973, some nine months after "Dudes," before they were finally able to unleash "Honaloochie Boogie," by which time they had already quit MainMan. Their reason? It simply wasn't working out.

Although Defries had initially been very enthusiastic about the band, he soon began having second thoughts about Mott's future. Part of the problem was the band's insistence upon putting up a democratic front. Defries was accustomed to dealing with artists on a one-to-one basis—if he had a question about the Spiders from Mars, he went to Bowie. If he had a question about the Stooges, he asked Pop. But Mott insisted that he call up all five members of the group and then sit on his hands until they'd all called one another to discuss the matter themselves.

There was another problem, too. Mott weren't Bowie. Neither, looking through the other artists whom MainMan represented, were Iggy Pop, Mick Ronson, Dana Gillespie, or Tony Ingrassia. But, for the moment, they weren't the issue. Mott were.

Zanetta explained, "Defries and Bowie had a very special partnership that worked...because of who they were. They depended upon each other for certain things, but not for other things. David was very much a self-starter and had his own support system away from Defries. Most of the other artists, maybe because they were in a secondary position to David, didn't have that characteristic. They didn't have that relationship with Defries. They were different kinds of people, or they expected too much from him. Bowie didn't expect Defries to do everything.

"Tony provided a certain space that David could function in. With other artists, Tony thought it would be the same thing: he'd provide the space and they'd get on with it. But they couldn't function, or they needed something else to make them function. Some of the things that Tony thought he was doing for David, he actually wasn't doing, David was doing. But because of their relationship, you couldn't see the divide."

Mott, Defries decided, couldn't function. It was time to say goodbye. By way of a farewell present, Bowie made some last-minute, and nobly uncredited, alterations to the "Honaloochie Boogie" lyric, while the band's choice of new management didn't stray too far from the family tree either—they signed with Lou Reed's old representative, Fred Heller, and marched on into a once-unimaginably bright future.

Lou Reed, on the other hand, remained stubbornly loyal to his past, both onstage, where the Velvet Underground repertoire continued to dominate his performances, and in the studio, where the songs that band never got around to recording continued to loom over his thoughts. "Men of Good Fortune," a melody he'd been toying with as far back as Nico's first rehearsal with the band, at the Factory back in January 1966; "Stephanie Says," a haunting lament for a speed freak; "Oh Gin," a rattletrap boogie condemning an abusive lover; "Sad Song," an exercise in English history that went out of its way to live up to its title; "Kid," watching as the authorities swoop on a rock-bottom mother and carry her children off into care...

Reed had never shied away from the notion of a conceptual body of work, for what, after all, were the Velvet Underground if not a singular notion that only developed with time? Now he was musing over the possibility of bringing that same line of thought and that same collection of songs together into a single long-playing cycle.

Transformer and "Walk on the Wild Side" had placed him in a position of considerable strength. After two such massive hits, it would be a brave label executive who would shoot down anything that the golden boy wanted to do next. But a concept album? "There was this big fight with RCA," Reed admitted, "[but] I shoved it through. I talked them into the veracity of the whole thing, of how astute it would be to follow up 'Walk on the Wild Side' with not just another hit single, but with a magnificent whatever."

And what was that whatever? A divorce set to music, from the opening rounds of strife and unfaithfulness, through to the bitterest denouement of all, suicide and regret, its own personal division set within the broader framework of cultural separation, the then-divided city of Berlin. "It was thought of as a concept right from the top," Reed admitted. From the moment he contacted producer Bob Ezrin, riding high at the time on the back of his groundbreaking work with the then-superhot Alice Cooper, "we just liked it. It was an adult album meant for adults, by adults for adults. And I think that's exactly what came out."

It was early summer before Reed could return to the studio. Talk of Bowie becoming involved in the album in some capacity, signaled to MainMan by Ezrin himself, had long been forgotten now. So had Reed's intentions of keeping the Tots together for the occasion; "I wanted to see whether I could have a hit single with a band, rather than me on my own." But the group fell away once the tour was over, together with his earliest ideas for the follow-up record. "*Rock N Roll Animal*, that's the title. I've got the cover shot, too. A black-and-white shot of me in leather. Yeah, say it's a backlash on *Transformer*. Maybe I'll do a song on it called 'Get Back in the Closet, You Queers.'"

Reed flew alone to London, home to all his first-choice studios. He was still enamored with that English sound. But his band this time was almost exclusively American, players whom Ezrin had long since learned to rely upon—guitarists Steve Hunter and Dick Wagner, a horn section led by Michael and Randy Brecker. Occasionally a local player might wander through the proceedings, Steve Winwood, Cream bassist Jack Bruce, keyboard player Blue Weaver, drummer Aynsley Dunbar... Later in the year, that pair would move on to Mott the Hoople and the Spiders from Mars, respectively. But this was Reed's circus, and he and Ezrin directed it with razor-blade precision. As Lou said later, "Bob Ezrin is as bad as I am. He insists on doing things the hard way."

And *Berlin* was hard work. Taking a break from the studio on July 3, Reed dropped by Bowie's end-of-tour party at the Café Royal, and you could see the tensions of the studio fall from his shoulders as he joined Bowie and Mick Jagger at their table where the three laughed, chattered, drank, and hugged one another. But the very next day it was back to work, on an album that retains all its emotive energy today.

Journalist Lester Bangs might have employed a *soupçon* of hyperbole when he described *Berlin* as possibly "the most depressed album ever made," but few listeners would disagree that it was "a gargantuan slab of maggoty rancor"; not even Reed, who later confessed, "*Berlin* was *real* close to home. People would say—'Lou, is that autobiographical?' And I'd say 'Mmmmm, not bad.' Jesus, autobiographical? If only they knew."

His marriage to Bettye was on its last legs—she would later admit that she never understood how she fell so hard for Reed, and he would more or less expunge her from his personal record book. But while there is little truth to those claims that the death of their relationship was the glue that bound *Berlin* together, there were similarities.

"During the recording sessions, my old lady—who was a real asshole, but I needed a female asshole around to bolster me up, I needed a sycophant who I could bounce around and she fitted the bill...but she called it love, ha! She tried to commit suicide in a bathtub in the hotel. Cut her wrists. She lived." Caroline, the presumably fictional antiheroine of *Berlin*, was not so resilient.

Neither was Reed's audience, although it would be asinine to say he didn't care about that; they were the people who ultimately paid his wages, after all, and it was they who ultimately decided whether or not he got to make another record. *Berlin*, however, was in trouble almost from the moment it was completed, and the RCA bigwigs settled back to play "spot the hit" with the ten songs Reed delivered—and found themselves instead listening to the screams and cries of Ezrin's children, moments after he'd led them into a well-miked room to tell them that their mother had died. Or so the scuttlebutt on the streets insisted. Reed and Ezrin have since denied the story, but the world would be a much more balanced place if they hadn't. Because now we need to wonder, what exactly he *did* tell them to make them howl like that?

Reed delivered what amounted to a double album's worth of material. RCA's first insistence was that he cut it down to a single disc. "*Berlin* was basically a movie in sound," Reed said later. "I'd love to see Polanski make a movie of *Berlin*." Now he and Ezrin were beavering away in the studio, cutting it down to a television program, a shade over fifty minutes, with perhaps another twenty left on the cutting room floor. But they were obviously happy with the results—true, the eight-track release salvaged a minute or so of jazzy piano from the tail end of the title track, but even when *Berlin* was remastered for CD, and every other artist in the land was scurrying around looking for bonus material to pin on the end of their old masterpieces, Reed allowed *Berlin* to stand as it always had, unadorned, unappended, unblinkingly pure.

Transformer was the sound of Reed skipping wide-eyed and guileless through the back streets of New York, eyeing all that the underbelly had to display with a sense of wonder that even his already laconic "seen it all" drawl could not disguise. *Berlin*, on the other hand, was a quixotically orchestrated descent into the belly that lurks beneath the underbelly, the rancid collapse of an already rotten marriage, with songs and scenarios that didn't pull a single punch.

But the reviews didn't see it that way. *Berlin* was not simply dismissed. It was destroyed. "There are certain records that are so patently offensive that one wishes to take some kind of physical vengeance on the artists that perpetrate them," announced *Rolling Stone*, and the critical establishment lined up to agree. An album that, today, we blithely accept as Reed's second post-Velvet Underground masterpiece (*Transformer*, of course, was the first) was for many years the pariah in the pack, with only 1975's *Metal Machine Music* capable of arousing deeper loathing.

"It was a very painful album to make. I had to do *Berlin*. If I hadn't got it out of my head, I would have exploded. Everyone was saying, 'Don't do it, you'll get killed.' It was insanity coming off after a hit single, but it was all written. *Transformer* is a fun album, and *Berlin* isn't."

It still made the U.K. Top 10, however, an odd bedfellow for the likes of Status Quo, David Cassidy, Slade, and the Rolling Stones; an awkward companion, even, for Bowie's *Pin Ups*, as that rose to No. 1 in November and looked down on Lou from there.

But Reed never lost his affection for *Berlin*, as he proved a full thirty-five years later. "A friend of mine at a place called St. Ann's Warehouse in New York had been asking me periodically to bring my band and play *Berlin*, but I never did it, obviously. And then one day I said, 'Sure. I'm not touring or making a record. Why not?'"

St. Ann's was tiny, 150 capacity maximum; intimate and so comfortable that, as Reed warmed to the project, he began casting around for ways to maximize it. Bob Ezrin was brought back to supervise the arrangements and the youth choir whose ethereal beauty would harmonize with Reed's rock-slide vocals; the band enrolled another veteran of those long-ago sessions, guitarist Steve Hunter; and artist and filmmaker

Julian Schnabel was approached to design the set and shoot some visuals. He agreed on condition that he could film the entire performance.

A snatch of the closing "Sad Song" became the opening overture, choir and orchestra added more to the music than one could ever have hoped, and Reed and Hunter sparred with exquisite and energetic delicacy. Suddenly, a one-off venture to fulfill an odd urge became a full-blown extravaganza, capable of being toured around Europe the following summer, screened at Cannes the year after that, and finally launched onto DVD in fall 2008, where its beauty blazes with such incandescence that you can even forgive Reed for having grown so old. The voice and the hair really aren't there, and he should maybe think about wearing a rollneck sweater, but *Berlin* stood timeless and inviolate regardless, as a magnificent album became a towering construct, faithful to the original but building upon it, too.

Vindication took a long time. But, as with all of Lou Reed's most valuable performances, from the Velvet Underground on, *Berlin* got there in the end.

14

A NATION HIDES ITS ORGANIC MINDS
IN THE CELLAR

"When you entered the theater, you must have seen the sign saying 'Artists at Work'? Well, you came to see us, and when you go to work, we'll come to see you. Until then—shut up."
　　　　　—David Bowie, onstage, to a heckler, Liverpool, June 1973

The Stooges album had been delivered now, but it hung in limbo while Columbia worked out what to do with it. The Stooges were hung out alongside it. Without an album there was no point in touring, but without gigs there was no point in doing much of anything. So they hammed, they jammed, they boogied, they demolished their favorite cover versions, and every evening they'd pack up a little earlier, to wander down Sunset to Rodney Bingenheimer's English Disco, where they suddenly found themselves the not at all unwilling center of attention for the local groupie scene.

Bingenheimer looked on proudly. At a time when the MainMan organization was thrusting glamour and glam rock into the gray, recession-bound world of the early 1970s, so the disco was bringing a vivid slash of that same peacock finery to Sunset Strip, and he made no secret of the fact that MainMan was his role model. A friend of Bowie's since the singer's first promotional visit to L.A., Bingenheimer had even moved to London in late 1971, to be closer to the action that he knew was about to explode.

The visit cost him his girlfriend—Melanie MacDonald met Tony Defries when they dropped by a Bowie recording session, and Rodney was suddenly history. But it gave him the next four years of his life. Glam rock, he knew, was never going to take off in the United States in the same way it had in Britain. There was no room at the American table for such treats as Sweet, Gary Glitter, Alvin Stardust, and Wizzard, and even T.Rex had stumbled after scoring one hit. But Los Angeles, with its built-in obsession with satin and tat—that was another matter entirely. When Bowie suggested that he open a club that catered exclusively to the glam rock scene, Bingenheimer knew what he had to do.

Back in L.A., Bingenheimer and his partner Tom Ayres opened their first club, E, on Sunset Boulevard in October 1972. Two months later, a change of address, to further up the strip, brought the new name, and for the next two years, Rodney Bingenheimer's English Disco was the loud and living epitome of all the magic that MainMan promised.

"The crowd at the club ranged in age from twelve to fifteen," Tony Zanetta told his *Stardust* memoir. "Nymphet groupies were stars in their tight little world. Some dressed like Shirley Temple; others wore dominatrix outfits or 'Hollywood underwear,' a knee-length shirt, nylon stockings, and garter belts. These stargirls streaked their hair chartreuse and liked to lift their skirts to display their bare crotches. As they danced they mimed fellatio and cunnilingus in tribute to David's onstage act of fellatio on Ronno's guitar."

Other commentators revealed further secrets. "Once inside," wrote journalist Richard Cromelin, "everybody's a star. The social rules are simple but rigid: All you want to hear is how fabulous you look, so you tell them how fabulous they look. You talk about how bored you are, coming here night after night, but that there's no place else to go. If you're not jaded there's something wrong. It's good to come in very messed up on some kind of pills every once in a while, and weekend nights usually see at least one elaborate, tearful fight or breakdown. If you're eighteen, you're over the hill."

If you were a dancer, maybe. But not if you were a star. Rodney's was the place to be, the place to be seen, and the place to go if you wanted some action, and the Stooges spent as much time there as they could—at least until it was time to head back to Mulholland, with some spangle-bedecked jailbait booty squirming on their arms.

Rehearsals continued in and around the entertainment. "Head on the Curb," "Johanna," and "I Got Nothing" came into being. "Cock in My Pocket"—"an Eddie Cochran thing," Pop explained. "Nobody sits down and writes a song called 'I Got My Cock in My Pocket,' but that was basically what I carried around to keep myself alive, so I just stood up at the mic and there it was." And "Open Up and Bleed," a howl of protest against Defries's restrictions, bitter and battered in equal proportions, and one of the greatest songs the Stooges ever performed.

By February 1973, the Stooges had half an album's worth of new material in the bag, and *Raw Power* was finally inching onto the release schedules. It was time, Defries decided, to bring the band out of seclusion. In L.A. that month with the Bowie tour, he took Pop out for a spin in a hired limo, and began outlining his plans for the singer.

"We want to start thinking about film projects for you," he said softly. "We see you as Peter Pan."

He got no further. "I ain't no fucking Peter Pan," Pop shot back. "We're gonna do Manson. I'm gonna be Charlie Manson."

Defries shrugged and let the matter drop. Besides, he had another piece of news for the group; a Stooges homecoming concert at the Ford Auditorium in Detroit at the end of March.

Rehearsal time suddenly leaped back into prominence. No matter that heroin had drifted back into the band's orbit, with all the debilitating drama which that entailed; or that they were so easily distracted by the antics of their groupie following, a coterie headlined by the diminutive fifteen-year-old Sable Starr, her sister Coral, and another high schooler, Evita Adura. They were going home in style.

On March 18, Iggy and the Stooges flew to Detroit to find MainMan's publicity machine in full flow. Cherry Vanilla was there, ensuring acetates of the new album were available for anybody who wanted to hear them, while Pop was booked onto WABX DJ Mark Parenteau's late-afternoon radio show, to preview the album to the world.

Home base was established back in Ann Arbor, the Stooges moving into the small studio belonging to old friend Scott Richardson, SRC, and getting ready for the show. Talk was already flying of this being only the first of several gigs. Even more excitingly, the American media was lining the Stooges up as the band most likely to break out next. In an era when everybody from Alice Cooper to Silverhead was vying with one another to produce the sleaziest, glammiest band in the land, the Stooges were the real thing.

Even Columbia got in on the excitement, ordering Pop not to play any selections from the new album on the Parenteau show, in case the bootleggers got the tapes on the street before the real thing came out.

Pop seemed to agree. He would not play the finished *Raw Power*, he pledged. He would play an earlier version of it, the pre-Bowie version that the band themselves still believed was superior, Williamson's guitars slashing and screaming and painting the serpentine figures that Pop knew so well, but which the listening audience would never have believed. Neither, it transpired, could the show's audience have expected to hear an overexcited Pop dancing half-naked around the studio, singing along with his creation, while his uncaged penis slapped against his flesh and echoed down the microphone.

Said Childers, "Iggy was totally crazy by now. He did a local radio interview; he took all his clothes off in the studio and started waving his naked body out of the window, telling passersby that he was the greatest dancer in the world. He was weird, he was abusive"—he was Iggy Pop.

The night before the show, Pop and Williamson disappeared. They were finally discovered crashed out in an alleyway, having pawned all their equipment, including the three-quarter-size guitar Pop had had custom built, to buy methadone. "I was really nervous..." Pop excused himself. "I wanted it to be really good. [That gig] was bigger than we had ever done on our own, and also in a nicer joint, and with a new repertoire."

He needn't have worried. A watching Lester Bangs described the gig as "the greatest show many ever saw them do. Absolutely twitch perfect, they sounded and looked as slick as a whip, and the audience was frothing floodtides down the aisles." If anyone ever doubted that the Stooges were set for stardom, the Ford Auditorium show sent them packing. The band even eschewed the opportunity to play an encore, leaving the rabid crowd howling for more while Tony Defries patiently counseled the musicians to stay backstage. If the Stooges wanted to be stars, he said, they should behave like stars.

Backstage, too, all was glittering. Defries was everywhere, collecting the plaudits of everyone he spoke to. Pop's parents looked on proudly and, perhaps, a little bemusedly after Pop introduced "Cock in My Pocket" as a song that he cowrote with his mom; and English journalist Nick Kent absorbed it all, from the heights of heroism to the dark depths that wound up all but wrecking the evening.

First, the Asheton brothers were refused entry to what Defries was describing as a press conference, but which was clearly the best-fed affair they had ever seen; then Pop, evading the attentions of a drunken well-wisher, wound up pushing the girl down the stairs.

Defries fumed as the room hushed in shocked horror. No matter that the concert itself was glorious; when the story of the show was written, it would be the backstage violence that would pass into legend, not the performance itself.

Flash points mounted, arguments sparked. Williamson turned ugly. Not for the first time, Defries found himself regretting the decision to allow Pop to surround himself with the old friends and drug buddies who had held him back in the past, but this time, he determined to do something about it. Back in L.A., with Childers in firm agreement with him, Defries gave the Stooges an ultimatum. Either they sacked Williamson, or MainMan would sack the band. Williamson was out.

There was no shortage of potential replacements. Defries had recently suggested that Pop try working with Hollywood scenester and maverick record producer Kim Fowley; Fowley now put forward Warren Klein, guitarist with *Easy Rider* sound track stars Fraternity of Man. Another friend, eighteen-year-old Doors confidante Danny Sugerman, recommended Ricky Frystack, a high school friend and guitarist with a band called Moonstack. "That was the first time I ever worked with Iggy," Sugerman said in an interview shortly before his death in 2005, "I knew he was looking for a guitarist, and I was looking for a way into MainMan, so it could have worked out really well. They went with some other guy in the end [Klein, who was renamed Tornado Turner for the occasion], but it didn't matter because the whole thing fell apart about fifteen minutes later."

Suddenly, there was any number of final straws snapping, most of them involving drugs, and all of them demanding money...more money...even more money. The Torreyson Drive house had, like every other place the Stooges called home, been trashed, and the repair bill was going to be astronomical. Even Bowie, the one person who could have put in a good word for his hero, seemed to have tired of his plaything, or at least, become so wrapped up in his own career that, whatever his personal feelings for the band might have been, it was easier just to agree with Defries. Shortly after the MainMan entourage arrived in Japan at the beginning of April 1973, for the Far Eastern leg of Bowie's world tour, Defries fired off one final telegram to Mulholland Drive.

"The Stooges are no longer MainMan artists."

Pop was not necessarily downhearted. "While [Defries] was managing me, I only worked twice in nine months. Most gigs [we were offered] weren't good enough for me because I was 'Iggy Pop.' If I wanted a $300 car, I couldn't have one. I had to go to the drugstore in a limousine. I have no idea why."

He also smelled a rat. "Bowie and his organization wanted to root out elements in my band who would stand up to them. It was too difficult to deal with. Unhappy people are difficult, and they made me an unhappy person."

The oft-voiced suggestion that MainMan's (and therefore Bowie's) chief interest in the Stooges was to keep them under wraps to prevent them from offering Bowie any active competition was no stranger, either. "Personally, I think David's a fine fellow," Pop told *After Dark* writer Henry Edwards. But there was a distinct caveat to his compliment. "There are so many who stole a lot of shit from me, but the way David did it, I minded. Look at photographs of me taken in 1970 and then look at the way David Bowie looks. Check out my lyrics and see how David Bowie has rewritten them." And listen to the way Bowie allowed his singing voice to shift, from the excitable pitch of Ziggy *Stardust* and *Aladdin Sane*, to the more sonorous tones that would creep in thereafter. Do you think he wanted to sound like Iggy? journalist Paul Trynka asked Mick Ronson once. Ronson laughed. "*Sound* like Iggy? He wanted to *be* Iggy!"

But it is MainMan president Tony Zanetta who best placed the dilemma in proportion. "The entire saga has reached such mythic proportions, and Defries is always blamed for sabotaging poor Iggy and the Stooges. [But] there are always two sides to every story. Defries took a recovering drug addict, got him a record deal, brought him to the U.K. to record and rehearse, and supported him in comfortable if not quite grand style. He eventually imported his entire band to the U.K. and supported them as well. During this time the twenty-seven-year-old Defries was breaking away from his employer, Gem, to form his own company, MainMan, and trying to break two other acts—Dana Gillespie and David Bowie.

"He moved the entire operation to the U.S. in order to tour Bowie and establish him in the U.S. While touring Bowie, he set up Iggy and the Stooges in a very nice house in the Hollywood Hills. All of their expenses were paid for, including unlimited rehearsal time. Within three months, they had repaid his largesse by reverting to their drugs of choice, causing constant mayhem, and stealing from their own house in order to buy drugs. If there was a leash that they were on, it was largely of their own making, because of their irresponsibility and passivity and inability to be trusted."

Ziggy returned to London following Japan, riding the Trans-Siberian Express to the end of the line and then greeting his subjects at Earls Court, a massive arena in the west London neighborhood of the same name, that had hitherto served only to house boat shows and exhibitions. It was a disaster, an overlarge, underamplified bear pit that took a two-hour show that was rehearsed to perfection and transformed it into a muddy blurge. Bowie was heartbroken in its aftermath; the media was simply unforgiving.

Few artists had ever ventured into arenas that size in Britain, and those that did at least made certain they knew what they were letting themselves in for. To those media observers who best enjoyed taking potshots at the all-powerful MainMan machine, booking the boy into a hall that had never previously staged a live show was simply one more example of their absolute naïveté. The fact that Slade would be playing the same cavern a short time afterward, and pulled off their show without a hitch, only added to the brickbats.

The remainder of the tour, however, was little short of triumphant. Of course there were the occasional disruptions. In Liverpool, overzealous security hurled a female fan off the stage with such brutality that Bowie left the scene in tears, and refused to return until the gorillas were penned, at which point the entire audience piled into the orchestra pit, then leaped out when the floor started collapsing beneath the weight. The only casualty turned out to be the venue's grand piano, but the show was halted once again.

In Salisbury, Bowie attempted an Iggy-like leap from the PA to the stage, and landed awkwardly enough that he was still limping at the next show in Torquay. Cue chaos as, while making his way along the lip of the stage, he stumbled and fell into the audience. Undaunted, the star bunny-hopped his way as far up the aisle as the mic chord would allow, then sat himself down and continued to sing.

Ticket demand was astonishing. Bowie was the first act to sell out the Salisbury venue since Led Zeppelin played there and, as late as June 26, he was still agitating for a third night at London's Hammersmith Odeon to be added to the two already booked (and sold out). MainMan ultimately chose not to, and so it was, that on July 3, 1973, Bowie "retired." Onstage at Hammersmith Odeon, facing an audience almost as breathless as he was, he announced that was it. "Not only is this the last show of the tour, it's the last show we'll ever do."

Behind the scenes at MainMan, the news was greeted with a polarized range of emotions. On the one hand, there was relief. But on the other, there was terror. What would happen now?

As Tony Zanetta put it, "From July 1972 until July 1973, there was very little time for any kind of thought; we were just too busy. We were always traveling, always on the road, we worked twenty-four hours a day. I lived in the office with Defries, and some nights, he'd wake me up at midnight and we'd go to work. The same thing with the band and with David. David worked constantly, so no one had time to consider anything, there were no problems other than how to get enough money to get through the next day. We did two American tours, we did the Japanese tour, we did the huge English tour...and then it all stopped. And that's when the problems started."

The first casualty, if it can be called that, was Bowie's scheduled next American tour, his third in a year and a veritable leviathan that stretched Defries's ambition, and Zanetta's credulity, to the limit.

"It was very grandiose," Zanetta shuddered. "Tony was looking at these big sports arenas, huge places, but it really wasn't coming together." Bowie's success in America at that time was still an illusion. It existed in the press, but it did not exist in sales, and it certainly did not exist in the live arena. He had still only played in seventeen cities total in the U.S., and most of those were very small houses.

"We had only played one big place," Zanetta continued, "which was Long Beach Arena, and a 10,000-seater in Cleveland. Other than that, it was 3,000-seater halls, so to go from that immediately into a massive long tour where he wanted to book the sports arenas and domes on 90/10 percent deals, was completely nuts. He just couldn't get the deals he wanted, so we decided to cancel the tour. We put out a press announcement that we were canceling the biggest tour ever, even though it only existed in our imaginations."

The final Hammersmith was filmed and, for a time, it seemed likely that a Bowie concert movie might hit the theater circuit instead of Bowie himself. RCA originally hired director D. A. Pennebaker to shoot thirty minutes' worth of concert footage for a new video disc format they were working on, called Select-A-Vision. But he filmed the entire show and was so blown away by the images he captured that it would have been criminal to leave two-thirds of the show on the cutting room floor.

Wheels within wheels. The movie was completed but the project was never completed. Around forty minutes of footage was leased out to the ABC TV network, which aired it as part of their *In Concert* television series, but the full movie continued to languish. It would be 1983 before *Ziggy Stardust: The Motion Picture* was finally seen in public, by which time it was too late to do anything but amuse a few nostalgics. A decade earlier, it could have changed everything.

While Ziggy's farewell was still sinking into the fanbase, Bowie traveled to Paris, and checked in at the Château d'Hérouville studio to record his next album, *Pin Ups*. It was, he declared, a personal tribute to the sixties. And from the other side of the English Channel, Wayne County quietly seethed. It should have been his record.

Although he had yet to formally sign a MainMan contract, County was convinced it would only be a matter of time before he was sent into the studio with either Bowie, Ronson, or both. Or so the two informed him. "So I gave David a demo tape of my songs, for the LP, only for David to decide it would be better to do this album of covers. He thought that was a great idea. We would do songs by Iggy Pop, Alice Cooper, the Velvet Underground, Nico, and one of his own. And it would probably have been a great album, but even that he just talked about for a few weeks before going off to do something else . . . which turned out to be *Pin Ups*."

In fact, Bowie was as surprised as anyone when Defries suggested that his next album should be an all-covers collection, at least partially because it was already well known that Bryan Ferry was then working on precisely the same kind of project. But Defries had his reasons: a bust-up with Bowie's publishers, Chrysalis, over a renewal of their contract.

Chrysalis refused to agree to Defries's new terms, so he hit them in the only place they would feel it, by announcing that Bowie would not record any more of his own compositions.

Still, County was right to have felt so aggrieved. Like Iggy Pop, he believed MainMan was going to work for him. Instead, he was sidelined to make sure that he didn't compete with the main attraction.

"David would get all these great ideas, or somebody would, and he'd use other people as sounding boards. He'd talk things over with them, letting them believe they'd be doing something for their own career, then once he'd got all their ideas, he'd run off and do it himself."

In an age when most observers still considered Bowie outrageous, County made him look like a trendy vicar, "a nightmare vision of a house-wife in a soap commercial," shivered the *Village Voice*, "white makeup under a gray/purple wig festooned with spearmint gum wrappers and the logo from a box of Tide, crimson lips and gleaming eyes, heavily mascara'd, a green flouncy dress, red stockings, and high heels."

Props included "my cock shoes—the heel was two balls, the shoe was a cock," a chamber pot, a toilet seat necklace, a plastic dildo filled with shaving cream for the use of dancer Via Valentina, and a large plastic vagina, which County would ritually abuse at the end of "Dead Hot Mama," a song about a boy forced to have sex with his dead mother so as to free her spirit from his father's body. And finally there were a few tins of dog food, which County would let drain through the back of his pants.

"I loved upsetting people," he said. "If I could see that I was really upsetting them I'd just give in and get even worse. You know what it's like when you're really aggravating someone—you do it more out of meanness. You say, 'Ooh, you're getting *upset*! I'd better do it some more then. So there.'" But hopes that he might be allowed to give British audiences a taste of the mayhem were doomed to disappointment.

"The first time I went to London, RCA actually offered me a record deal, but MainMan said no, 'Wayne's not ready to record yet.' They just fucked me all down the line. I really believed they were going to work for me and . . . [a]nd by the time I woke up, it was too late. But when I came over, I'd get so much publicity and David would simply flip. He once said he couldn't pick up one of his own reviews without reading about me."

In October 1973, home from Paris, Bowie launched into the filming of *The 1980 Floorshow*, a one-off neo-comeback for American television's

Midnight Special, and County was on particularly fine form. "It was meant to be his show, but there was half a page about me in the papers. Because I'd talk to the writer, I'd go to the bar with him and drink with him and hoot with him, and David would be locked away in his dressing room or whatever, not having anything to do with anybody. I'd be running around going, 'Wheeee, wheeee, party party,' and David would be furious! 'How come everything I read is about Wayne?'"

Staged over three days of filming at the Marquee Club in London's Wardour Street, a venue Bowie had graced on several occasions during his own 1960s apprenticeship, *The 1980 Floorshow* was alternately the theatrical climax of everything Bowie had been working toward over the past two years; an early taste of his next project, a musical version of George Orwell's *1984*; and the final death knell of Ziggy Stardust and Aladdin Sane.

Either way, it was a riotous occasion. Before a live audience drawn from friends and the fan club, Bowie was bidding his final farewell to the painted, costumed creations he had nurtured through the last eighteen months of superstardom, an unspoken encore for the Hammersmith Odeon farewell, for the benefit of his American followers.

The statuesque beauty Amanda Lear was peeled off the latest Roxy Music LP cover, and invited to compeer the event; a handful of guests were on hand to help entertain the masses—sixties survivors the Troggs and Marianne Faithfull, and an Anglo-American flamenco rock band called Carmen, currently being produced by Tony Visconti. They were complete unknowns so far as the public was concerned, but a sprinkle of Bowie stardust would surely alter that.

Carmen frontman David Allen recalled, "Tony arranged for Bowie, Angela, and friends to meet us at his house for dinner one night a couple of weeks into our first album. We offered to cook and [we] made Mexican food . . . and the night went well. The following week, Bowie asked Tony if he could bring the head of *The Midnight Special* down to the studio to hear some of our music, as he was interested in including us. Tony said sure, and played them a rough mix of 'The Bulerias' when they arrived. They let us know right then and there that we were on. We were very cool and said thanks. Then—once they'd left—we went down to the pub and got drunk!"

The Spiders were there, still clinging on after Bowie at least hinted that they'd work together again sometime, but looking just a little lopsided after Woody Woodmansey departed. Veteran blues rock drummer Aynsley Dunbar, fresh from Lou Reed's *Berlin* sessions, filled his place nicely. There was room, too, for the Astronettes, the backing singers whom Bowie had first unveiled at the Rainbow. Bowie was about to take them into the studio to record an album, but listening to them squawk and flap at the Marquee microphone, it was difficult to see what he saw in them.

And that was the problem. Bowie was bored, so he looked for things to do, regardless of whether he intended seeing them through or not. *The 1980 Floorshow* itself was a fiasco, poorly thought out, badly executed, and produced in far too great a hurry.

Up to that point, everything that Bowie put his mind to was rehearsed to the edge of perfection. There was sufficient room left for a degree of spontaneity, but the nuts and bolts of every production were thoroughly tightened beforehand. Now, however, he was looking for shortcuts. In the past, before fame came knocking, the most arduous task was worth undertaking because this might be the one that proved the breakthrough. But once that breakthrough was made, why should he work so hard?

Like the Beatles when they were let loose on *Magical Mystery Tour* without the guiding hand of Brian Epstein to rein in their indulgences and force them to look closely at what they were attempting, Bowie stepped into *The 1980 Floorshow* believing that he was invulnerable; that he needed only wave his magic wand at a project for it to fall from the sky fully formed.

Instead, *The 1980 Floorshow* emerged looking grubby and tired. No matter how many hours MainMan invested in the project, attempting to improve the video quality on a rented Moviola machine, there simply weren't enough. NBC had their broadcast date and they weren't going to postpone it for anybody. *The 1980 Floorshow* aired as scheduled, and it did nobody any favors.

Bowie's interest in Carmen and the Troggs lasted the length of *The 1980 Floorshow*, and he never mentioned them again.

Marianne Faithfull fared a little better—her own relationship with Defries went back to 1970, when she'd hooked up with Gem house producer Mike Leander for the sessions that very belatedly became her *Rich Kid Blues* album, and though nobody at MainMan (including Defries) could understand why Bowie had invited her along ("he could have had anybody"), still she pulled off the visual shock of the show. Resplendent in a backless nun's habit, dueting with Ziggy through "I Got You Babe," her voice a smoky croak, her eyes two sunken orbs, she was fabulous. Bowie rewarded her with a berth on the slowly lengthening list of artists whose careers he intended kick-starting with a quick production job, but nothing ever happened. Like so much in his universe at that time, simply having an idea was enough for the mercurial Bowie. Once he'd worked out the details, it was time to move on.

Sixties pop idol Adam Faith, now carving his way through seventies legend via a clutch of well-chosen television and movie roles, was talking about making a musical comeback. Bowie promptly offered his services as guitarist—"and maybe a little saxophone—I'm much better at that!" It didn't happen.

Another sixties survivor, Lulu, was promised an LP, although she at least got into the studio with Bowie and Ronson, to cut her biggest hit single in years, a cover of Bowie's own "Watch That Man." For a few weeks in March 1974, a woman celebrating her tenth year of hits was up there with the very best new talent that the British pop circus could throw into the ring: Leo Sayer, the Wombles, the Bay City Rollers, and Lena Zavaroni—a child star who wasn't even eating solids when Lulu scored her first hit single.

The Astronettes seemed to be on course as well, locked into Olympic Studios in December, and laying down most of their projected debut album before Bowie tired of it and announced he wanted to make a solo Ava Cherry album instead. But that, too, went by the board after just a handful of sessions, and the Astronettes ascended to the annals of Bowie legend for the next thirty years—until a mid-1990s release for the project revealed he'd been right to can it in the first place. Generously, one can trace the evolution of the blueprint that would one day become Bowie's *Young Americans* to the Astronettes. Honestly, one never needs to listen to the record again.

He hooked up with folk rockers Steeleye Span, to wheeze saxophone across their version of "To Know Him Is to Love Him"—Steeleye bassist Rick Kemp had figured in a passing incarnation of Ronson's pre-Bowie band, the Rats, and might even have been recruited to the Spiders from Mars had he not had the misfortune to be losing his hair at a time when Defries wanted Bowie's band to have hair to spare. (At least, that's the story. The truth may be less—or even more—prosaic). According to drummer Nigel Pegrum, Bowie arrived at the studio "in a big American car full of transvestites," then vanished with them once his job was done.

He championed a rising young American named Bruce Springsteen. Upon launching his last American tour in New York in February 1973, Bowie was thrilled to discover Biff Rose was playing Max's—the same Biff Rose whose pen had provided him with "Buzz the Fuzz" and "Fill Your Heart." He was opening for a local newcomer named Bruce Springsteen, although Bowie had little interest in that. "He came to see me," Rose recalled. "He'd never heard of Springsteen—not many outside New York had. Bowie came up to me.... [H]e had such admiration... awe... in his eyes.... I was grateful he'd done the song."

Springsteen, on the other hand, was simply "loud, very loud, so it was easy to think something was happening." Bowie certainly thought so. He scooped up Bruce's "Spirits in the Night" for the Astronettes album, and history records him as the first artist ever to cover a Springsteen song— and then abandon it.

Other projects came and went. There was talk of a Cherry Vanilla album—while Mick Ronson regularly inspected the New York club scene in search of musicians who might be right for her band, Bowie and Angela actively encouraged Cherry's writing abilities. It was Angela who, at the Springfield Rock Festival in Missouri (dedicated in its entirety to Bowie and his music), persuaded Cherry to present one of the performing bands with her own lyrics for inclusion in their set. And, interviewed in 1974 by *Penthouse* magazine, the couple were amongst the most vociferous supporters of *Compositions*, a book of Cherry's poetry published as a limited edition in the U.S. Like Wayne County's projected LP, however, a Cherry Vanilla record never happened.

Yet if Bowie had really wanted to salvage a career, to extend a helping hand to a drowning man, or even simply pull an old friend out of the abyss, he needed only look back at the Stooges.

15

CAGED LIKE A WILD RAT BY FOOLS

"Iggy is stupid. Very sweet, but very stupid. If he'd listened to David or me, if he'd asked questions every once in a while . . . He's just making a fool of himself, and it's just going to get worse and worse. He's not even a good imitation of a bad Jim Morrison. . . . I'd say, 'Man, just make a one-five change and I'll put it together for you. You can take all the credit. It's so simple, but the way you're doing it now, you're just making a fool out of yourself.'"
—Lou Reed (to Lester Bangs), 1975

The Stooges were not left without a safety net, even after they were expelled from Mulholland Drive. Jerry Wald, husband and manager of the Australian songstress Helen Reddy, had been sniffing around the group recently, convinced that all the Stooges needed was a manager who could actually remain on top of every situation, rather than swan off around the world with another client entirely. Unfortunately, as Childers succinctly puts it, "Jerry Wald thought Helen Reddy was weird. He hadn't seen anything yet!"

Pop, too, dismisses Wald's efforts. "It took a big person to manage the Stooges. And Defries was, I'll give him that, he had a big vision, that man." Wald remained on the scene for little more than a week, Childers exaggerated. The Stooges lived on the street for the rest of the year. "It was a ridiculous situation," Childers sighed. "They were on the street, I was living in a four-bedroom house with nothing to do. Suzi HaHa was still coming up every day to be my secretary; we'd just sit around by the pool. Dana Gillespie came to stay. She sat by the pool for two weeks, then went home. It was all a total waste of time."

Raw Power finally hit the streets in May 1973, and Pop remembered the day vividly. He was so broke at the time that he had to borrow the money from Kim Fowley to purchase a copy for himself. His record label hadn't even bothered sending him one.

With no heavy-hitting management company to push the label into working the record, it was destined to sink like a stone. By mid-June, British sales amounted to a paltry 2,500 (Bowie's *Aladdin Sane*, by comparison, had done 189,000), and the only people who appeared interested in Iggy Pop that week were the Hampshire police, who wanted to speak to him with regard to an underage runaway.

The lineup was in disarray. Tornado Turner played one show with the Stooges, at the Aragon Ballroom in Chicago on June 15, then admitted that he wasn't working out. By the time the Stooges returned to Los Angeles later that week, to open a five-day, ten-show season at the Whisky a Go-Go, James Williamson was back in the saddle.

Danny Sugerman caught as many of the Whisky shows as he could. "They were on fire every night, and you kept going back because every show would be different, and there'd be something else that would burn itself into your memory. Pop being groped by every woman in the front row, getting a blow job while he was singing, and then singing about the blow job. Being carried around the room by the audience, being passed across the kids' heads to the back of the place and then back to the stage. Blood. He'd always come off stage bleeding from somewhere or another."

"I did it to the point of parody," Pop laughed in 1993. "Other people drove their cars into swimming pools. We couldn't afford a car, so we drove other people's cars in. Then, when others started doing that, we went beyond it again. We'd throw ourselves into the pool and drown." He smiled nostalgically. "We were a very nasty little band. The only people who responded to what we did were the avant-garde and the deviants, the arty sickos. And kids and high school dropouts, the real dregs, the young sickos."

The sickos were out in force now, even if the Stooges remained in chaos. Two nights into the Whisky residency, the keyboard player the band had recruited for the occasion, Bob Sheff, walked out after roadie John Myers refused to pay him. The following night, Pop executed one of his trademark swan dives into the audience, and crashed onto the dance floor, injuring himself so badly that he had to cancel the band's second set of the evening. And so on.

"You didn't feel like you were watching a rock concert," journalist Greg Shaw remembered. "Because rock concerts are artifice and the suspension of belief. There was no playacting with the Stooges—everything they did, they did for real."

He recalled the drama with which a typical evening began. Prior to his departure, Sheff took the stage first, a string of tiny red lightbulbs wound around his head and hair, and kicked off the rhythm of the opening "Raw Power." The Ashetons and Williamson would follow him a few minutes later, picking up the riff, while behind them a film loop played and replayed one single sequence from the 1964 movie *The Killers*, Lee Marvin gunning down Ronald Reagan. Finally Pop took the stage, striding to the microphone but not touching it yet, nor opening his mouth, just staring out at the audience while those groping hands roamed over his skinny legs and torso. It was a moment that could last forever, it seemed, or at least until Pop finally grew bored with all the attention, kicked away his admirers, and started to sing.

Shows were sporadic to begin with. Following the Whisky, the band had only one more date in their itinerary, in Lake St. Clair, Michigan, before moving to New York at the end of June, for a week of shows at Max's Kansas City. Bob Sheff had been replaced with Scott Thurston by now, and his introduction to the band was as chaotic as their reputation warned him it might be. Pop had not even sung a note at the Michigan show before one audience member was carried out, concussed—Pop had thrown a watermelon into the crowd, and it hit a girl on the head. Further into the set, the singer took a dump behind the speakers, then hurled that out at the onlookers as well.

The band arrived in New York on July 28, two days before their opening night at Max's, and two flights ahead of Pop, who had gone to sleep the previous night with a bottle of Valium for company. Assuming he would turn up sooner or later, the rest of the Stooges took up residence at Columbia's rehearsal studios and began reworking their set, before Pop finally showed up. "I remember we were playing without him, just music, and he just came running in and running up to a microphone and started to do his thing like nothing had happened," Ron Asheton recalled.

In front of an audience of wall-to-wall celebrities, from Alice Cooper to the Dolls to Todd Rundgren, with Lou Reed watching carefully, and a host of old friends from the Stooges' first visit to New York as well, the band were greeted onstage as returning heroes, even if they weren't quite sure precisely what they'd done that was so heroic. Dancing on the edge of their own grave, perhaps? Backstage, Jackie Curtis dropped by to talk to Lou and Pop together. The conversation was not recorded, but *Rock Scene* magazine published a fabulous photograph of the three of them together, with Ron Asheton a glowering presence alongside the centerpiece. The Stooges were home, and Reed celebrated by asking Pop if the Stooges would like to record one of his songs. Pop turned him down. They wrote their own material.

New songs "Rubber Legs," "Head On," "Cry for Me" and "Pinpoint Eyes" were all readied for action, alongside "Heavy Liquid," a radical reinterpretation of Gary U.S. Bonds's "New Orleans." A disheveled beast, a thrashing monster, "Heavy Liquid" stood proud within that underworld of atmosphere and adrenaline that was the roar of the Stooges, its very transience a hallmark of the unrepentant dishevelment that was the band's final dying glory.

They copped some new stagewear. Pop recalled, "James and I had acquired some really hideous costumes from a designer named Bill Whitten, who designed for Neil Diamond, among other people in L.A. James had this sort of Spiderman outfit and I had this . . . strange human fly outfit. It was kind of cool in a way, but I don't know what I was thinking."

Iggy's first impressions of Max's, in 1973, were poor. It had degenerated from its prime, transformed from a place in which to hang out with like-minded freaks, to a straightforward rock 'n' roll club, with its visions of grandeur reduced to mere the point of parody. You know you're in for a long evening when the most exciting event on hand is the sight of Mike Montgomery, the guitarist with Bloontz, throwing chick peas at Lou Reed, and then feigning innocence when accusatory eyes circle the room in search of the miscreant. According to Montgomery, his target was usually so out of it that he could never figure out who was accosting him.

"I didn't feel that it was really a music venue," Pop complained. "I remember I was pretty unhappy when we got to the gig to find that the entire room was organized with folding chairs. It was like going to a Pentecostal church or something."

The audience, too, took some getting used to. In among the old friends, Pop gasped, "I don't think I had ever seen so many rock critics in one room in my life, nor will I ever. If they weren't rock critics, they looked like rock critics. It was just wall-to-wall."

Pop's reputation for self-destruction had of course preceded him, and he was in no mood to disappoint. Wayne County recalled watching Pop leave the stage midset, and pick his way through the audience via their chair backs and tables, until he finally tumbled from his perch and landed chest-down on a table stacked with glasses. As he rose from the shattered mass, his chest was slashed to ribbons, with one cut so deep that, every time Pop moved his left arm back, a jet of blood shot out. So he kept on doing it.

"It was horrible, like a Roman arena," County shuddered, but the show went on, Pop still singing even as roadie Bob Czaykowski attempted to patch him up with duct tape. But Pop was bleeding so heavily that the tape couldn't adhere to the flesh. Another night, he threw a glass on the stage, then rolled in the shards. "My heart is broken," he told the crowd; then he picked up more glass and tried to show them the shattered organ.

The following evening's shows were postponed to allow Pop to recover from his injuries, but there was more blood to be spilled regardless, as he headed along to Madison Square Garden's Felt Forum to catch the New York Dolls, and collided with a glass door. Dazed and bleeding, he was finally discovered lying in a heap by the Dolls' producer, Todd Rundgren, and his then-girlfriend, Bebe Buell. The pair found themselves putting him up at their Horatio Street apartment for the remainder of the Stooges' New York residency.

From New York, the Stooges zigzagged a precipitous route across North America; a couple of nights in Vancouver, Canada, followed by stands in Phoenix and St. Louis, before they arrived in Washington, DC, opening up for Mott the Hoople as they, too, adjusted to life away from MainMan.

Mott were undergoing their own crises at the time. MainMan was behind them; "Honaloochie Boogie" was a hit, their new album, *Mott*, was on the verge of release. But guitarist Mick Ralphs was on his way out, and this was his last show with the band. It was, the rest of Mott believed, a time for solemnity and respect. Unfortunately, nobody told the Stooges.

Pop spent most of the preshow crashed out on a toilet seat, after a proffered line of coke turned out to be something considerably more potent. An hour late taking the stage, the Stooges launched into the signature power chord intro to "Raw Power"—and kept it going for fifteen minutes while they waited for Pop to emerge. Finally he arrived onstage, unceremoniously scooped up and then dumped down by one of the road crew. He could scarcely stand, he could barely sing, and when he attempted to step out into the audience, he fell from the stage, straight into a peanut butter and jelly sandwich that somebody had thoughtfully brought along to the show. The oozing red thickness of the jelly looked just like blood.

The beginning of September found the Stooges back at the Whisky in Hollywood, for a string of shows that seasoned Stooge-watchers later described among the most "enjoyable, and together" shows they ever witnessed. "You still felt as though everything could fall apart any moment," Greg Shaw reflected. "It was still like watching a bunch of psychopaths who someone had shoehorned into a pop group, and taught to play 'Louie Louie.' You knew that what you saw was not an act, it was real. But Iggy never crossed that line between sanity and madness, and that gave everything an extra thrill because you were always waiting for it to happen, and when it didn't, you'd stay for the next set, then come back the next night."

"For me, every show was like I was in the audience," Scott Thurston agreed. "I had no idea what [Pop] was going to do. I was as interested as the audience as far as what was going to happen next. For me, every show was kind of like going to a show. I had the best seat in the house."

"We were still trying to forge ahead," Pop insisted. "We weren't standing still for all the chitter-chatter about the band in that period. We were trying some things. That's what I remember more than anything else, being a little bit out there, but also very concerned about the music."

On October 5, the Stooges returned to Detroit for a couple of shows at the Michigan Palace; then it was down to Atlanta for six nights, including one show that promptly found its way into Iggy mythology. Elton John was in Atlanta at the same time, midway through his own spectacularly successful tour of the U.S. John was an avowed Stooges fan, and the rumor that he might be producing the next Stooges album was enough for Ben Edmonds, editor of *Creem* magazine, to suggest Elton make a special guest appearance at one of the shows, dressed in a rented gorilla suit. A photographer was hired for the event, and a few friends were on hand to bellow their applause; in fact, the only principal players who didn't appear to know what was planned were Iggy and the Stooges.

Pop was not in the best state that evening. As showtime approached, he was still sleeping off the massive dose of Quaaludes that he'd taken the previous evening, so his bandmates shot him up with an invigorating dose of methamphetamine sulphate. That did the trick, but Pop remained so far out in space that, when the gorilla appeared onstage, he completely freaked. "It scared the hell out of me," he admitted later; probably because "[I] was . . . stoned to the point of being barely ambulatory."

While Pop stood stock-still and stared, undecided whether to run for the hills or rip the beast's head off, Elton remained calm, smiling as he finally removed the head, and remaining onstage to dance with Pop. "I simply can't understand why Iggy's not a huge star," he mused afterward. But while Elton's manager, John Reid, did at least talk with the Stooges about possibly signing them to his Rocket label, the Stooges' date sheet left them little time to even think about the studio.

Florida, Tennessee, Indiana, New Jersey—the Stooges toured throughout the end of 1973, clearly heading for a crisis of one form or another. Andy Warhol was even spreading the rumor that their final show of the year, opening for the Blue Oyster Cult at New York's Academy of Music on New Year's Eve, would be the band's last ever performance. "I heard Iggy's planning to kill himself on stage," he murmured. "I wonder if I could get a camera in to the show." Past suicides among his coterie had bothered him, he liked to say, because nobody ever caught the final moments on film. This time, he'd like to remedy that.

Pop didn't kill himself, but the Stooges died a death anyway. Pop introduced every song as "Heavy Liquid," maybe to amuse himself, but possibly to harpoon Columbia's intention of recording the show for release as a live album. The taping went ahead, but the result was so shambolic that not only was the album canned, Columbia announced that the Stooges were as well.

Cut adrift from their last association with the music industry, the Stooges moved into the final month of their life, tattered, torn, and utterly beaten down. There was talk of Todd Rundgren coming in to produce them, but like so much else in the Stooges' universe, talk was cheap. They would do the job themselves, scheming the screaming which became the unwritten rule of the band's immediate future.

There was no shortage of material, a welter of songs that still exists in a twilight zone that is uniquely its own, a land of desperate nihilism shot through with a rage so tangible that you can still touch it, almost forty years on.

One by one, the band's lifelines had vanished—Bowie, their friend; MainMan, their management; Columbia, their label. On the road, shows booked in the first flush of optimism were degenerating into weird, wired violence. The Stooges had a reputation for drama, danger, and destruction, and audiences wanted nothing less. What could the band do but oblige?

Beaten, battered, and bruised, the Stooges were sinking, and they not only knew it, they almost welcomed their fate. Songs like "Rubber Legs," "Till the End of the Night," and "She Creature of the Hollywood Hills" captured the band at its most drug-crazed and disillusioned, offered a giant fuck-you to the world, and would ultimately establish the Stooges' worst reputation.

The desultory autobiography of "Open Up and Bleed" oozed fresh disillusion and despair. The Stooges regularly ended their live set with this song, drifting from harmonica-fueled slow blues into a cacophony of protesting feedback as the band left the stage but didn't tell their instruments. In the rehearsal studio, Armageddon crept in far more quietly. It was there all the same, though, wallowing in energies and emotions that were already old when the world was still young. But there was a slovenly majesty to the proceedings all the same, a sense that the world might have trampled across the Stooges' dreams, but at least the band could still dream if they wanted.

Quite what they were dreaming of, however, was to be left unsaid.

In July 1973, in the aftermath of Bowie's onstage retirement, Mick Ronson told writer Michael Benton, "I can tell you, Mick Ronson will continue. He may even go out on the road as Mick Ronson one day, and a solo album is pretty likely." No sooner were Bowie's *Pin Ups* sessions complete than Ronson and the rest of the band—Bolder, Dunbar, and pianist Mike Garson—were sequestered in Trident Studios recording that solo set.

Ronson pulled songs from wherever he liked. Three Bowie contributions were joined by an Elvis cover and a piece written by another of

MainMan's passing infatuations, jazz singer Annette Peacock. The title track, "Slaughter on Tenth Avenue," was the old movie theme, spiced up with some archetypal Ronno guitar beauty, and "Only After Dark" was written by Ronson himself, in tandem with sometime Stooges associate—and Angela Bowie's latest lover—singer Scott Richardson.

Ronson's first album was released on March 1, 1974, at the outset of his first solo tour, a thirteen-show British outing that opened, incredibly, at London's Rainbow Theatre, a baptism of fire and a veritable lion's den as the nation's press poured out to cast their eye over the man already being touted as a surrogate Bowie.

The event epitomized MainMan's mania for promotion. The buildup to the show began in the foyer. Posters, album sleeves, and blowups of Ronson's photograph littered the area. Fan club membership forms cluttered every surface (Ronson, like Angela and even little Zowie, had had a thriving fan club in operation for over a year). Of course it was simply a microcosmic re-creation of the stunts used to publicize Bowie during his early days; the slick way in which the audience were led to believe they were part of the family, encouraged to participate in the carnival and generally assist MainMan in launching Ronson as what some critics were already calling the Surrogate Bowie. David wasn't touring, so his guitarist did instead. Ten years before, it would have been his car that pulled in the punters. (Well, it worked for Elvis Presley.)

Onstage, a film crew prepared to capture the show in movie form. Out back, a mobile recording studio was ready to hatch a commemorative live album. And backstage, Bowie watched with mounting envy as Ronson took center stage for the first time in his life—all of which was scant consolation for Ronson himself, who looked increasingly dismayed as the stalls continually erupted with calls for the singer, and when "Moonage Daydream" garnered the evening's biggest response.

By the time Ronson was ready to play an encore, it was all that Defries could do to hold Bowie back from racing out there as well, to break his own in-concert silence by usurping his old lieutenant. On the road, Bowie was exhausted. Off the road, he was restless. He finally allowed himself to be restrained and the concert played out as scheduled. But it was clear that Bowie could not remain inactive for much longer.

The film of Mick Ronson at the Rainbow was Cherry Vanilla's brainchild. Operating now out of her own loft in Chelsea, she convinced

Defries that MainMan needed to diversify. The company had paid a small fortune for director D. A. Pennebaker to shoot Bowie's final Hammersmith Odeon concert the previous July, but the projected theatrical release never came, and they'd been forced to lease a seriously edited one-hour version to America's ABC television network, simply to recoup some of the expense.

The Pennebaker film had been a waste of money. Surely there were enough people around the MainMan setup already who had the knowledge and the ability to make a movie? Plus, if the company made the movie, the company would control it as well. Defries listened to her pitch, thought about it some, and then nodded. Go ahead.

Potential projects began flying immediately. Bowie insisted that MainMan finance a movie of Czech defector Peter Sadecky's comic strip heroine Octobriana. He had long been a fan of the eponymous strip, and in his mind, he had already cast Amanda Lear in the title role. She seemed enthusiastic too, even writing a couple of songs for the project, "To Be a Star" and "Octobriana," while taking singing lessons (at MainMan's expense, of course) from the same teacher that Ava Cherry was using. But though Defries did look into obtaining the necessary movie rights, *Octobriana* was never got off the ground.

Doomed, too, was the film division's next effort. Wayne County was writing for *Rock Scene* magazine now, dispensing sexual advice to the readers via what must have been the most subversive self-help column ever to appear in a mainstream American magazine. With a nationwide readership hanging on (or from) County's every word, Tony Zanetta decided that it was clearly time to push him into a more fitting spotlight.

"I put the live show together for a pretty reasonable budget of about $10,000. The idea was to create a theatrical/rock 'n' roll evening that could be presented in a theater. Cherry then persuaded Defries that the entire evening, and the process of creating the show, should be documented and put out as a film on the midnight movie circuit. We all thought that this could be a new way of breaking an artist and would be something that would be worth quite a bit in years to come."

Named for what Wayne County described as "an area of New York, very depraved, very S&M," *Wayne County at the Trucks* was a ludicrously theatrical study of the neighborhood and its denizens, seen through the eyes and music of County and his latest band. Produced by Tony Ingrassia and Zanetta, it was filmed live at the WestBeth Theatre on the west side, close to the New York docklands, on January 17, 1974, and, County continued, "it was a piss take on that sexual thing, taking sex to the extreme. It was an incredible movie, very long, very funny, not at all serious...a much slicker, more theatrical version" of what he had been doing with his regular band, Queen Elizabeth, with extra added direction and order.

Borrowing from the *Pork* set, the back of the stage was lined with doors, decorated with a vast portrait of County with his mouth wide open. From the audience, his appearance onstage looked as though he'd vomited himself into view, a vision in silver hair and green lamé, festooned in half-inflated condoms, resplendent in the most lifelike cock shoes he had ever worn, "huge cocks with balls the size of oranges, big blue veins going down the side and a big red knob at the end. Incredible!"

And it was all doomed to obscurity. "It got out of hand," Zanetta lamented. "Defries was not very keen on Wayne and basically got involved with him because of Leee and me. I think he thought that he was doing it as a favor to us, and as long as we did all the work and it did not cost him too much, he didn't mind. But he was never committed to the project, so when conflicts arose and a real budget was done in order to edit the footage into a film, he abandoned the project."

The tapes were shelved, the film was forgotten, and when a fire swept through the warehouse where the recordings were buried, that was the end of the tale. Or was it? Fast-forward thirty years, and somebody passing by a recently closed-down New York studio found an old acetate disc in a box on the street corner. Of course they listed it on eBay, from whence one of County's U.K. fans purchased it for $600, and passed it back to County. More than thirty years after *Wayne County at the Trucks* threatened to send Wayne County exploding onto the silver screen, its sound track snuck out on a tiny Spanish record label.

The MainMan movie division was in trouble the moment Defries canned County. The Ronson movie became the final straw. Defries pulled the plug on the entire operation, but the ideas kept flying.

MainMan considered branching into publishing, purchasing a Los Angeles teen magazine, the close-to-moribund *Star*, and relaunching it as, essentially, a MainMan propaganda machine; among the incentives being offered to prospective distributors was an exclusive David Bowie photo book.

There was talk of venturing into legitimate theater, with Tony Ingrassia being brought on board to direct the MainMan assault on Broadway. There were so many ideas, and they had all the time in the world in which to essay them. It was early 1974, and MainMan and its main man were at their peak.

The New York offices had shifted out of the east side duplex now, into swish new surroundings on Park Avenue—Defries had always hankered after such an address, and now he had one. Yes, there'd been talk of a less conventional setup—shortly before Zanetta flew to London for *The 1980 Floorshow* in October 1973, Defries sent him out to locate a loft that might become MainMan's own Factory-style home, just around the corner from Warhol's own original. Designers were recruited, decorators were hired... but then the Park Avenue premises came onto the market and there was no looking back.

Why should there have been? MainMan was the most famous management company in the world, and the staff was growing constantly, not only from the traditional *Pork* crew, as Zanetta recruited Jaime Di Carlo (or Jamie Andrews, as he now called himself), but from elsewhere in the world of business, too. Real accountants, real advisers, real paper pushers and pen-cap chewers. The mavericks were now legitimate, and Defries could only see his world growing larger. He talked openly of buying a record company (the slowly-fading Decca was a distinct target), or at least persuading RCA to buy it for him. And Bowie was now planning a tour that would dwarf any he had ever dreamed or schemed before. That Mick Ronson concert in London in March had affected him more than anyone could ever have imagined. He didn't simply want to get back onstage—he *needed* to. He needed the adrenaline, the excitement, the activity. He picked up the phone and started making calls.

16

YOU CAN HIT ME ALL YOU WANT TO

"The Dolls were playing upstairs at Max's, and David Bowie was downstairs at the round table. I was DJ that night, and the Dolls kept saying, 'Bring him up, he's got to see us.' So I went down and said, 'David, the Dolls are going on in a minute and they insist you come upstairs.' And David went, 'YUK! I don't want to see the Dolls.' So I went back and told the band he was eating, and David Johansen said, 'Okay, we'll hold on about another ten minutes.' And I couldn't tell him Bowie had said, 'YUK,' so I was just running up and down the stairs between Bowie and the Dolls about a dozen times. In the end, I had to tell them David was stoned and couldn't get up, and his bodyguards were insisting he didn't move.
—Jayne (Wayne) County in conversation with the author, 1987

Bowie's covers album, *Pin Ups*, was still new on the racks when he began work on his next project. For months he had been considering a musical version of George Orwell's *1984*, that most deliciously dystopian vision of a future world. He worked for a while on it with Tony Ingrassia, and although that collaboration eventually fell apart, victim to the two men's very different methods of working, Bowie already had much of the project mapped out and written. Then word came back from Orwell's widow, Sonia.

"Why would anybody want to set *that* to music?" she demanded, and without waiting for a reply, she refused permission for it to go ahead. Bowie shrugged, either scrapped or reworked the songs he'd already composed, and effectively decided to remake *Metropolis* instead. Only this time, he kept his mouth shut about it.

The postapocalyptic splendor of what became 1974's *Diamond Dogs* album remains very much the sound of a second choice struggling to become the mainline attraction. So much of Bowie's attention was focused upon *1984*, both the album and the attendant stage play with which he intended showcasing it, that he barely had the energy to expend on any new ideas.

The album itself came together better than it ought to have under those circumstances; no matter that the best songs ("We Are the Dead," "Big Brother," "Sweet Thing," "Candidate," and "1984" itself) were those that were most clearly left over from the earlier project, judicious recording and the addition of the storming "Rebel Rebel" propelled the album's contents to classic status regardless, at the same time as Defries realized one of his fondest dreams. Three years before, he had talked about establishing Bowie as a "one-name superstar," like Dylan and Lennon and Elvis. The "Rebel Rebel" single was credited to Bowie, plain and simple.

More alarming for Bowie was having to abandon the stage play. No matter how serious Bowie may have been about retiring from the concert arena to concentrate upon his other creative interests, he remained a showman at heart. A stage show, static in a single theater for as long as audiences demanded it (or until he tired of it, whichever came first) was an easy solution to the restlessness that was now growing inside of him. Well, if he couldn't put on forty shows in a single venue, then he would perform a single show in forty. The *Diamond Dogs* tour was not only the longest single outing he had ever committed to—he would ultimately play eighty shows across the United States between mid-June and early December 1974—it was also the most extravagant that *anybody* had pulled off.

A quarter million dollars was sunk into the set; a crack band was hired and then hidden out of sight of the audience—Wayne County had pulled that same stroke at the Trucks, and it looked amazing, one man controlling the entire expanse of stage, while the music arose unbidden from the void.

Backing vocalists were retrained in choreography, as Bowie conceived a series of set pieces unlike anything ever seen on a rock stage before, boxing rings and Shakespearean puns, elevated chairs that launched him into orbit over the audience, vast mechanical hands that opened and closed on cue. Simply setting up for each show was a major undertaking, while rehearsals for the opening night, taking over a Port Chester, New York, theater to run through a "typical" set, revealed that the invention was not confined to the visuals alone.

Songs were stripped back and reborn, "All the Young Dudes" freshly cast as a doo-wop lament; "The Jean Genie" reduced to Quaalude pace, "Changes" reinvented with pianist Mike Garson's jazziest inflections playing it in and out. There was even a story line of sorts, if one cared to pay sufficient attention, although again, any hope that the presentation might have had of truly elevating itself above the rock 'n' roll norm was smothered by the haste with which Bowie insisted on putting it together.

On more than one occasion, Defries raised the possibility of hiring professional show writers to come in and make sense of the ideas that were swirling around in Bowie's head—great ideas, crazy ideas, ambitious ideas. But Bowie refused. It was his show and he was going to do it his way. And in so doing—in so selfishly grasping onto every iota of detail, the tricks and flourishes that he had once happily allowed Defries, Ronson, Angela, *whoever*, to contribute—he discarded the very thing that had actually made him a star to begin with: the mystique and the illusion of magic.

But when Defries tried to intercede, or suggest another course of action, Bowie either ignored him or didn't seem to hear him to begin with. Communication, the one thing that had always been so easy for the two men, was at an end, to be replaced by paranoia. Bowie was trying so hard to stay ahead, to maintain his reputation as one of rock's most visionary figures, that he'd forgotten how he'd gained that reputation in the first place.

It was a role that had once come easily to him, not only through his own creative talent (and that of the people with whom he surrounded himself), but also by synthesis. In 1971, 1972, the names of the Velvet Underground and Lou Reed, and Iggy Pop and the Stooges were little more than irrelevant footnotes, and Bowie's own stock rose as he both assimilated and promoted their reputations. By 1974, the situation had changed considerably.

The Stooges were not a threat. "The name Iggy Pop was synonymous with 'shit,'" Pop himself admitted. "The guy who'd be tied up in a bag and thrown out of a window two floors up at a Deep Purple gig. The guy whose girlfriend ran off with Robert Plant. The guy who Ian Hunter said would never make it because he had no talent." It would be another four years before Pop could relay all that to an English journalist, then smile the smile of the truly triumphant. "But I'm still here. Where's Ian Hunter today? Up with the raccoons somewhere, counting the money from his Barry Manilow covers." Right now, in early February 1974, the Stooges had a date with their own inevitable destruction.

Monday, February 4, found the Stooges playing the Rock and Roll Farm, in Wayne, Michigan, a tiny bar capable of holding no more than 120 people, and best known in the area for entertaining the local bikers with regular rock 'n' roll revival acts. And they were out in force that night, fighting among themselves, lobbing eggs at the band, and when Pop wandered out into the audience, eyeball-to-eyeball with one of the bikers, he was rewarded with a fat fist in the face. The blow knocked him flying, the biker's buddies roared their approval, and that was the end of the show. "That's it, we're gone," Pop swore as he made his way back to the stage—and they were.

But they were not going to take the matter lying down. The following day, Pop turned up at WABX radio in Detroit, "and I challenged the entire gang, the Scorpions, of which the guy was a member, to come and do their worst at my [next] big show in Detroit, at the Michigan Palace [the following weekend]. Which they proceeded to do."

The show was opened by what Lester Bangs, reviewing the evening for *Creem*, described as "three dogshit bands," one of whom was a barely known East Coast rock group called Aerosmith. Then the Stooges took the stage to the clatter of "Heavy Liquid," and Bangs's day was made. "The Stooges are back and I'm happy...because they're such a great, great band, a distillation of beautiful fury that could tear your head off. I believe in the Stooges."

"Riot in the Motor City!" Pop cried, but the crowd didn't rise to the bait. If the Scorpions had turned up, they weren't making their presence felt. But more than a few souls in the audience had heard about the last show, and they came equipped for action. So did Pop. "Our next selection, for all you Hebrew ladies in the audience, is entitled 'Rich Bitch.' And I don't care if you throw all the ice in the world. You're paying five bucks and I'm making 10,000. So screw ya."

Pop hurled insults; the crowd began to throw things back. Eggs, ice cubes, shoes...James Williamson only narrowly missed being smacked in the head by a flying Nikon camera. Pop, on the other hand, seemed to be hurling himself in the path of every projectile he saw.

"You can throw your goddamn cocks if I don't care. You pricks can throw every goddamned thing in the world, and your girlfriend will still love me. You jealous cocksuckers...

"Anybody with any more ice cubes, jelly beans, grenades, eggs they wanna throw at the stage, c'mon. You paid your money, so ya takes your choice.

"Thank you for the egg. Do we have any more eggs? More eggs, c'mon, try it again, c'mon. Is it time for a riot, girls? RIOT!

"Lightbulbs too? Paper cups? Oh my, we're getting violent. Oh, there's two guys left of stage, we'll have to leave, see you later...."

The last song the Stooges ever performed live was a manic "Louie Louie," debauched and deflowered, an E-flat mutation of its joyous prototype that was prefaced by Pop perhaps realizing precisely what was going on around him, seeing for the first time the carnage that was exploding throughout the ballroom, and unable to keep himself from making one final, despairing observation. "I never thought it'd come to this, baby."

Except those weren't his last words. His last words, as he half crawled, half staggered off the stage, beaten half senseless as the blood poured from a head wound, were one final gesture of defiance aimed at whomever had hurled the Stroh bottle that shattered across Scott Thurston's piano. "Thank you the kind person who threw this glass bottle at my head. It nearly killed me, but you missed again. But keep trying next week."

There was no next week. The band split, disillusioned and angry, and Pop was left alone.

"That night was probably the most violent and paranoid, probably the height of paranoia and violence of that edition of my group. In fact, too paranoid for my taste and a little too violent. But I liked the record." Released a little less than three years later, *Metallic KO* captured the last half of the concert, leading up to its bloody, savage denouement.

"It was a faithful recording of what actually happened that night," Pop smiled. "Actually, it was much stronger had you been there." But still, Lester Bangs hit the nail square on the head when he declared, "It's the only rock album I know where you can actually hear hurled beer bottles breaking against guitar strings."

Lou Reed, on the other hand, was about to unleash the only rock album where the guitar strings are hurling the beer bottles back at you.

As Reed worked to piece together the band that would accompany him out on tour that fall of 1973—guitar players Steve Hunter and Dick Wagner, bassist Prakash John, keyboardist Ray Colcord, and drummer Pentti Glan—he already knew the impression he wanted to leave on anyone brave or foolhardy enough to stray into his path. He may not have used his *Rock 'n' Roll Animal* title for his last album. But next time...

The tour that followed, driven across Europe and the U.S. through the last months of 1973, and then preserved on wax as *Rock 'n' Roll Animal*, remains seared into the memory of anyone who saw it, the sonic and scenic successor not only to everything Reed had ever threatened in the past, but also to all that other people had borrowed from him. If there was any single impetus behind Bowie's decision to so utterly sterilize his upcoming tour, it was surely the knowledge that it was the only direction left to him. Lou Reed had swept up all of the others, and even created a few of his own. Asked by journalists to sum himself up, Reed delighted in describing himself as the "Hamlet of Electricity." Six months later, at the height of his own show, Bowie was tongue-kissing a plastic stage-prop Yorick's skull every night, as though desperate to draw some of Reed's magic from its mouth.

His dark curls shaved mercilessly close to the bone, then drenched in vivid peroxide, his habitual costume of leather jacket and denim switched for a sleeveless black T-shirt and black leather pants, his customary body type slimmed to malevolent stick-insect proportions, Reed exuded power and malevolence. He carved Germanic crosses into his stubbly hair, prompting Lester Bangs to compare him to a "bubblegum Kenneth Anger," and Rona Barrett to marvel, "They said it couldn't be done, but somebody's finally managed to invent a totally new hairstyle." Photographer Mick Rock described him as looking "skinny as a syringe," and that was no exaggeration.

Reed's show opened without him, guitarists Hunter and Wagner dueling out an overture that only slowly resolved itself into "Sweet Jane," just as Reed ambled out onto the stage for the first time, the lights picking him up as he stepped toward the microphone, a military aerobics instructor from hell on his way to the darkest S&M basement in town. Queen Butch.

He communicated to the audience with glares and stares. No matter that he disguised them beneath those omnipresent shades—you knew his eyes were pinpricks of rage. Between songs, words were reduced to

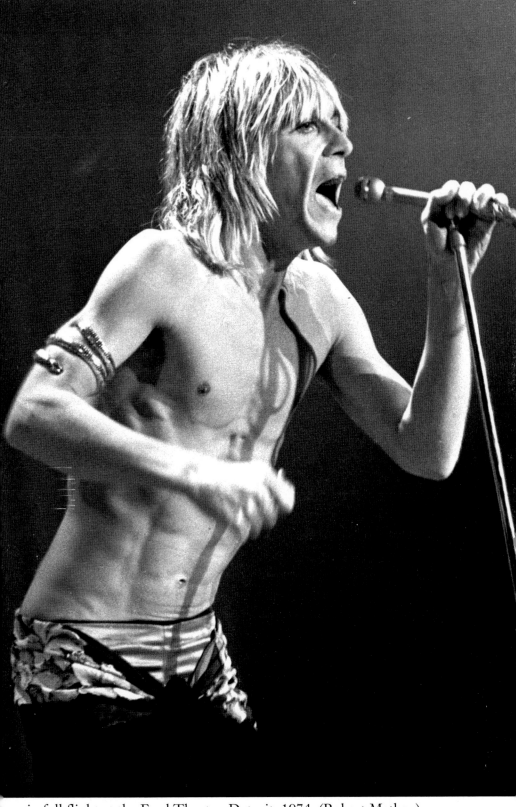

ggy in full flight at the Ford Theater, Detroit, 1974. (Robert Matheu)

David Bowie and Lou Reed enjoy a cuddle at the Dorchester Hotel, July 1972. (Photo copyright Mick Rock 1972, 2009)

The couple of the year, 1973—David and Angela Bowie. (Smith/Getty Images)

David Bowie and Lou Reed onstage at the Royal Festival Hall, July 1972. (Photo copyright Mick Rock 1972, 2009)

ggy Pop and James Williamson at the Stooges' second and final show as MainMan
tists, at the Ford Auditorium in Detroit, March 1973. (Robert Matheu)

Marc Bolan, the biggest star Britain had produced since the heyday of the Beatles. (Photofest)

Three of the young dudes: Mott the Hoople's Ian Hunter, Overend Watts, and Mick Ralphs. (Jorgen Angel/Redferns)

David Johansen and Wayne County backstage at Max's Kansas City. (Leee Black Childers/Getty Images)

Iggy and Bowie, *TV Eye Live*. (Theresa Kereakes)

Panic in Detroit: A pugilistic Bowie on the 1974 *Diamond Dogs* tour. (Robert Matheu)

ou Reed, walking on the wild side, 1976. (Theresa Kereakes)

Iggy, '77 style. (Theresa Kereakes)

disinterested introductions, as though he was wondering why he even bothered. If the packed halls before him didn't already know that this was a Velvet Underground song, and that one was from *Berlin*, then what the fuck were they doing in the audience in the first place?

Beneath the arrogance, however, there was a sense of pride, and behind that, even a smidgeon of humility. "I wanted to get the Velvets stuff known," he admitted three years later. John Cale might have murmured darkly how "Lou ended up doing album after album of reissues of the same song," and Velvet Underground purists might have reeled away from the elongated "Heroin" that haunted every night, with Reed miming a mainline to the whoops of the crowd. But he knew what he was doing, all the same. "The 'Heroin' that got popular," Reed agreed, "it's just desecrated. It's so blasphemous it's horrifying. I understand why people like it, but it almost killed me. It's so awful." He persisted, however, because he had to. "I had to get popular. People love that album," and he wasn't yet self-assured enough to believe that his fans would follow him wherever he went.

Maybe that was why his next release, scant months after *Rock 'n 'Roll Animal*, was such a dire disappointment, not only to the fans, but to the artist himself. "I slept through *Sally Can't Dance*, that's no big secret. They'd make a suggestion and I'd say, 'Oh, all right.' I'd do the vocals in one take, in about twenty minutes, and then it was goodbye."

But the crowds that discovered him on the last American tour, and who were already block-booking the venues for his next one, didn't know that when they raced out to buy his new record, and they probably wouldn't have cared if they had. "Of course Sally Can't Dance, the tourniquet's too tight," snarled the *New Musical Express*, and Reed apparently agreed. The man who that same organ described as looking like "a ravaged monkey" called his latest album "cheap and tedious. But," he reasoned, "the worse the albums were, the more they'd sell." *Berlin* had barely even bothered the American chart. "The record sales, compared to *Transformer*, were a disaster for a normal person, but for me it was a total disaster." *Sally Can't Dance*, on the other hand, "went Top 10. What a horror! It goes to No. 10 and it sucks...."

Reed was back on the road with *Sally Can't Dance*, and the live show reflected his lack of interest; more than that, it offered a harrowing glimpse inside Reed's personal life. *ZigZag* magazine caught him opening for the Who in London in May 1974, and put into words the disappointment that a lot of Reed's British fans were feeling.

He had another new band—guitarist Danny Weiss, keyboard player Michael Fonfara, bassist Prakash John, and drummer Pentti Glan—but it was "utterly unsuitable...as he butchered 'Sweet Jane' and turned 'Heroin' into a lousy, sadistic B-movie melodrama completely devoid of the incisive phrasing and objectivity that so distinguishes the original version. I couldn't take more than a couple of minutes of it."

Six months later, following a desultory show at the Felt Forum in New York, his old friend Lisa Robinson found herself in agreement. "What a tacky gesture," she said of the rubber-hose-and-syringe routine. "He never had to do that when it was the spellbinding antidrug song it used to be.

"I remember," Robinson mused on, "when some of his intimates almost jokingly suggested that he be put back on speed during the days of scotch and Valium...to help him get his energy back. But this skin-and-bones is ridiculous."

But the look, and the savage depletion of Reed's musical resources, according to John Cale, was not an act. The night before that London show, a limo pulled up outside Cale's apartment and disgorged Reed and his latest companion, a half-Mexican Indian named Rachel.

Cale described her as "a long-limbed, long-haired transvestite," whose real name was Tommy; Lester Bangs called her "a grotesque creature... that might have grovelingly scampered in when Lou opened the door to get the milk and papers in the morning, and just stayed around. If the album *Berlin* was melted down in a vat and reshaped into human form, it would be this creature." But she would remain alongside Reed for the next three years.

Reed and Rachel came in, were introduced to Cale's wife, and then made the purpose of their visit clear. The gig was taking place at a soccer stadium, but, to overwork the most obvious analogy, there was only one thing Reed was interested in scoring this particular evening. So the Cales agreed to help and, having completed the necessary business, the little group headed back to Cale's apartment, "fully loaded and ready to party," Cale smiled.

Lou took himself off to the bathroom while the others relaxed to some Beach Boys records. Half an hour later, he was still in there. With everybody growing increasingly concerned, Cale said, "I opened the loo door and saw a strange sight. Lou's arm was punctured in several places and blood ran down his arms from each. The needle was crimson and looked clogged. He was perched on the john as if mesmerized, not moving. It looked like a scene frozen in time, a statue of a sitting figure trying to control an uncontrollable object about to fly away from him . . ."

Cale walked in and removed the needle from Reed's arm.

"Oh man," Reed murmured. "Oh man, oh man, oh man . . ."

"I quickly tied his arm off, inserted the needle into the best vein I could find, and let it rip. Removing the needle, I washed it swiftly in the sink and stepped out to the astonished, frightened faces in the living room. I too said, 'Oh man.'"

And people wondered why Reed did not always appear at the top of his game.

Bowie, too, was beginning to discover that a project which had originally seemed like a good idea had considerably less to hold his interest than he originally intended.

The *Diamond Dogs* stage sets were impressive, but prone to malfunction. Costs were spiraling out of control. Transportation fees were skyrocketing as an international gas crisis hit. Ticket sales were sluggish in the most unexpected places. The band was bitching about their anonymity, and rumor insisted that they were rebelling against their wages as well—by the time the tour touched down in Philadelphia, and word filtered through that they'd be recording a live album, the mood was allegedly approaching rebellion.

But worse than all of that, Bowie was miserable. The longer the tour went on, the more he missed the interaction that had once been such a vital and spontaneous part of his live show. Dancers Gui Andrisano and Geoffrey MacCormack (now traveling under the name Warren Peace) played their part in the performance, of course, but choreographer Toni Basil had so nailed down their movements that there was scarcely any room in which to maneuver, and if Bowie decided to move in *this* direction, rather than *that*, it could throw an entire routine off its stride.

Gone were the days when he could revise the set list in midperformance; gone, too, the nights when an idea could hit him as he walked out onstage, and be incorporated into the act on the spot. The show *was* a brilliant spectacle, and the band behind the screens was nothing if not steaming—even if older fans could (and did) denigrate the rearrangements that so disguised certain favorites. But it was hollow and, ironically in view of the directions Bowie's musical tastes were moving, absolutely soulless.

As he lost faith in his creation, so Bowie lost interest in so many of the other things that had once sustained him. When the drive for stardom had been simply an experiment, it was fun. But then it became real, and with it arrived the realization that now he was playing for keeps. There were no second chances. One false move and he was dead in the water, and he didn't have far to look for justification of that fear.

In 1971 and into 1972, Marc Bolan was the biggest star Britain had produced since the heyday of the Beatles. Two years later, where was Marc now? Growing fat on Courvoisier and cocaine, and for everybody who sniffs into the air and says you can't get fat on such a combination, Marc's former manager Tony Secunda, who ran into him in Los Angeles in 1974, could have told you very different. "He was bloated, he looked disgusting. He was constantly drunk and permanently coked up. It was horrible to see him."

It was difficult to listen to him too, turning out records that were so far from the joyous raw ramps that he had once spun out with such ease that even he no longer seemed to believe in them. "Whatever happened to the teenage dream?" Bolan had asked in T.Rex's most recent hit single, but he might as well have been asking what happened to his own dreams. If Bolan could fall, then so could Bowie, and he knew it.

The extravagant live set was the first to go. The *Diamond Dogs* tour closed for a summer break in July 1974, before picking up again in Los Angeles in early September. But aside from one night when the BBC was in town, to film the live portions of the *Cracked Actor* documentary, the albatross that Bowie had once named "Hunger City" never came out of its boxes again.

Anything could set Bowie worrying. Frank Sinatra was among the special guests at one of the Los Angeles shows, and that in itself was an accomplishment. The grand old man of American music was not one of rock's most fervent fans, and the fact that he could be prevailed upon to attend any show was little short of a miracle. But it wasn't enough for Bowie. He wanted Sinatra to come back for a second show, and when his wish wasn't fulfilled, it left him close to despair—so much so that, when

Iggy Pop attempted to contact him, first at the venue and later at his hotel, the ragged little man was turned away empty-handed. Bowie did not want to see him, in case he caught a glimpse of his own frightening future.

He turned to his friends for support, the old chums who had always rallied around him, but new ones as well. Mick Jagger and John Lennon, the wise old men of rock 'n' roll, had treated him like a curio at first, as they watched him encroaching upon their superstar territory, but they had come to accept him since then. Or so Bowie thought—other voices in the MainMan camp warned that they were also trying to nullify him, filling his head with self-defeating ideas while stuffing his system with self-mythologizing drugs.

Cocaine raised its head. Tony Defries kept a very tight ship where drugs were concerned; roadies were dismissed for daring to take a toke of weed in his presence, and the inner sanctum watched in horror as Bowie started flaunting his rebellion.

For rebellion is what it was. Why, both Jagger and Lennon demanded, did Bowie need a manager growing fat on his hard work? They reminded him of Defries's apprenticeship, legal-eagling away on behalf of one of the sharpest operators in the game, Allen Klein. Both had had their run-ins with Klein, and they bore both the emotional and the financial scars to prove it. Defries, they suggested, had learned well at Klein's knee, and when Bowie mentioned the terms of his MainMan contract, just two years into its ten-year life span, they did not even need to speak. Because they knew that Bowie believed them.

But what did he believe? That everything that had happened for him in the years since Defries first walked into his life would have happened anyway? That both his fame and the fabulous nature of that fame were preordained, and that Defries was just some lucky chancer who happened to catch a ride on his coattails as he prepared to take off? That he had done the whole thing on his own?

"Up until that point, Tony and David never had a real reason to question one another, because they were too busy doing it," Tony Zanetta observed. He was on the road with Bowie for the *Diamond Dogs* tour, and watched with mounting dismay as the relationship between Bowie and Defries grew icier. "They needed each other, they were good together. But they had reached the top of a mountain, and they didn't necessarily need each other to get down the other side. Tony was a superstar manager, David was a big rock star, and at last they had a chance to live out that fantasy."

The difference was, Defries knew how to do that. Bowie was still too scared.

MainMan was reveling in the kind of lifestyle that most people associated only with the Hollywood dream factory of the thirties, and which seemed more than unreal in the cold light of 1974.

While the west suffered from a gasoline shortage, MainMan chartered fleets of limos.

While the music industry complained of a vinyl shortage, MainMan shipped records by the truckload.

While mainstream pop grew pastier and ghastlier, as record companies seized upon any even passably good looking young man to throw into the market, in the hope of launching the next teenybop sensation, MainMan released one album (Bowie's *Diamond Dogs*) with its cover star disguised as half a dog, another (Ronson's) with its maker in tears, and a third (Dana Gillespie's) that might have been an ad for a high-class Victorian bordello.

The grapevine abounded with tales of Bowie's road crew inviting total strangers in off the street, then charging them $10 to order the most extravagant meal on the hotel menu. The bill would go to MainMan; the cash would go in the roadies' pocket.

Another day, another rumor. Certain MainMan employees had their back teeth filed down so they could give better blow jobs. The bill would go to MainMan.... At one point, half of the staff were spending their weekends on Fire Island, the setting for that so-long-ago *Island* stage play, then hiring a seaplane to take them back to Manhattan for work on Monday. At the Beverly Hills Wilshire Hotel, the same gang ran up a $30,000 bill.

Dana Gillespie looks back on those days with an affection that still borders upon amazement. She cut two albums for MainMan—*Weren't Born a Man*, which included her superlative version of "Andy Warhol"; and the possibly bitterly titled *Ain't Gonna Play No Second Fiddle*. Neither sold, but still she lived the life of a superstar.

"I was forever jetting off places. I was totally unconcerned about money. Every time we stayed in New York it was at the Sherry-Netherland. Angela and I would be flitting about in a big red limo with a bar and a TV in the back—life was sublimely luxurious. It was so outrageous. If you rang up a restaurant and booked it as MainMan, you always got the best seats.

"It was a fabulous era, and what was so great was that Tony had to work out where the funds were going, but the rest of us were like children romping in the fields. I never questioned the price of anything, and Angela certainly didn't. She was always buying clothes for herself, for David. He might say he liked something, but it was Angela who would actually go out and buy it. She'd go to the High Heel Shop and come back with ten pairs for herself, five more pairs for me, all in different colors. There were all these great clothes coming out and we used to have great dressing-up sessions with everybody in the room having to join in, all the men, everyone. We just used to get bunkered in and nobody was spared. Which is when David used to leave the room...."

Cherry Vanilla continued, "It looked to the outside world like there were many more millions of dollars than there actually were. It was a very magical thing, a combination of people who were doing it with their whole heart and soul in it.

"It's like... in old Hollywood... they knew that when times were hard, all anyone wanted to see was fantasy and make-believe and someone saying, 'Everything's divine! We're drinking champagne and riding in limousines all the time!' People wanted to believe in that. We had so much love and belief in the project, David Bowie especially, that we had the energy to slave all day and get the work done and still stay out all night. We'd show up at Max's Kansas City and buy champagne for five tables. Defries was living a high lifestyle, and we appeared to be living a very glamorous and expensive lifestyle as well. But a lot of it was done on credit. Everything was only temporary, it was all rented."

The story best loved by disapproving outsiders is the one about Leee Childers's teeth. Defries had decided to grant everybody in the organization a single wish, which he would then grant. He then watched on as his staff heaped up the material possessions, without a single thought for anybody else, or even for the future. Cherry Vanilla asked for shoes, piles and piles of shoes. Mick Ronson went out and bought a load of shirts. Suzi HaHa ordered a boob job, and Childers had his teeth fixed.

"I was vice-chairman of MainMan and my teeth needed straightening," Childers defended himself. It was a totally legitimate expense—they do it at some department stores for their employees, and Tony cleared it because, after all, I was representing the company and I had to look presentable. It only caused such a big sensation because Lisa Robinson thought it was so funny."

Defries even saw the fruition of one of his own fondest dreams, in which he took over the Chrysler Building and renamed it in his own image. For Christmas one year, his staff presented him with a huge photograph of that distinctive Manhattan skyscraper, the MainMan logo proudly, and realistically, placed over the front door.

The bubble, outsiders predicted, had to burst. Murmurings from the now fiercely divided Bowie camp had the star bitterly counting the pennies, wondering how MainMan and Defries could be reveling in luxury while he scarcely had a pot to piss in. It would be a very expensive pot by most people's standards, of course, but that was not the point. He believed he had made an awful lot of money. Where had it gone?

Minor flash points. He planned bringing the latest tour to Europe once it wrapped up in America at the end of 1974, and was already picturing his London homecoming in his mind when word came down from on high. The shows were off, because costs were too high. MainMan, too, had made an awful lot of money. Where had it gone?

Bowie cast his mind back over the past year or so. Well, some of it had gone on Mick Ronson's album and tour, and some of it had gone on Dana Gillespie. Some was spent on the Astronettes, and some had been wasted on Wayne County. But he only needed to pick up the *New York Times* to discover which black hole the last wad had been flung into, and Bowie had had enough.

Enfolding Tony Ingrassia into the MainMan empire was something that Zanetta felt should have been done long ago. Without him, after all, he and the core members of the team—Leee Black Childers, Cherry Vanilla, Jamie Andrews, even Wayne County—would never have come together in the first place, and would certainly never have embarked upon this fabulous adventure together.

"In some sense, I felt indebted to him, and I also believed in his talent. I thought that MainMan could help him get his career off the ground. Defries agreed to take Ingrassia on as an artiste. He could coach the other MainMan artists, and Defries would own any work he created while under contract."

Now the company was producing *Fame*, a comedy based upon the life and times of Marilyn Monroe, at a time when Monroe herself was approaching something of a cultural rebirth, a dozen years after her death. Elton John had already scored with "Candle in the Wind," while American actress Sandra Dickinson was touring the U.K. in what could be construed as a rival production, *Legend*.

Ellen Barber, an actress with television and Broadway credits, was cast in the main role, alongside Michael Nader, who would later play Joan Collins's husband on *Dynasty*. The remainder of the cast were unknown, but nevertheless legitimate stage players.

The production was conceived as an off-off-Broadway showcase, presented in a downtown theater that met the Equity criteria for both off and off-off Broadway. This meant that while the budget of $25,000 was expensive for an off-off production, it could easily become an inexpensive off production—"most off-Broadway productions at that time cost about $75,000," Zanetta explained.

Fame was not a success, and closed after just a short run. Ingrassia, however, continued to believe in it and, according to Zanetta, "he was able to bulldoze Defries into going for a full Broadway production, at a cost of around $250,000." The John Golden Theatre was booked for an indeterminate run; the media was blitzed with promotional material. Opening night was November 18, 1974.

It was a disaster. Cast, crew, and MainMan employees had barely started tucking into the opening night party at Sardi's restaurant when the first review came in. It was *New York Times* critic Clive Barnes's dismissal of "this wet rag of a comedy" with the words "it was *Fame* but not fortune." There would be no second night.

Bowie was furious. Two hundred fifty thousand dollars would have made all the difference in the world to his own tour plans, and would certainly have returned many times that amount had it been left at his disposal. He had already recorded his next album, ducking into Philadelphia's Sigma Sound Studios with Tony Visconti during that summertime break from touring, and pouring out six months of exposure to the soul sounds then sweeping the American chart into a new album. It was cruel coincidence alone that decreed that Elton John should have arrived at much the same conclusion on his latest tour, and was already crafting "Philadelphia Freedom." But still, the record that Bowie and Visconti created, *Young Americans*, was scheduled for release in March 1975, and Bowie's head was abuzz with visions of all it might portend. But what was the point of any of that if he couldn't be out on the road to promote it?

He didn't know where to turn. MainMan itself had changed immeasurably in recent months, and not for the better. The new offices on Park Avenue were only the beginning of Defries's personal dream. He had established the company, and within its manifold divisions a travel department, an art department, a press office, and so many more little divisions were created. Now it needed to behave like a company, and Zanetta, too, watched in dismay as "one by one, the original family were being replaced by so-called professionals."

Childers and Vanilla had gone; so had many of the other staff that Zanetta called friends. In their place came a succession of strangers, usually culled from market research positions, and the odd thing was, Zanetta wryly noted, a lot of them were brought on board by Jamie Andrews— the actor friend he'd introduced to the company, because that was how you treated your friends, and who had now risen so high up the hierarchy that he was extending the same largesse to his own pals. The difference was "they knew their way around the office, so instead of these mad, passionate, theatrical people who would do anything, they were being replaced by these bureaucratic clerks. Which really wasn't the way to go."

Defries himself was so inaccessible that Bowie stopped even trying to reach him, sick of being frustrated at every turn. He had his supporters in the office, of course—Corinne Schwab, the onetime typist who had now risen to the rank of Bowie's personal secretary; Tony Zanetta, who really was doing his best to keep the lines of communication open; a handful more. But it wasn't the same and it certainly wasn't enough. So he turned inward himself.

Hanging out with Lennon one evening, a week or so after the debacle of *Fame*, the pair made their way down to the Electric Lady studio to see what they might come up with. Bowie was fuming as they traveled there, and still steaming as his guitarist, Carlos Alomar, began playing around with an old James Brown riff, "Footstompin'." Without even thinking about it, Bowie began scatting the word that had been haunting his thoughts all week—*Fame*—and the sentiments that were coalescing around it. "I reject you first...what you get is no tomorrow...what you need you have to borrow."

Across the studio, eyes flickered toward the ad-libbing Bowie. Nobody said it, but they all knew what the song was saying. Two months later, in February 1975, Bowie lodged a writ of summons against MainMan, ultimately demanding, amongst other things, an accounting for all funds, estimated at several million dollars, earned by him over the preceding three years. He had seen how quickly money flowed out of MainMan; he knew how quickly he and Angela had spent it, let alone everybody else. Now he wanted to make sure it hadn't been his money so willfully frittered away.

"Fame" was added to the running order of the *Young Americans* album, together with a Beatles cover that Bowie and Lennon also knocked out that evening, a painfully hollow wallow through "Across the Universe." To make room for them, two of the originally scheduled songs, the vast, orchestrated ballads "Who Can I Be Now?" and "It's Gonna Be Me," were dropped, and MainMan flipped; even tried to convince RCA that the company had no right to release the revised version of the album. But their protests fell on deaf ears, while Tony Visconti, too, found his objections overruled.

He loved the two songs that had been dropped, and had devoted a huge amount of time to perfecting them. Now they were being dumped in favor of a couple of spur-of-the-moment knockabouts that Bowie probably wouldn't have even remembered recording if John Lennon had not been there with him. He was furious, Bowie was hurt, and the pair would not truly reconcile for close to another two years. Bowie and Defries, on the other hand, would never work together again.

Perhaps surprisingly, given the glacial nature of the law, a legal settlement between Bowie and MainMan was arrived at within less than six months. It essentially retained the same 50-50 split between Bowie and his former management as had been in force since the outset of their partnership, and ensured Defries would also enjoy an interest, financial if not creative, in all Bowie's future recordings for the remainder of the life of their initial contract—until March 31, 1982.

The dream was over.

Part

CABARET

17

DOWN BELOW WITH THE REST
OF HER TOYS

It's 1975 and Lou Reed is a star. The Velvet Underground, the New York band he powered through four years of obscurity, is a legend. "Walk on the Wild Side," his solo hit from two years back, is an AM radio staple and will one day help sell Suzuki motorcycles. His last album made the Top 10 and now his record label is on the phone, demanding a follow-up.

"Okay," says Lou. "I can do that."

He rummages around for a cassette player. "I've got something here I wanted to do way back when. I had to wait a while to get the equipment, but now I've got it and it's done." He depresses the play button. "It's a double album. Wanna hear it?"

The record company man can scarcely control his excitement. "Are you kidding? Hey, c'mon, Lou, baby, let me have it."

At the other end of the line, Lou smiles. "Okay."

For a moment, silence. Then it begins. ZZZZZZZRRRRRRRRRRRRRE EEE EEEEEEGGGGGGGGRRRRRRAAAAAAAAAARRRRRRRRRRZZZ ZBBBBBBBBBB.

By the time Lou's ready for side two, the line's dead. By the time he reaches side three, so is his commercial potential.

A lot of lines went dead when Metal Machine Music *was released. A lot of loyalties, too. Four sides of eardrum-shattering feedback. Lou could rabbit on forever about it being the ultimate guitar solo . . . tell folks that if they listened hard enough they'd hear all sorts of little tunes dancing around in there . . . he could even say they should be grateful he released it in the first place.*

But the fact is, Metal Machine Music *HURT. And not in a wimpy "Oh my God, that's so awful that it's painful" way, or "If you don't turn off the fucking Doobie Brothers, I'm going to rip my tongue out."*

It hurt in an "Oh shit, I think my brain just exploded" way. Most people returned their copy before they got to the end of side one. Others got to side four, and then they returned it. "It's the only recorded work I know of seriously done as well as possible as a gift, if one could call it that, from a part of a certain head to a few others," Reed's liner notes mused politely. "Most of you won't like this, and I don't blame you at all."

News of Bowie's split with MainMan traveled fast and hit hard. The two names had been synonymous for so long, certainly for as long as most fans had been aware of Bowie, that it seemed incredible that either could even exist without the company of the other.

Nobody doubted that they would, however, and while Bowie geared up for the release of his final MainMan album, *Young Americans*, in March 1975, Tony Defries prepared to take his own first steps into an unknown world. He was going to manage Lou Reed.

Bemused by the success of *Sally Can't Dance*, but intent on maintaining the high, Reed continued touring, continued shocking audiences and outraging critics with his ever more explicit mime of drug use, degradation, and disgrace—did he really once hand a loaded syringe out to a member of the audience? Did he really once shoot up *for real* in front of 10,000 baying fans?

Rumor insisted that every outrage was true, but when Reed was asked about them, his silence and the pinpoint pupils that bore back into his inquisitor's eyes were unreadable. Debauchery has always been in the eye of the beholder, but what if the beholder is too scared to press for evidence? Reed did not *give* interviews, he occasionally tolerated them, and even then you never knew if he'd actually answer. It was the ultimate mindfuck, for fans and critics alike, and the only thing that anybody knew for sure was nobody really knew what Lou Reed was thinking.

He remained, however, unhappy—some would even say bitter. He was popular, but his audience was limited. He was successful, but his fame was infamy. And no matter how many plaudits his own tours received, he could not help but notice that Bowie's latest outing, soulless though it was, had won even more.

Other artists might have said that was unfair—Reed's fans certainly did, and a lot of Bowie's agreed with them. But Reed himself took his dismay even further. The dichotomy was disgusting; worse than that, it was disrespectful, not only to Lou, but to everyone. Bowie wasn't a rock star. He was an actor, playing at being a rock star. There was a difference.

Lou had told him as much as well, or something very much like it. Meeting with Bowie in New York, a casual conversation suddenly erupted when Reed threw his drink across the table—the prelude, according to Dennis Katz's assistant Barbara Falk, to a big fight. Lou was jealous of Bowie's success, she said, "but he also said he [Lou] was the cool, underground, credible one. David stomped out screaming."

So far as Reed was concerned, he was still screaming. Why else had Bowie thrown away the management who made it all possible for him? Reed might have studiously avoided signing with Defries in the past, but that was because it suited him not to. He was not (in the wry words of Dana Gillespie's latest album!) *gonna play no second fiddle*, not to Bowie, not to Iggy Pop, not to Mott the Hoople.

Well, they had all gone now, but Defries was still around...just like he had always been around when anybody needed him. And Lou certainly needed *someone*.

Relations with manager Katz were crumbling fast, a process that climaxed in Milan on February 13, 1975. Reed was in Italy to launch the first leg of a world tour but took the stage to find the arena on the edge of pitched battle. The Masters of Creative Situations, a Communist action group, chose the gig as the venue for a confrontation with the police, which necessarily spilled over onto the stage.

Choking through a thick pall of tear gas, while screwdrivers and bolts rained down upon the band, Reed first fled from view, then fled the country. With Barbara Falk alongside him, he headed to Zurich, Switzerland, then demanded to know where his manager was. And when he didn't receive the response he required, he told Falk to call Defries.

Tony Zanetta took the call, and his heart sank. "None of us were that keen on Lou," he admitted, and throughout Defries's first pursuit of the singer, he, Childers, and Vanilla did "little to encourage" him—whenever the topic came up in conversation, they would simply change the subject. "I disliked Lou's amphetamine use and his amphetamine personality. He was super smart-alecky and could be quite vicious. He also was quite erratic as a performer and could be absolutely brilliant one night and embarrassing the next, depending on what drugs he had consumed.

"He was also quite a handful from a managerial point of view."

Falk's call was short and to the point. "She said that Lou was ready to make a change, he wanted to talk with Defries, and could Defries get on a plane right away?"

You bet! Convinced that his chance to manage Reed had finally arrived, Defries caught the next plane to Zurich, made his way to Reed's hotel—and spent the rest of his visit waiting. Reed would not meet him, would not see him, would not even speak to him. Maybe it had all been a ploy to try and get Dennis Katz back on track; maybe he'd simply had second thoughts about working with Defries. Maybe the amphetamines that Falk believed he was devouring so hungrily had upped his paranoia even higher than usual. Whatever it was, Defries never got to meet his man and, shrugged Zanetta, "returned rather sheepishly to New York. We never heard any more about Lou Reed again."

What was interesting was the fact that Reed now seemed intent on ensuring that nobody else would want to, either.

He first started thinking about *Metal Machine Music*, he claimed, "as far back as when John [Cale] used to work with La Monte Young. I had also been listening to Xenakis a lot. You know the drone thing? It took a long, long time. It's way more complex than people realize, but that's all right." Originally he made the tape for his own amusement alone. "I wasn't going to put it out, I made it for myself. John and I were always making tapes; we made sound tracks for underground movies of the time."

But then he changed his mind.

"There are some frequencies on there that are dangerous. What I'm talking about is like in France, they have a sound gun. It's a weapon. It puts out frequencies that kill people. They've had this weapon since 1945. Maybe that's why they play such bad rock 'n' roll."

Metal Machine Music, on the other hand, had nothing whatsoever to do with rock 'n' roll, bad or otherwise. It simply *was*, and in years to come, some remarkably intelligent critics would come up with some remarkably asinine "excuses" for its presence in Reed's back catalog, four sides of extravagantly, exquisitely packaged vinyl, with a cover pic that looked so close to an extension of *Rock 'n' Roll Animal* that even Reed smiled, "It looked like a live rock 'n' roll album."

But he wasn't going to apologize to anybody who fell for it. "Nobody has ever been able to put their finger on me, because I'm not really here,"

Reed cautioned shortly before the album's release. "At least not the way they think I am. It's all in their heads. What I'm into is mindlessness. I just empty myself out, so what people see is just a projection of their own needs. I don't do or say anything." *Metal Machine Music* epitomized those words.

"Just because some kid paid $7.98 for it," he said the following year, "I don't care if they paid $59.98 or $75 for it, they should be grateful I put the fucking thing out and, if they don't like it, they should go eat rat-shit." And two years later: "I don't like any of my albums except *Metal Machine Music*. Why? Because they're not *Metal Machine Music*."

Such sentiments made little difference, of course, to a marketplace that was simply staring in aghast disbelief at Reed's offering. *Rolling Stone* described *Metal Machine Music* as "the tubular groaning of a galactic refrigerator," and that was one of the more complimentary reviews. Lester Bangs was simply grateful to discover that his pet hermit crab, Spud, enjoyed dancing to it.

Thirty years later, however, while Reed's opinions on the album's worth remained constant, the rest of the world changed its colors completely. *Metal Machine Music* was a cult classic now—no less than the Velvet Underground (of whom Eno made much the same observation), *Metal Machine Music* might only have been appreciated by a hundred people, but they all went out and formed industrial bands. They loved it.

"The guy who made it loved it as well," Reed smiled. "I made up phony liner notes, and I was whacked out of my head, but I believed in it. I still believe in it." And to everybody who continued to believe *Metal Machine Music* was a put-on, a piss-take, a monumental goof designed to scare off his fans and say "fuck you" to the record company, Reed was genuinely dismayed. "Oh no! No! I would never do that and have someone buy my 'fuck you,' that's ridiculous. I don't know why people think that."

Maybe because you've suggested as much in the past?

Maybe. But he continued, "I love feedback and distorted guitars. And that's what *Metal Machine* is. The record company was supposed to put a big disclaimer on it that said, 'This is all instrumental, it doesn't have any songs, it doesn't have any vocals,' but instead they...they're money-hungry grubbers, so the little fucks put this tiny, tiny print that I probably can't read now, which said, 'This is an electronic composition,' and no one saw that.

"People thought it was a rock album with songs on it, and they went crazy when they found it wasn't. That album was almost a career end for me...yet another career end." Almost.

The last words on the subject, though; and the last laugh as well, belong to *Metal Machine Music* itself. In March 2002, the Berlin Festspielhaus played host to a very special performance: the eleven-man German avant-garde group Zeitkratzer plus special guests Lou Reed and Mike Rathke came together to perform, in its near entirety, *Metal Machine Music*.

Reed chuckled, "[They] got in touch with me, 'Can we play *Metal Machine Music* live?' I said, 'It can't be done.' They said, 'We transcribed it. Let us send you a few minutes of it and you tell us.' They sent it, I played it, and there it was. It was unbelievable. I said, 'My God! Okay, go do it.' They said, 'Will you play guitar on the last part of it?' So *Metal Machine Music* finally got performed live at the Berlin Opera House. It's extraordinary."

It was. Some people will still argue that it's easy to understand *Metal Machine Music* in theory, but it remains a bitch to live through. Love the machine, though, and Zeitkratzer's performance was incredible. With the metal stripped back from its electronic origins to an almost exclusively acoustic base, Zeitkratzer's violins were now the dominant instrument, but every different frequency, every pulse and squeak and barely audible burble, was recaptured by a different hand, each one recreating the peaks and troughs of the original soundscape and even drawing in those fabulous sequences where you think...you're sure...you'd almost swear... that there were actual snatches of music dancing in the distance, backward classics and the ghosts of riffs. In fact, the only failing that immediately came to mind was, the live performance was about fifteen minutes shorter than the original album. But there were some folks who might call that a blessing.

"You may not recognize me, but my name's Iggy Pop. I've just been worked over for a week by a Transylvanian masseuse in San Francisco...." And so Iggy Pop broke a silence that stretched back more than two years, turning up unannounced at a Patti Smith gig at L.A.'s Roxy in January 1976, and then vanishing back into legend again.

What a legend it was becoming, though. More active in obscurity than he'd ever been when he had a record deal, Pop had had his name attached to more abortive possibilities than probably even he was aware of: a U.K. tour in May 1974; an album for Elton John's Rocket label; a new band with the Doors' Ray Manzarek; maybe even a full-fledged rebirth replacing Jim Morrison at the helm of a reunited Doors.

Released in America in 1974, The Phantom's *Divine Comedy Part One* album was to the memory of the Doors what Klaatu later became to fans of the Beatles, a dramatic, and so utterly convincing recapitulation of the band at its peak that even Morrison's own associates were initially taken aback. "It was weird," remembered Danny Sugerman. "Ray Manzarek and I heard it on the radio and we just went, 'Fuck!'"

The Phantom himself turned out to be an absolute unknown; Manzarek remembers only "a guy named Ted something-or-other. He was from Detroit, and he sounded like Jim." Manzarek met him in L.A. in July 1974, when the Phantom guested at the Jim Morrison memorial concert at the Whisky, to perform a spine-chillingly perfect "Riders on the Storm" with Manzarek himself on keyboards behind him. "He was a weird guy; he dressed in black and would only wear silver jewelry. What's funny about that is, there's now a story going around that it was actually Iggy Pop on the record, who was also at the show, who was also from Detroit, who also sounded like Jim."

There are other tales as well, vaguely implicating Pop as a willing partner in any number of Living Jim rumors. But Pop himself never had time for such tales, a point he made at the Morrison memorial itself, performing a poignantly revised "L.A. Woman" with Manzarek on organ alongside him. "Jim Morrison died today," he sang, "Jim Morrison was more beautiful than any girl in this town. And now he's dead. Now I cry." Got that? He's *dead*.

"And that was all I ever did," Pop affirmed. "I never had any interest in being that guy. I never had discussions with anyone about being that guy, never did anything more than come up and sing that song at the memorial, which I thought was correct given my feelings about his music. You know, I did go to his grave, more because a friend wanted to go and talked me into it that day, but basically, I really like the music, I really checked out the music, but I never had an unnatural, morbid fascination with that guy—he just did some great stuff that I was checking out. He was big for me, but I'm really not into all the rest of that stuff, you know?"

Besides, he was scarcely in a fit state to do anything. He attended the New York Dolls' Death of Glitter festival at the Palladium. He wrote a play, *Murder of the Virgin*, and then gouged a hole in his own chest at the opening night, while being whipped with a length of electrical flex. And he started work on a new album with Stooges guitarist James Williamson.

The sessions, though, barely stumbled along, fading in and out of focus according to Pop's external commitments, and Williamson's ability to keep his charge in order. When Pop shambled out of the studio leaving nine tracks unfinished, he probably thought that was the last he'd ever hear of them.

Weird scenes inside the mixing room. Williamson alone would complete what became *Kill City*, for release a full two years later, taking an album's worth of essentially unusable and certainly commercially unlistenable noises and transformed them into a thing of beauty. Historically, *Kill City* was no more a part of Iggy Pop's career than an airbrushed Picasso would be a part of his. But maybe that was for the best. Pop was at his lowest ebb when *Kill City* was recorded. Short of having wiped the tapes clean immediately, filling in the dots between the flashes of brilliance was the kindest thing anyone could have done.

So far as Pop was concerned, however, unfinished music was the order of the day.

In May 1975, David Bowie and Warren Peace dragged Pop into Hollywood's Oz Studio to record an archetype for what would one day become the gratuitously autobiographical "Turn Blue," a rambling tune hinged around the confession "Mama, I shot myself up." They tackled one of the abandoned *Kill City* tracks, "Sell Your Love," and a couple of new songs, a Bowie effort titled "Moving On," and "Drink to Me," a raw vocal improvisation over a backing track that Bowie had spent nine hours laboring over. And then they left them on the shelf.

The pair had reconnected just days earlier. Bowie had been living in L.A. for a couple of months now, first at Deep Purple bassist Glenn Hughes's house, now at a rental home on Doheny Drive. There, he slipped into the archetypal mid-seventies L.A. routine of coke, paranoia, and sleeplessness; a year earlier, shooting the BBC documentary *Cracked Actor*,

Bowie had complained about the "underlying unease" that permeated the city. Every time he visited, he observed, "I've...been aware of how dubious a position it is to stay here for any length of time."

Now he was living that dubious position, and bombarding friends with the fears and hallucinations with which the city seemed to cram his mind. During an interview with *Rolling Stone* writer Cameron Crowe, he swore he'd just seen a body hurtle past their high-rise window. In conversation with his increasingly estranged wife Angela, he told her he'd been kidnapped by two witches and a warlock. He lived in mortal fear of sundry black magicians whom he had somehow offended, and he spent his time engrossed in books on the occult and fascism.

But it was a sunny day when he was driving down Sunset and suddenly spotted Pop.

Bowie was well aware, from the grapevine if noplace else, of all that had befallen Pop over the past year or so. Pop, for his part, simply thought Bowie looked ill, his naturally pasty skin not only unaffected by the Los Angeles sunshine, but maybe looking even more pallid than usual. He, too, had heard rumors, but if the pair had any traditional rock 'n' roll habits in common, they weren't about to share the secret.

Neither was their reunion to last long. Pop walked out and, though he promised to return to the studio later, he never did. Afterward, when he phoned his mentor to apologize, Bowie told him to piss off. "I hope he's not dead," Bowie mused later on. "He's got a good act."

He wasn't dead, but he was close. Thrown out of James Williamson's apartment after one transgression too many, Pop scored a fistful of downers from an obliging L.A. doctor, stopped by a local diner, and dropped into somebody's dinner.

The cops gave him a choice—jail or hospital. He chose the hospital, then discharged himself and hitched a ride out of town. The next thing he knew, he was puking vivid green bile on a sidewalk somewhere. That's when even he knew he'd had enough. He checked himself back into medical care, at the Neuropsychiatric Institute at UCLA, even though the staff there was dubious about admitting him—"usually you have to be a certified loon," Pop explained. "But it was a sort of experiment for them." There he was diagnosed with, and treated for, a bipolar disorder known as hypomania. His psychiatrist Murray Zucker has since reassessed that opinion, preferring now to consider that drugs and a simple drive for creativity lay at the root of Pop's psychological problems. But the treatment worked, regardless

Pop kicked heroin, together with whatever other substances were driving him downward, and then proved his resolve one weekend in New York. Dropping by CBGB, Pop allowed Johnny Thunders to spend three days trying to coax him back onto smack, and resisted every entreaty. Finally Thunders collapsed in tears.

Which is when Bowie picked Pop up again, hauling him away from the Transylvanian masseuse in spring 1976, to join his latest tour entourage.

A year had now passed since Bowie quit MainMan, a period during which he scored his biggest hit to date with the bilious exorcism of "Fame"; saw the soul of *Young Americans* push him as far afield as the *Soul Train* music awards; cut a freakishly gaunt and scary figure on songstress Cher's eponymous TV show; and finally made the movie debut that rumor had been pushing him toward since 1972.

Back then it was a filmed version of Robert Heinlein's *Stranger in a Strange Land* that seemed most likely to place Bowie on the silver screen. Further away from the headlines, meanwhile, Tony Defries was in negotiation with filmmaker George Lucas about placing the singer in a starring role in a new science-fiction project called *Star Wars*. In the end, Lucas declined. The role in question, he determined, required a new face, a young face, a name without any baggage attached to it, and the part of Luke Skywalker was ultimately passed to Mark Hamill.

But other directors were less squeamish about the burdens that Bowie might add to a film shoot, and when Nicolas Roeg offered him a part, Bowie bit. It was Roeg, after all, who first filmed Mick Jagger, placing him center stage in the gangster-noir seediness of *Performance*, and those were not shabby footsteps to be following in.

Ultimately, *The Man Who Fell to Earth* was scarcely the glittering spectacle that it could have been, and while it certainly ignited the sporadic film career that would keep Bowie ticking over into the next millennium, it was another movie project altogether that first drew his thoughts back to Pop.

Interviewed by *RAM* magazine's Anthony O'Grady, Bowie claimed to have no fewer than nine screenplays littering his mind, dating back to his first abortive attempts to stage the *Ziggy Stardust* cycle on screen, and forward to *Diamond Dogs*, and even a vague approach toward *Young*

Americans. The closest to fruition, however, was an untitled piece written specifically for Iggy Pop and Joan Stanton. And why Pop? Because "Iggy should never have been a rock 'n' roll singer. He's an actor. David Johansen is an actor. I've got nothing to do with music, I've always interpreted or played roles with my songs. [But] rock 'n' roll is a very accessible medium for any young artist...."

The screenplay itself, he insisted, was bleak; the movie would be shot in black-and-white. "I don't really want to go into the story," he hedged, "but it's very violent and depressing. It's not going to be a happy film. It will probably bomb miserably." In fact, it didn't even happen. Bowie was already planning his next album, to be titled *The Return of the Thin White Duke*, as he talked about the film, while the one *after* that was also in hand, after Bowie's proffered sound track to *The Man Who Fell to Earth* was rejected by Roeg. Both would be informed by the fresh expanses that had opened up in Bowie's mind.

The Return of the Thin White Duke would eventually be retitled *Station to Station* (the original name lived on in the opening lyric of the title track), but it remained a "return" all the same, Bowie's return to rock, shot through however with an intangibly European flavor. New musical influences had ridden into his life. The soul music of the previous year's *Young Americans* album ("plastic soul," as he preferred to describe it) had never sat easily on his shoulders; had sounded as forced and fearful as its maker looked, as he turned out at the *Soul Train* awards to help hand out the awards, or standing alongside Cher as they hammed through a medley of oldies and moldies. So he dropped it. Not completely, because it had sold a lot of records, and would probably continue to do so. But it was morphing into something else, an icy beat, a Spartan landscape, a world of cinematic darkness miles removed from the theatrical presentations that had once laid so heavily across his writing. He had discovered Kraftwerk.

Today, Kraftwerk are a legend. They are the robots who rode the Trans-Europe Express to *Skylab*; the autobahn-crazed Krautrockers who breathed life into showroom dummies everywhere. They are the operators with the pocket calculators. In 1975, however, they were simply another name percolating in the ferment of a musical movement that British critics had labeled beneath the somewhat distasteful brand of Krautrock, a pair of classically trained musicians, Ralf Hütter and Florian

Schneider, who had already cut three albums (four if you count the pre-Kraftwerk *Tone Float*) before they decided to cut loose all pretense at being a rock band and convert their instrumental arsenal to electronics.

It took them three days to construct their first electronic instrument, a bizarre contraption which newly recruited drummer Wolfgang Flür described as "sticks on wires which you could touch and make noises with, and I could play it standing up without sweating." They debuted it on a German TV program, and Flür remembered "all the cameramen with the big lenses were running up to film me playing that crazy instrument which no one had seen before. It looked so unusual, a little bit scary, a little bit funny, and that was it for me. I was proud of it, it worked, and once we started recording what became *Autobahn*, of course, I loved it more and more."

History has not recorded whose idea it was to edit the original, twenty-two-minute title track to the fourth Kraftwerk album down to a snappy three minutes; nor does it recall the look on the faces of the sales reps who were handed advance copies of it and told to do their job. But few records have ever seemed so unlikely, so unsuited, so *unsingle-like* as "Autobahn." And few have turned all those presumptions so thoroughly on their heads, and done the complete and utter opposite.

Top 30 in America, Top 20 in the U.K., "Autobahn" (and in its wake, its parent album) became the surprise hit of the year, of the decade. In Britain, the record was popularly known as *Dr. Who* music, out of deference to the BBC Radiophonic Workshop's pioneering electronic sound tracks to the long-running science-fiction television series. And elsewhere, a surprisingly popular misinterpretation of the record's lyric (it really *did* sound as though the group were singing "fun fun fun on the autobahn") conjured up visions of grinning Teutonic Beach Boys.

Flür laughed. "That is wrong. But it works. Driving is fun. We had no speed limit on the autobahn, we could race through the highways, through the Alps, so yes, '*fahren fahren fahren* [drive drive drive] . . . fun fun fun,' but it wasn't anything to do with the Beach Boys! We used to drive a lot, we used to listen to the sound of driving, the wind, passing cars and lorries, the rain, every moment the sounds around you are changing, and the idea was to rebuild those sounds on the synth."

"Autobahn" completely rewrote the rock rulebook. There was simply nothing to relate it to. Nothing except—it really did sound like a road trip. Trucks raced by, horns sounded, there was the lash of the windshield wipers, and the splash of another puddle. If you really thought about it, it was almost frighteningly mundane. But it was also exquisitely exciting, a fact which two continents' worth of record buyers were quick to pick up on. "Some of the American stations were playing the short version," Flür celebrated, "but some were playing the whole track. It sounded really good on car radios, I was told."

With both single and album storming the chart, Kraftwerk were one of the hot tickets that summer of 1975. The quartet played shows across Europe and America, but the fascination cut both ways. Bowie was so impressed by the group that he promptly arranged a meeting with Hütter and Schneider in Düsseldorf, to suggest any number of possibilities—a musical collaboration, a tour, anything. Nothing came of it in the end, to both Bowie and Kraftwerk's disappointment, but as Bowie prepared to head back out onto the road to promote *Station to Station*, he amused himself by compiling a tape of his favorite Kraftwerk music to be played before he took the stage, as audio accompaniment to a screening of surrealist director Luis Buñuel and Salvador Dalí's eyeball-slicing *Un Chien Andalou*.

For many of his audience, it would be their first exposure to anything the group had accomplished beyond the hit "Autobahn." But it was an experience they would not forget, and when they looked around for other leads to take, Brian Eno was awaiting them.

Eno was three years out of Roxy Music now, but only just placing the first tentative toes into musical forms that were unrecognizable from the skewed pop of Roxy's first two LPs: his calculated aversion to convention had already bristled across one electronic symphony, his *No Pussyfooting* collaboration with King Crimson's Robert Fripp. The next time Eno met Bowie, when they found themselves sharing neighboring studios at Olympic, Eno was astonished to learn that the singer could hum great chunks of the album. "I know his work quite well," Bowie defended himself.

It was Eno's ability to harness those same disciplines to more traditional song forms that fascinated, and Bowie had certainly loaned one ear to Eno's work as he conjured up *Station to Station*, even as the other sought to untangle Kraftwerk's conundrums.

"I'd got tired of writing in the traditional manner that I was writing in in America, and coming back to Europe, I took a look at what I was writing, and the environments that I was writing about, and decided I had to start writing in terms of trying to find a new musical language for myself."

His aborted sound track for *The Man Who Fell to Earth*, panned even by former associates as an unlistenable slab of commercial suicide, dabbled deepest in those waters. But the pulsing guitars and locomotive rhythms of "Station to Station," the new album's title track, and the convoluted danceability of "TVC 15," its most distinctive single, posited directions in which his heart was certain to follow. It didn't hurt, either, that "TVC 15" was inspired by a story Iggy Pop told him, about the night that his girlfriend was eaten by her television. The machines were taking over.

Now Pop was back on the scene, turning up at Bowie's hotel when the *Station to Station* tour ground into San Diego on February 13, 1976. He was clean, he was happy, he was pleased to see Bowie again, and that feeling, this time, was mutual. By the time the pair retired for the evening, they had already made plans to start recording again. There was a bass line that Bowie and Carlos Alomar had put together during the tour rehearsals, a funk riff slowed to foreboding menace, but so far boasting just a single Bowie verse, a few rhymes built around the opening line, and an awkward stab at falsetto call and response. He titled it "Calling Sister Midnight."

They'd played it live for the first time the previous evening, and the audience at the Forum in Inglewood had been suitably bemused. Even on a stage that size, it was clear that they were listening to a work in progress, a spiky rhythm that was surely more of a showcase for a blinding guitar solo than anything else.

Elsewhere, the set pulsed with power, vivid beneath the blinding white lights that echoed some vast Man Ray photomontage...or was it Michael White's London production of *Cabaret*, with Judy Dench tiny and vulnerable beneath the stark white bulbs? Or even the harsh monochromatics of Lou Reed's *Rock 'n' Roll Animal* outing?

The opening "Station to Station" rode in on a guitar overture as great as any of those that preluded Reed on that same three-year-old tour, before resolving itself into the shifting collages of the song itself. There was a moody "Word on a Wing," a plaintive "Five Years" and "Life on Mars?," a lascivious "Waiting for the Man." But "Calling Sister Midnight" remained a cauldron without its contents, and Pop knew it. So he listened once, and then extemporized the rest. "Sister Midnight" was reborn that night and both Bowie and Pop knew that Pop had a new single. More than that, the speed with which Pop then reeled off enough material for half a dozen more songs convinced Bowie that they should set their sights on an album.

"Bowie gave me a chance to apply myself, because he thinks I have some talent," Pop reasoned. "I think he respected me for putting myself in a loony bin. He was the only guy who came to visit me—nobody else came. Not even my so-called friends in L.A. But David came." In fact, that wasn't quite true—a number of friends and admirers dropped by. But the point was made. The bond between the two men was strong.

Pop leaped aboard the Bowie tour the following morning, joining an entourage that barely numbered half a dozen people beyond the band and road crew—a far cry from the sprawling organization that had kept the *Diamond Dogs* tour on the road, but a comfortable crowd, one that knew instinctively what their individual duties were, and stuck to them.

Bowie himself was overseeing everything, even taking time out after every show to go through tour photographer Andrew Kent's latest proofs, to decide which pictures would be issued to the local press. Anything he missed would then be hoovered up by Corinne Schwab, who now doubled as his eyes and ears in every situation—a role, it seemed, for which she was born.

Hugh Attwooll, MainMan agent in the earliest days in London, recalled, "I hired her as a secretary. She came in and within thirty-six hours she concluded that I was a complete dickhead, she could do the job far better, and she convinced Defries of that. Tony sent me on holiday and when I came back there was a letter [of dismissal] from him on the desk." Soon, Schwab was working the same persuasive magic on Bowie, and long after he'd placed the MainMan years behind him, Corinne was still there at his side.

If Pop's role within this tightly knit crew was essentially undefined, nobody doubted what his purpose was. He was Bowie's friend and, sitting together as they crossed America by car and train, the two listened to the music that seemed to have the most in common with the directions in which both either were moving, or had already passed through.

Tom Waits was a favorite, but so were the Ramones, the New York speed minimalists whose debut album was due to hit American stores just as the tour wrapped up. But it was Kraftwerk's latest album, *Radio-Activity*, that hit them both the hardest, and the only question either of them had was whether their core audience, the fans who constituted the die-hard heart at the center of their appeal, would ever permit them to move so far from their perceived roots. But what, they now wondered, if they were working together, on a project that took past reputations and threw them up in the air?

Bowie was in a strange mood. "That whole tour was done under duress," Bowie admitted later. Burned up by the year he had spent in Los Angeles, a year of coke-fueled craziness that had built him up to new heights of paranoia, he described himself as "out of my mind, totally, completely crazed."

He turned to books for escape and bound himself up in the legends that lurked behind the Nazi regime, the mythology that convinced Adolf Hitler that he was right, even when the whole world was screaming that he was wrong; the Nazi search for the mythical Holy Grail, bound up with the Nietzschian values of racial purity that hung heavy over German folklore; the works of Wagner, the legends of King Arthur. And all bound together into one vast melting pot of crazed, but strangely cohesive confusion that would peak, finally, when Bowie arrived at London's Victoria Station for his first U.K. shows in three years.

Standing in the back of his hired limo, smartly suited in what really could have passed as the regalia of a visiting fascist dignitary, Bowie waved to the crowds with one arm outstretched—flash went a camera and there was Ziggy Stardust, proffering a Nazi salute to the masses.

18

A DIRTY SKY FULL OF YOUTHS
AND LIQUORS

In 1969, working toward his second album, the unpromisingly titled Man of Words, Man of Music *(later reissued as* Space Oddity*), David Bowie found himself writing the longest song of his career so far—and still an epic by any of his subsequent achievements.*

"Cygnet Committee" was meandering and, compared to some of his later writings, unstructured. There are moments where it feels as though at least two songs have been shoehorned together, and possibly even three.

There are certainly enough ideas adrift for any other artist to have fashioned an entire concept album around it, but Bowie somehow holds it all together, and does so with such apparent ease that one could believe he penned such behemoths every day.

He didn't, and "Cygnet Committee" stands alone in his canon as quite possibly the most important song he has ever written, and not only for what it says. Even at literal face value, the song is the most venomous indictment he has ever written. It is important because of what it would *say, if you played it again a decade or so after its original release, and viewed those words through the eyes of plaintive hindsight.*

First he describes himself, tying his shoelaces and listening to birdsong. He is Everyman. But then he meets the Thinker, a man who gives life, gives all, to those he considers his companions; who "ravages" his bank balance for their well-being, who guides their cause and throws all his resources ahead of them, because he believes so fervently in what they have to offer.

Bowie himself would soon be meeting a man who fulfilled all of those services and many more besides; who "opened doors that would have blocked [his] way"...who raised his charge from Everyman to Superman. And then— "we let him fill our needs, now we are strong."

David Bowie in 1976 was strong. But he was also cautious—not for himself (although his finances remained parlous) or for his music, because he'd always had that. He was cautious because he knew that great changes were coming, changes that would *ultimately affect both his life and his music.*

"The road," he wrote back in 1969, "is coming to an end," and what manner of prescient flash did he experience that prompted him to name-check both the Damned and the "guns of love" . . . the Sex Pistols, of course . . . in the very next line of the song?

Punk rock was approaching, and in its fiery wake a wholesale revolution that might not change the face of rock as we knew it . . . for some bands and institutions could never be blasted away that easily. But a new hierarchy was arising regardless, and so many of them were Ziggy's own children, either by example or default.

The Pistols claimed to have stolen their earliest equipment from the Hammersmith Odeon when Bowie played there. Slaughter and the Dogs guitarist Mick Rossi received his first Les Paul as a gift from Mick Ronson. Even closer to home were the latest activities of a clutch of MainMan mainstays. Wayne County and Cherry Vanilla had both moved to London to ignite recording careers of their own; Leee Black Childers was back in New York, managing Johnny Thunders and the Heartbreakers.

Punk was not only a musical phenomenon, however. It also set in motion a chain of cultural events, ones that would irrevocably alter the austere social landscape that Ziggy Stardust had only chipped at, "the ruptured structure built of age," to replace it with a brave new world of tolerance, obedience, and, ultimately, conformity. The distorted dystopia of political correctness, the liberal fascism that became so concerned about not offending anybody that it dismantled every other right they had, was born of punk.

"The lovers were slain," Bowie cries as "Cygnet Committee" approaches its conclusion, "because they knew not the words of the Free State's refrain," and how many others have been murdered or worse because they were not quite au fait *with the demands of their peers? A misplaced racial slur that past generations would never even have noticed; a slip of the tongue in the wrong kind of company, a sexist jibe or an ageist stumble. Or maybe even a photograph, catching its subject at just the wrong moment, one arm raised to wave to his fans, but locked before bending, with palm and fingers rigidly extended. . . .*

"He looks terribly ill," wrote the *Daily Express*'s Jean Rook. "Thin as a stick insect and corpse pale, as if his lifeblood had all run up into his flaming hair." But then she pounced. A few days earlier in Stockholm, still adrift in Nazi mythology, Bowie had mused to a local journalist that Britain, his homeland, needed a fascist prime minister, and that he was the man to fill those jackboots. "Bowie would blush if he could spare the blood," Rook observed, and Bowie merely squirmed. "If I said it, and I've a terrible feeling that I did . . . I'm astounded anybody could believe it. I'm not sinister. I'm not a great force. I don't stand up in cars waving to people because I think I'm Hitler. I stand up in my car waving to fans."

But Pop, with his sharp eye for detail and a gift for wrapping that detail up in song, recalled the event regardless and, a few months later, singing "China Girl" for the first time, he surely had Victoria Station in mind as he wrote of stumbling into town, "just like a sacred cow . . . visions of swastikas in my head and plans for everyone." Maybe Bowie tried to suppress that line, for fear of what he knew it could do to Pop's reputation; or maybe he didn't, because he wanted to see what would happen next. But Pop wasn't taking shit from anyone, and when a disabled Belgian reporter made his very first question, "How can you feel sympathy for Hitler?" Pop made him leave the room.

The American leg of the *Station to Station* tour wrapped up at Madison Square Garden on March 26, 1976. The following day, Bowie left for Europe, while Pop hung on in New York, catching up with old friends. CBGB staged a reception in his honor, feting a man whose influence upon the now-bristling New York "punk" scene had never been in doubt, but the stay was only ever intended to be a brief one. By mid-April, Pop was back at Bowie's side, the first round of shows in Germany and Switzerland at an end, and preparing for a railroad trip to Moscow, arranged on a whim as a way of killing time before the next scheduled show in Helsinki.

They had already stepped off the beaten track once, taking advantage of a couple of days halt in West Berlin by throwing themselves into the city's nightlife, the same sordid mix of sex and drugs and all pleasures in between that had constituted the former (and future) German capital's underbelly since the Weimar years. Backstage at the final Forum show in L.A., Bowie was entranced when author Christopher Isherwood appeared backstage—the same Isherwood whose short story *I Am a Camera* had become the stage show *Cabaret*, whose revolutionary lighting effects were clearly on Bowie's mind as he designed his latest concert presentation.

They talked for what seemed hours, Bowie diving deep into Isherwood's memory, intent on drawing out every last corner of prewar Berlin. Isherwood laughed a lot; Berlin, he told his tireless inquisitor, was nowhere near as exciting in real life as he had made it sound in his writings. But his writings conjured a powerful image, and Bowie wanted to see it for himself. Even more importantly, he wanted to live it—even if it was from the comfort of a Mercedes 600 that once belonged to the president of Sierra Leone.

They crossed through the Berlin Wall, the vast concrete barrier that then separated democratic West Berlin from the Communist East, the archetypal strangers in a very strange land, and they adopted those same roles again as they traveled to Moscow, gawking out of the windows as the train passed through Germany and Poland, posing for photographs in Red Square, and hitting the rest of the Muscovite tourist trail too, before reboarding the train just seven hours later, to make the journey back to Finland.

The tour rolled on—Scandinavia, London, the Low Countries, France; ten nations in six weeks before it all wrapped up in Paris. Then it was off to the Château d'Hérouville, where Bowie had recorded *Pin Ups* three years before and where, he told Pop, they would now be recording *his* record.

Laurent Thibault recalled their arrival. The bass player with the French progressive band Magma, Thibault was the new owner of the Château d'Hérouville, and initially thought Bowie was visiting simply to get away from the massed throng of fans who had discovered the hotel he was staying at. "I received a phone call from Corinne.... [A] lot of people were trying to see him and it was very disturbing, so she asked if David could come to the Château to be protected. Of course, yes."

The party arrived that same evening, and Thibault was only a little surprised when Bowie led Pop straight up to the second-floor studio to show him around. *That*, Bowie announced, is a true rock 'n' roll studio, and the following evening, he told Thibault that he wanted to book it for around six weeks, leading up to mid-July. He even wrote a personal check to confirm the booking, while he waited for RCA to cough up the funds.

Sessions for what everybody now knew as "Jimmy's album" kicked off at the end of May 1976, Bowie and Pop accompanied with an electric piano, a Plexiglas guitar, an ARP synthesizer, and a Marshall amp. Bowie had already recorded rough instrumental sketches of some of the songs onto cassette, while "Sister Midnight" had been expanded beyond that, into something approaching its finished state during a stopover at a London studio earlier in the month. Now, while Bowie and newly recruited drummer Michel Santangeli worked on the backing tracks, Pop slumped in the control room, scratching down lyrics to the music he was hearing—it was that spontaneous. Pop later compared making the album to "a couple of little old ladies with knitting needles or something." Other musicians would eventually file through the sessions, but the basic tracks were Bowie and Pop alone, "just the two of us on that whole album."

Bowie brought out the guitar, playing the instrument in anger for the first time since the *Diamond Dogs* sessions. "[Bowie] plays better Angry Young Guitar than any Angry Young Guitar Player I've ever heard, including James Williamson," Pop genuflected. "The only guy who cuts [Williamson] to pieces. When Bowie plays guitar, he gets nuts."

Twisting the instrument through "Dum Dum Boys," Pop's lament for all his past fallen bandmates, Bowie tortured out a tone that sounded almost like it was calling his name, an anguished wail of "bowe-waaaaahh." "That's his part," Pop revealed. "That's David doing that. He struggles with that thing when he plays. Struggles! His fingers start cramping after a while and we have to stop halfway through and he's yelling, 'I don't know why the fuck I'm doing this for you, you jerk!'"

He was doing it because it was liberating. He was doing it because it gave him the chance to make a record without the accountants at the record company breathing down his neck, to make sure there were enough future singles on the disc. He was doing it because he could.

Thibault supplied the bass without once being told what he was expected to play, but Bowie laughed when he expressed concern about his performance. Neither Thibault nor Santangeli were ever content with what they heard back of their contributions. Both were convinced that with a little more time, and definitely some more rehearsal, they could nail the performances to perfection. But Bowie did not want perfection. He wanted looseness, raw and angry. If a mistake dropped onto the master tape, chances were good that it would be left there.

Only once did Bowie step forward to correct one of Thibault's improvisations. Having played through what the bassist recalls as "a very long song called 'Borderline,'" Thibault was told it wasn't quite what the song required. "Try this," Bowie told him, and he started humming a new bass line. Thibault followed along "and that became 'China Girl'"—a lyric, ironically, that Pop wrote following a brief but passionate fling with Kuelan Nguyen, the wife of another of the Château d'Hérouville's residents, French singer Jacques Higelin.

Bowie could do no wrong, it seemed. Every song he brought to Pop was a diamond. All except one. "People get annoyed with each other's persona, so at one point he composed one on acoustic guitar called, 'Oh Iggy Pop, When Are You Gonna Stop?' But I wasn't going for that, I'm not recording that, I'm not interested."

With Bowie spending so much time in the studio, Pop was free to wander. He would tour the château's grounds if he didn't want to travel far, venture further afield if he fancied it and, every so often, journey the twenty-five miles into Paris, to spend time with his old girlfriend Nico.

Nico had maintained her nomadic existence in the years since they last met. A year earlier, she was in London, reuniting with Lou Reed for a short time, and posing with him for photographer Mick Rock at the Blake Hotel—Lou had suggested they make an album together, Reed writing and producing, Nico singing and playing. It never happened, and she moved on. West Berlin, Amsterdam, Los Angeles...now she was in Paris, and Pop reappeared just days later.

"It was wonderful to see Jimmy again—we were like two old lovers reunited after so long apart and wondering why we ever broke up," she laughed gently. She was only marginally curious to learn that he was working with Bowie. The last time she had seen *him*, she said, was in London sometime around the end of 1973 or early 1974.

"He said he wanted to produce a record with me, and was going to introduce me to his manager Tony Defries and make me a star. But, of course, he said that to all the women he wanted to take to bed and I already had a manager and a new record."

It was a short-lived renaissance. Nico's label, Island, dropped her, apparently after misconstruing a remark she made about Jamaicans as a slice of racist rhetoric (*another* slice of racist rhetoric; her remark about Lou Reed's Jewishness was not forgotten), and by the time she arrived in

Paris, she was as low as she had ever been, suicidal and strung out on smack. Patti Smith ran into her one day and discovered to her horror that Nico had even lost her harmonium—possibly it had been stolen, possibly sold. Smith bought her a new one, but still there seemed to be no way back. And though the reappearance of Pop at least brought her some happiness, that lasted only until Bowie learned where Pop was spending his time.

"He told Jimmy not to come to see me anymore. He told Jimmy that I was a bad influence and was trying to get Jimmy hooked again," Nico mourned. "But I think he was just jealous because I wouldn't sleep with him." Bowie later claimed he arrived home one day to find a note from Nico demanding, "I need to see you." To which he responded with one insisting, "Well, I don't need to see you," while Pop tells another story altogether:

"Forget the state she was in, she just desperately wanted to get in touch with me. Maybe with Bowie more, but hell, I'd suffice and she had me followed. Had radio monitors scanning my every move. Taxi drivers were bribed, just everything. Anyway, when I found her, I just rejected her immediately.... And she got that look that the Deutsche get when they're about to bite into a pig. She got that vampirism in her eyes. She wasn't about to be defeated outright, or so she thought. Because her next number was to slyly offer me a snort of heroin. She laid out a line, figuring that heroin would get me into her little web. But just as the enticing line came close to my nostril, I blew it off the mirror, all over the floor, got up and said, 'So long, baby, nyah nyah, fooled you.' And that's the last I've seen of Nico."

Nico, however, shrugged off such remarks. "I know what happened between us and so do they, and that's all that's really important."

At the end of July, the team—Bowie, Pop, and the now integral Thibault—moved on to Munich to complete the album and finally lay down Pop's vocals. The backing tracks were all but complete now. All that remained was for some additional guitar to be added in by a young unknown whom Tony Visconti had been raving about, Phil Palmer.

He received one of those legendary calls where the phone rings and a voice on the other end announces, "Hi, my name's David Bowie...."

Palmer didn't believe it when his mother handed him the phone and told him who was calling, and he didn't believe it once the stranger started to speak. But finally his suspicions were calmed, and just days later, Palmer found himself walking through the deserted shopping mall which housed Musicland Studios—deserted because the session kicked off at midnight—to find instead of the calm, collected demeanor that he might have associated with a Bowie-run studio, the chaotic carnage left behind by the studio's other residents, Thin Lizzy.

"David Bowie and Iggy Pop, what a racket," Lizzy's Phil Lynott grimaced a couple of years later. "We didn't see that much of them to be honest, but somebody played us the tapes, and we just looked at each other and said, 'Well that's it, he's blown it.'"

Palmer spent five nights in the studio, wrangling unimagined sounds from his guitar. Sometimes, Bowie or Pop would make a suggestion. Layering his instrument over "Nightclubbing," Palmer was told to imagine that he was walking down Wardour Street in London's Soho. "Now play the music you hear coming out of the door of each club." Other times, he found himself harmonizing with the guitar lines that Bowie had already laid down once, or trying to make melodic sense of the tape loops that Thibault was creating to filter through "Mass Production," a symphony of industrial crashes and bangs that became a percussive field unlike any he had heard before. Pop, however, said they reminded him of home . . . of growing up in Ann Arbor, in the heart of America's industrial soul.

"I always found myself fascinated by the industrial home that was always around me. Everything from my father's electric shaver to the electric space heater in our metal trailer. And when I was about nine years old, I was taken on a tour of Ford's main assembly plant in River Rouge, and there I saw my first machine press. I loved that sound!"

That love enfolded his vocal performances. It had been three years since Pop last made a record that he genuinely intended completing, and that was a long time to wait. From the moment he opened his mouth, he was in better voice than he'd ever been, sonorous and sensual, commanding and melodic. And his words just blew Bowie away.

"Jimmy would make up lyrics on the spot," Bowie marveled at the time. "[He'd] keep everything he did, and occasionally change a line after he had recorded. I've never seen anybody able to make up lyrics just out of his head to a track. He'll hate me for this, but it's more like the beatnik era. It's a very spontaneous kind of lyric, it's not...a writing thing for Jimmy. With mine, I spend months writing one word, then I have to look it up to see how to spell it." Pop, on the other hand, didn't even need to think about it. He just opened his mouth and the lyrics spilled out.

The recording was complete. It was time to shift operations once again. That weekend taste of West Berlin earlier in the year had left both Bowie and Pop wanting more. When they discovered that the Hansa Studio was available, an office block on the Kurfürstendamm, Bowie booked as much time as he could get. And then he rented a place to live. West Berlin became Bowie and Pop's home for the next two years.

The author Günter Grass once described divided Berlin as the city that stands closest to the "realities of the modern age." Talking to *Vogue* magazine, Bowie professed himself to be in full agreement. "Berlin is... the center of everything that is happening and will happen in Europe over the next ten years," he predicted. "It's such an ambiguous place, it's hard to distinguish between the ghosts and the living."

Pop was less poetic, but just as enthusiastic. "I always wanted to come to Germany, even when I was a kid," he raved. "I read everything about it. I always knew I wanted to come here, just like some guys always knew they wanted to wear a dress." He celebrated his arrival in the city of his dreams by walking, walking everywhere. "When I first got here, I just walked and walked. Not thinking about anything. Just talking to myself."

Pop adored West Berlin. It was one of the few cities he'd ever visited, after all, that was as crazy as he was, and whose craziness (like his) extended across so many different levels. One night after an evening spent at the Jungle nightclub, Pop stepped into a phone booth to make a call, and was promptly locked in by the same mysterious miscreant who, according to the local police, had already caged ten other people the same way.

"He sneaks up on people and locks them in," Pop laughed, "and watches the police come and get them out. I didn't know that, I was just trying to make this phone call.... [S]omebody saw me in there and they were slipping me cigarettes under the door. I was in there for a half hour...."

Home was a second-floor apartment at 155 Hauptstrasse, in the same Schöneberg district that Christopher Isherwood had called home when he lived in the city in the 1930s.

With seven rooms, including an office and a studio that Pop quickly commandeered for his painting hobby, Bowie, Pop, and Corinne squeezed into the apartment, and immediately converted it into the center of operations for a host of activities, only a few of which seemed to revolve around work. Pop later claimed that of the seven days in a week, two were spent partying, two more were spent recovering, and only the last three were devoted to worrying about the music.

Naturally, some days would be spent quietly, particularly those which Bowie devoted to the seven-year-old Zowie, or when other business called him away. There were clouds on Bowie's personal horizon, after all. No sooner had he disentangled himself from the labyrinthine tentacles of MainMan than he was embroiled in another legal dispute with the short-lived manager who took the company's place, Michael Lippman. He was also dealing with what was clearly the irretrievable breakdown of his marriage to Angela, one whose ramifications were only complicated by her apparent replacement in his life with Corinne Schwab.

Occasional evenings, too, would pass gently by, Bowie and Pop sitting and listening to music, or settling down excitedly to watch the once-a-week television show that was broadcast in English. "Very mundane activities," shrugged Pop. Or he would read. Pop was a vociferous reader, and Bowie had a library that you could lose yourself in. They made friends: a Romanian filmmaker, an artist, a local clothing designer and her carpenter husband—it was he who hand-made new beds for Bowie and Pop. A bar opened beneath the apartment, the Anderesuhfer, and they hung out there. And if they ever got homesick, there was an expat American and British community that was always good for a few hours of nostalgia.

"There were local characters you would meet," Pop celebrated. "And instead of the constant, insane, mindless, American drug culture, there was an artsy-crafty weekend drug culture. So on the weekends, you'd go meet an eccentric character who was interested in the arts and knew other people, and maybe you'd have a little coke and get drunk and go till four in the morning to three or four clubs, which would run the gamut from . . . there was a big rock dance club called Tribe House, and it would go right down to places that didn't open until breakfast, the full-on Berlin nightlife."

They befriended Romy Haag, the Dutch transsexual whose eponymous cabaret was one of the hippest nightspots in town, a playground for the rich and famous, and a flash of delightful nostalgia for anyone who regretted the passing of the old Max's Kansas City. It was no surprise at all when they discovered Tony Ingrassia was both living in West Berlin and close friends with Haag. It was more shocking that they didn't find more old friends in the neighborhood.

Rumor stalked Haag like a faithful hound. It was she, insisted one pervasive legend, who had lured Bowie to West Berlin in the first place, so they could continue the affair they had allegedly ignited the first time he visited the city. But Bryan Ferry, Mick Jagger, Lou Reed, and German superstar Udo Lindenberg also numbered among her alleged conquests, until it seemed that Haag needed only talk to a recognizable figure for someone to assume they were passionate lovers.

Wayne County, who had made his own way to West Berlin to complete the gender reassignment that transformed Wayne into Jayne, was another Cabaret Romy Haag regular. And although he never met up with Bowie there, his old rival's presence was still palpable. Haag and Bowie had fallen out, County heard, "because she thought he was nicking her ideas." County would preserve his memories of the city in his own song "Berlin," and in doing so captured the menace and dichotomies that were the pulse beat of the nocturnal city. He was not at all surprised to discover Bowie distilling those same attributes into his music. No less than New York seven years earlier, West Berlin was a hotbed of psychosexual artistry that danced so far to the left of the mainstream center that it sometimes seemed impossible that the two could ever collide. The very same energies that had attracted Bowie to Max's were now living large at the Cabaret Romy Haag. "Berlin was a great place for transsexuals," County laughed.

Bowie called Tony Visconti in to mix the record that they had decided to title *The Idiot*, the first time they'd worked together since falling out over *Young Americans*.

All that was forgotten now, and Visconti's first thought upon seeing his old friend again was how much healthier Bowie looked than the last time they'd spent time together, and how much more invigorated he seemed, by life and by his music. Indeed, no sooner was Pop's album mixed—into a listening experience which Eno later compared to "being encased in a block of concrete"—than the entire crew was packing up again and, in late August 1976, shifting back to the Château d'Hérouville, to work on

Bowie's own next album—a record that was to be unlike any he had ever attempted before.

His regular bandmates Carlos Alomar, George Murray, and Dennis Davis were on site, while both Pop and Tony Visconti had made the short leap from West Berlin. Visconti introduced yet another unknown guitarist, Ricky Gardiner, and a rock 'n' roll pianist named Roy Young completed the band. But Brian Eno was along as well, to twist and tease Bowie's ideas into new landscapes altogether; to build a musical experience that would shed all the skins Bowie had adopted in the past, strip them down to the barest minimum and rebuild from there.

The notion of Bowie and Eno teaming up was first raised when they met backstage at one of Bowie's Wembley gigs in May. Robert Fripp, too, was to be involved, and Bowie pondered vaguely on the possibility of that being the dream team that would create the then-gestating Iggy Pop album. But Fripp was unable to make it, and Eno was tied up for a few months more, so the idea was shelved. Now he was free again, and the plans shifted accordingly.

Half the songs that Bowie brought to these new sessions were little more than vignettes, and it was Eno who suggested they remain such. The remainder were virtual paintings in sound, instrumental notions and passages that would now be expanded beyond the simple riff or chord sequence that Bowie originally envisioned, into what became a side-long symphony of wordless atmospherics, impressions of places he'd passed through in recent months. The strange thing was, Bowie found it easier to explain what each track was about than he'd ever managed with his lyrical efforts.

"'Warszawa' is about Warsaw, and the very bleak atmosphere I got from the city. 'Art Decade' is about West Berlin, a city cut off from its world, art and culture, dying with no hope of retribution. 'Weeping Wall' is about the Berlin Wall, the misery of it. And 'Subterraneans' is about the people who got caught in East Berlin after the separation, hence the faint saxophones representing the memory of what it was."

Sometimes he would return to the aborted *Man Who Fell to Earth* sound track, to salvage whatever the pair thought was worthwhile. Other times, however, he would absent himself from the proceedings altogether, and leave Eno to work undisturbed. The result would be an album, originally titled *New Music Night and Day* but now slimmed down to *Low*, that was destined to polarize everybody who heard it.

"I had no statement to make. It was low in profile in its own way, and it was a very indulgent album for me to find out what I wanted to do musically. The strange thing that came out of *Low* is that in my meanderings in new processes and new methods of writing, when Eno and I listened back to it, we realized we had created new information without even realizing it, and that by not trying to write about anything, we had written more about something or other that one couldn't quite put one's finger on, than we could have had we actually gone out and said, 'Let's do a concept album.' It was quite remarkable."

It was also utterly dislocating.

Watching from afar, no longer Bowie's manager but still an interested party, Tony Defries was outraged. Anxious to safeguard his financial stake in Bowie's future recordings, he simply could not see how *Low* could possibly be to anybody's advantage.

Neither could RCA. Having already had their fingers severely burned by *Metal Machine Music*, a year old and still turning up on the returns sheet, the company fought so hard against *Low*'s release that one executive allegedly offered to buy Bowie a house in Philadelphia if he would only make another *Young Americans*.

Bowie, however, would not be budged. Not only did he believe in the new album, both as a disc in its own right and as the blueprint for what he intended doing in the immediate future, he was also adamant that, having earned his freedom from managerial interference the hard way, he wasn't about to kowtow to similar interests now. He made just one concession. If RCA would only release the album, he would not count it against his contractual obligation.

Behind his resilience, however, Bowie knew that *Low* was taking a chance; that an audience that was still divided over the stylistic changes of his last couple of albums was scarcely going to welcome another sideways twist—particularly one that so deliberately undervalued the two attributes for which his records were most prized, the songcraft and, across the instrumental side two, his singing. When RCA asked how he intended promoting the record, he announced that he didn't. There would be no tour, no television performances, and only a handful of carefully selected interviews. *Low* would be left to sink or swim on the strength of Bowie's name and reputation alone. How was he, or anybody else, to know just how vast that reputation would become as a consequence?

Britain in late 1976, early 1977, was firmly in the thrall of punk rock, a musical discipline (although some would say indiscipline) that bubbled up off the streets in the first part of the year essentially as a grassroots reaction to the increasingly pompous attitudes of the era's biggest rock names—the Rolling Stones, the Who, Genesis, Pink Floyd, Yes, Elton John, Rod Stewart. Bowie too could have slipped into that ill-starred company. He was certainly on a similar plateau to them all, and on the rare occasions when he even deigned to tour the U.K. (the Wembley shows in 1976 were his first British gigs since 1973), ticket prices were as high as anybody else's.

But his music had also sound-tracked so much of the decade so far that even punk's most outspoken acolytes could not help but nurture a soft spot for him—all the more so because, if you pried away the surface stardom, Bowie's own attitude toward his fame appeared to be as confrontational as that of any punk rocker. Why else did he keep changing musical direction?

Respect by association, too, clung to Bowie's cloak—just as he had known it would six years earlier, when he first started singing the praises of the Velvet Underground and the Stooges. But even he could not have realized just how heavily those acts, too, would impact upon the newborn punk movement; nor could he have known that the rebirth of Iggy Pop under Bowie's current tutelage would dovetail exquisitely with an entire new generation's discovery of the albums he'd made in the past.

The first two Stooges albums might have been available only as comparatively costly French imports. *Raw Power* was seldom seen outside of the highest-priced collectors' emporiums. But *Metallic KO*, the live album culled from the Stooges' final tour, and culminating with three songs recorded at the last ever show, with the bottles shattering and Pop being pummeled, had been released just a couple of months before, to the shock and awe of everyone who came into contact with it.

If any single record could be said to have coalesced the new energies of punk rock with the themes and streams that the past had to offer them, it was *Metallic KO*, and the news that Bowie was bringing Pop back into contention could not help but turn ears toward his own current work as well—especially after somebody leaked the news that Pop was also involved in *Low*, "hover[ing] in the background," as Visconti put it, "a very positive influence, feeding the project with creative energy."

Publicly, Pop's involvement was minimal, confined to turning in some backing vocals on a song that had originally been intended for *The Idiot*, "What in the World." In the studio, however, he was a constant source of entertainment, particularly on the night that he sat spinning yarns for Bowie and Visconti while they fired questions about the life and times of the Stooges. "The stories were both decadent and hilarious," Visconti understated.

Low was released in January 1977, with the RCA executives already piling into some metaphorical bomb shelter to protect themselves from the inevitable critical blast. But the blast never came. "Sound and Vision," the album's first single, soared to No. 2 in the U.K., despite riding in on an instrumental intro that lasted longer than the song itself. At one point, BBC television was even harnessing an excerpt for its in-house promotional spots and trailers.

It was enormous. "Sound and Vision" became Bowie's biggest U.K. hit with a current release since "The Jean Genie" in 1972. Only a 1975 reissue of "Space Oddity" had climbed any higher, and with *Low* selling through the ceiling as well, suddenly the worst misstep Bowie had ever taken in his life was beginning to look a lot like a stroke of unalloyed genius.

Yet he continued downplaying his own career. He maintained his insistence that he would not tour. But Pop would, and Bowie astonished everybody, perhaps including Pop himself, when he announced that he would be joining his friend on the road, not as a simple companion, but as an integral part of the band, playing keyboards. Then, with Ricky Gardiner hanging on from the *Low* sessions as guitarist, and the brotherly rhythm section of Hunt and Tony Sales—sons of comedian Soupy—completing the lineup, rehearsal time was booked at the old Universum Film AG movie lot in nearby Potsdam-Babelsberg, the legendary home to such classics as *Metropolis*, *The Blue Angel*, and *Dr. Mabuse*.

Word of Bowie's presence on the stage was intended to be secret. Especially in the U.K., it was felt that Pop would have no trouble selling out the chosen venues to his own fan club, without complicating matters by throwing Bowie's following into the ticket queue as well.

In any event, everybody seemed to have at least heard a rumor long before the tour opened at Bowie's traditional low-key haunt, Aylesbury Friars, and the audience in every ticket line harbored its fair share of

Ziggy clones, Thin White Dukes, and Philadelphia soul boys, each of them blending almost imperceptibly in with the shock of color and imagination that was the punks' chosen mode of dress.

In the face of such glamour, it was scarcely surprising that the Friars' own security goons were so nonplussed by Bowie's jeans-and-shirt-clad appearance that they tried to prevent him from entering the building, convinced that there was no way on earth that he could be who he claimed to be.

Besides, anybody hoping that the skinny guy chain-smoking behind the piano might get up and do something more than tickle the ivories was in for a disappointment. From the moment the band took the boards and kicked into a stuttering but so powerful "Raw Power," it was Pop's stage, and if, as a few reviewers later remarked, there was a hint of disappointment registered when he *didn't* swan dive into the audience, or carve his flesh to collops, still it was impossible to take your eyes off him for a moment, for fear that he *would* do something.

For seven years, British fans had been reading about the legend that was Iggy Pop; for seven years, his name had been a byword for manic self-destruction. Simply seeing him strain his sinews against the mic stand was enough to send your heart racing into your mouth in anticipation, and through a set that seemed only half aware that there was a new album to promote, so many older classics were there already on hand, Iggy Pop left his reputation in the dust behind him.

"What about the annihilation of self?" asked the *New Musical Express*, in an interview published the weekend of the London Rainbow shows.

"I have tried that in the past—with some success, I might add."

But you gave it up?

"I do it on weekends."

19

THE PLAYS HAVE GONE DOWN
AND THE CROWDS HAVE SCATTERED

A tiny cellar in Copenhagen, September 1977

Iggy Pop is in town to headline Daddy's Dance Hall, but right now the band are at the House, a tiny musicians' hangout in what could be called the local answer to Greenwich Village. There's no more than fifty people inside, chatting away while a local jazz rock band tootles through its paces. And Pop's bored.

He looks around the room. A champagne bottle candleholder on a neighboring table catches his eye. He leans over, a beer bottle clutched in one paw, and swings it toward the candle, judging his aim so precisely that, even when it seems certain that the two bottles will make shattering contact, there's an eighth of an inch or so clearance. Again he swings, again you see the champagne bottle tremble in anticipation of the impact that never comes, while Pop's eyes bore transfixed into the glass.

Finally his publicist, Barbara DeWitt, steps over and confiscates the bottle. Pop looks at her blankly, surveys the scene once again, and then leaps onto a table and starts to sing "Deutschland Über Alles."

Up on stage, the jazz rockers stumble to an astonished halt and ask if he would mind shutting up. Pop just ups the volume. The more they cajole him, with humor, threats, and sarcasm, the louder he gets, until somehow word reaches them that the only way to really shut him up would be to surrender the stage to the upstart and his band. They agree, and Pop is so overcome with gratitude that he completely forgets his hostility toward the band—and turns it upon himself instead.

Pop does everything that evening. He swan dives onto a table littered with glasses, bottles, and burning cigarettes, and illuminated by a low-hung metal lamp. Still clutching the mic and singing "Sixteen," he begins swinging from the lamp while his eyes swivel across the room, to alight upon a young girl.

He crosses over and begins to serenade her. She ignores him, staring fixedly ahead and avoiding his eyes. But Pop will not be deterred. First howling, then screaming into her impassive face, he finally grabs her by the neck and shakes her furiously. Then, clocking the cavalry riding to her rescue, he releases his prey and bounds back to the stage, while his roadies and entourage form a barrier around it, prepared to repel the outraged locals.

And Pop calms down after that, and eventually returns to his hotel. But the beast will not remain caged.

"For just five minutes," he screams aloud the following day, while demolishing a TV studio filled with plastic plant life. "For just five minutes, can't you treat me like an animal?"

A funny thing happened after Pop's British tour wrapped up. David Bowie climbed aboard an airplane.

For five years, he had been refusing to fly. For five years, his face had turned pale at the thought of entrusting his life to a membrane of metal, poised precariously tens of thousands of feet up. But if he wanted to tour with Iggy Pop, he didn't have any choice in the matter—the last British date, and the first American one, were so close together that flight was the only choice.

Of course, few people truly believed that he had really spent all those years defiantly earthbound, particularly after sundry ex-MainMan personnel told the world about the day when they scored a bunch of tickets to an Elvis gig at Madison Square Garden. Bowie was a huge Presley fan—they shared the same birthday, for goodness' sake!—and they only called him up to tease him: "We're going to see Elvis, and we've got a spare ticket. Shame you'll never get here in time." Bowie couldn't have been by their side any faster if he'd miraculously sprung wings and flown in himself.

There was something else, as well. The refusal to fly had been a heaven-sent opportunity when it played into a certain image. But Ziggy and Aladdin were long dead now, and Bowie was another man entirely. His fear was an affectation that had finally run its course. Nobody, Bowie included, cared how he transported himself around any longer, which meant that once the tour was over, too, he could board another flight back to West Berlin, preparing to follow up *The Idiot*.

It was a fractious period. Friends and collaborators still, Pop and Bowie had spent a lot of time together over the past twelve months... had, in fact, seemed virtually inseparable. It was time for Pop to regain his independence.

Back in West Berlin, he moved out of the apartment he and Bowie were sharing, into his own flat in the same building, a fourth-floor, three-room pad at the back of 155 Hauptsrasse. With him went girlfriend Esther Friedmann, the daughter of an American diplomat who had never even heard of Pop before they met in a bar one evening, and together they used Pop's RCA advance to furnish the apartment to their precise tastes. "Nice rugs," Iggy boasted, "wallpaper, and an oak table with the German eagle motif for the four legs, and huge oaken chairs with leather backs that had an arcane symbol of some secret German clan."

He took over the recording sessions, too, scrapping any notion Bowie might have had of pursuing the visions laid down with *The Idiot* by retaining the Sales brothers as a manic rhythm section, and making sure that the guitars were on stun from the start. For *The Idiot*, Pop had been content to allow Bowie to dictate the pace of the songs and the sessions. The tour, however, had reawakened his rock 'n' roll restlessness, and the new songs, though they shared the same Bowie-Pop writing credits as before, were to reflect Pop's own heritage. The album title said it all— he'd come up with it almost before he knew he needed it: *Lust for Life*.

Abandoning the civilized surroundings of Hansa's main studio, the party alighted instead at the same owners' newly opened Hansa-by-the-Wall, a wartime concrete bunker set, as its name suggests, in the shadow of the Berlin Wall. Through the windows of the studio, the gun towers and searchlights cast dark silhouettes against the lights of the city; through the windows, too, the discerning eye could catch sight of the lovers who would make their trysts in the shadow of the wall.

Bowie would write the song "Heroes" about one such encounter (Tony Visconti later claimed that he was one half of the spied-upon lovers), a song that bleeds directly out of Lou Reed's "Berlin" to paint a portrait of the city as the soul of doomed romance. Pop, however, had no time for such emotion.

For him, West Berlin brought craziness to his music, exuberance and sexuality, unbridled love and lust shot through with only the occasional glimpse of the sobriety that lies behind the neon and glamour. Only one song, "The Passenger," might have fit onto *The Idiot* without too much rearrangement, and even it bristled with a joie de vivre that shone through the lyric's nocturnal moodiness.

Elsewhere, the glam-soaked pounding of "Fall in Love with Me" could have been lifted wholesale from the nightly sound track of the Cabaret Romy Haag, fed through any of its Weimar-era counterparts. Step into the wrong side of town and the tight, coiled menace of "Neighborhood Threat" and "Some Weird Sin" might wrap themselves around your throat; and the heart-stopping reinvention of the once-abandoned "Turn Blue" saw Pop turning the spotlight full upon his own vivid legend. Even "Lust for Life" looked to West Berlin for inspiration, as Bowie lifted its percussive fanfare from the Morse code rhythm that opened the daily Armed Forces Network radio broadcasts.

The song that truly epitomized the new album, though, was "Success," kicking off the vinyl's second side by nodding reverentially to all the great call-and-response songs of the past. Delightfully, contagiously spontaneous, "Success" sounds as though it were made up on the spot—which, given Pop's preferred method of working, it may well have been.

He'd sing a line, his bandmates would bark it back at him, and the whole thing descended into uproarious farce as Pop conceived ever more absurd lines for them to parrot—"I'm gonna do the twist..." "I'm gonna hop like a frog..."—and finally, as the entire room sounds set to simply disintegrate with laughter, "Oh shit." "Oh shit," the band chorus back, and it would be a few months more before even Bowie realized that much the same melodic sequence, slowed and pumped to fresh heights of grandeur, had a new life ahead of it as "Heroes." Over the years, Bowie would rework several of the songs that he and Pop cowrote, with varying degrees of success (or otherwise). "Heroes" was the one time it truly worked.

Bowie drove the sessions as usual, but Pop worked his balls off to wrestle control away from him, working around the clock to make sure he had the final say on everything. "See, Bowie's a helluva fast guy. Quick, quick. Very quick thinker, very quick action, very active person, very sharp. I realized that I had to be quicker than him, otherwise whose album was it gonna be? The guys and he'd leave the studio to go to sleep, but not me. I was working to be one jump ahead of them for the next day."

He remained one jump ahead, too, until the end of May 1977, with the album finally completed—and then it all came crumbling down. He quit the apartment and holed up instead at the Hotel Gerhus, to work his way through a small mountain of cocaine, and silently and increasingly unhappily ponder what he'd created.

He started at the beginning and worked his way in. RCA had sent proofs of the projected cover, a grinning close-up that looked more like the cover of *Mad* magazine than any street-walking cheetah whom Pop'd ever heard of. "I stared at the cover over and over, waiting to like the picture." He failed. He played "Lust for Life" over and over, "waiting for it to be faster." It wasn't. "And things only got worse after that."

Finally, Bowie and Corinne stepped in, with an American couple they'd been hanging out with. "There was practically an intervention between the four of them," It was, Pop laughed, very polite. First there was a ruse to get him over, an anguished call from Corinne—"We're cooking some fish and we don't know how to scale them properly, we absolutely have to have your help." He arrived, and immediately, "they were checking my shape, and then they got the Americans.... 'Listen, you're having an Italian vacation, take him with you and get him to have a bath and a haircut, for Christ's sake.' I went to Capri, and that was an experience I treasure."

While Pop vacationed, Bowie went back to work, stuffing the same Hansa studio with his own crew—Visconti, Eno, Alomar, Murray, and Davis, plus, at last, Robert Fripp—to record the follow-up to the most eye-opening hit of his career, albeit one that was less informed by the pastures laid bare by *Low* than those that bristled and prickled through *The Idiot*.

Punk was a major market force in Europe now—the United States would follow soon enough—but, more than that, it was a serious revision of what made music matter, away from the dollar bills and spreadsheets and sales reports that were the record companies' only take on the subject, and back into the realm of artistry and creativity. As so often before, Britain was taking the lead in revitalizing rock, and though Bowie remained content to call West Berlin home, he was well aware of the impact that revitalization could have, not only upon his career, but upon that of every artist that he cared about.

Eno was already working on a new album that was distinctly informed by the spikiness of punk, as it morphed into what would later be marketed as new wave. Released the following year, *Before and After Science* was the fourth and final of Eno's rock albums, and the scratchiest one of them all. The ideas that Eno was feeding into *"Heroes"* would spin off from the same mind-set that was already at work creating "King's Lead Hat" and "RAF," and would themselves be highlighted across the marketplace once *"Heroes"* was complete, when RCA launched a new marketing campaign that claimed, simply, "There's old wave, there's new wave, and there's David Bowie."

But *"Heroes"* was more than a simple reaction to all that was going on in the outside world; more, too, than the succession of deeply private ruminations that past Bowie biographers have painstakingly set into stone—that "Blackout" concerned the heart attack that he allegedly suffered in late 1976, but which was actually a misreported case of diarrhea; that "Sons of the Silent Age" reflected in some vast, obtuse manner on the sad state of Bowie's half-brother Terry, a diagnosed schizophrenic; that "V-2 Schneider" was nothing more than a honking tribute to Kraftwerk, answering the Germans' own reference to Bowie and Pop in the title track to their latest album, *Trans-Europe Express.*

The songs on *"Heroes"* have been allied to all manner of events and influences, and they may well have been all of those things. But Bowie has never been one to imbue his own songs with more meaning than the listener wants to draw from them, and he shrugged off suggestions that *"Heroes"* was any exception.

"It was just a collection of stuff that I and Eno and Fripp had put together. Some of the stuff that was left off was very amusing, but this was the best of the batch, the stuff that knocked us out." Eno, meanwhile, was happiest pointing out that most of the backing tracks were recorded in just one take. "We did second takes, but they weren't nearly as good."

Bowie, too, was in spontaneous mood, lifting from Pop the notion of stepping up behind the microphone and simply letting rip. He had, he said, "absolutely no idea" what the songs were really about; no sense of the "consequences" of individual lyrics, "and no preconceptions of any kind." In the past, he had enthused about one particular lyric writing device that he employed, the William Burroughs–esque "cut up" technique of penning a verse and then cutting up the page and rearranging individual lines or words.

Now, however, he was capable of creating the random couplets and imagery that he sought without resorting to this device.

If the recording was swift, the album's actual gestation was somewhat more relaxed. Bowie and Visconti were still mixing *"Heroes"* in August 1977, just weeks before its scheduled release in October—which in turn placed it on the streets just a couple of weeks after Pop's *Lust for Life.*

Hopes within the audience that Bowie might again accompany Pop onto the road, as he set out to promote his second album in six months, were doomed to disappointment. Retaining the Sales brothers, plus guitarist Stacey Heydon and replacing Bowie with former Stooge Scott Thurston, Pop was back on the U.K. circuit at the beginning of September, with gigs across Europe and the U.S. to follow.

Support on the British dates was provided by the Adverts, one of the—if not simply *the*—best of the punk bands that had arisen over the past year or so. It was a well-heeled pairing. Adverts bassist Gaye Advert was a longtime Stooges fan, had owned both *The Stooges* and *Fun House* since she was introduced to them at college in 1971, and could be numbered among the very select band of fans who had also picked up *Raw Power* on release. That album's cover photo of Pop adorned her bass guitar, and when *Record Mirror* asked for her top ten albums, Pop was responsible for five of them.

"I loved doing that tour," Gaye recalled. "Iggy was really great. The first night, in Manchester, we were just sitting around in the dressing room thinking that we wouldn't even get to see him apart from onstage, when he just walked in and said, 'Hi, I'm Jimmy,' and we ended up spending the whole time with Iggy and his band. Iggy to me is what Elvis Presley is to some people."

While Pop toured, Bowie was televised. Having ignored every attempt to draw him out of his shell behind the release of *Low*, he now threw himself into a string of television appearances—albeit to the strains of strangely tragic coincidence. Just days after the cameras witnessed Bowie's reunion with Marc Bolan, stepping out as special guest on the last episode of his old friend's eponymous teatime TV series, Bolan was dead, killed when the car in which he was riding crashed into a tree in the early hours of the morning of September 16, 1977.

Two days after the Bolan show, Bowie guested on Bing Crosby's *Merrie Olde Christmas* special, dueting with the old crooner across a medley of "Peace on Earth" and "Little Drummer Boy." Bing, too, would be dead before the program was broadcast.

Bolan's death hit Bowie hard. So close throughout their years of struggle, their relationship fell on hard times around the same time Bolan's star began to ascend. In January 1970, Bowie thought nothing of inviting Bolan to guest on his latest single, "The Prettiest Star," then ensured that Mick Ronson retained the spirit of that original solo when they rerecorded the song for *Aladdin Sane*.

Since that time, however, the opportunities for their friendship to continue had declined precipitously, as producer Tony Visconti explained. "That was the only time they could have worked together, the only time their egos would have allowed it. But you could tell the rivalry between them was there."

That rivalry only grew angrier over the next few years, with Bolan, his friends all say, far more intent on maintaining it that Bowie ever was. "I don't think Bowie ever understood why Marc seemed to hate him so much," said Tony Secunda, Bolan's business manager during the T.Rexstatic peaks of 1972. "Bowie never said anything bad about Marc, but Marc didn't miss a single opportunity to make some kind of sly comment."

"What they tried to do with Bowie was create another Marc Bolan," was a typical Bolanic jibe, unleashed to the magazine *Creem*. "But the interest with the kids was not there. I don't think that David has anywhere near the charisma or balls that I have. Or Alice has. Or Donny Osmond has got. He's *not* gonna make it, in any sort of way." The same month the interview was published, July 1973, Bowie "retired" at the peak of his fame. The two events were likely not related.

Secunda's belief was, "He knew that Bowie was beginning to get bigger than he was, and would continue to do so," so perhaps Bowie could afford to be magnanimous. It's intriguing, after all, to compare Bolan's attitude toward Bowie with the rising Ziggy's occasional digs toward the mercurial ascent of Elton John—not least of all his barely concealed scorn for the manner in which Elton's breakthrough hit "Rocket Man" so echoed the premise of "Space Oddity."

Yet Bowie and Bolan never truly fell out of contact, and when the pair found themselves spending time in Los Angeles in 1975, they were soon writing together, too. Nothing concrete came of the collaboration—they did complete one song, a vaguely disco-themed number called "Walking Through That Door," complete with period falsetto vocals, but they did nothing with it. They had higher hopes for their next encounter, though, in March 1977.

Bolan had just released his latest album, the return-to-form *Dandy in the Underworld*, when Bowie breezed into London with the Iggy Pop tour. Instantly Bolan invited him to visit; Bowie accepted, and though the twenty minutes of music that they recorded together was rough and raw, there are few more exhilarating noises in the (post-Ziggy) Bowie catalog than the short, but joyously boisterous tape that emerged from their union. One of the songs even became a solidly stupendous single, after the post-punk glam revivalists Cuddly Toys took a rambling riff and a few half-finished lyrics and transformed them into "Madman," a shimmering pop jewel.

Would that Bowie and Bolan had been afforded the same opportunity. As much as Bowie's collaboration with Pop reinvented the world's most forgotten boy and earned Bowie fresh kudos with the punkier crowd, so Bowie and Bolan united as performers could have rewritten their personal histories. Indeed, Bolan was happy to talk about the album they were going to record, writing one side apiece, but performing side by side. "What a combination it's going to be, the two greatest musical influences of the seventies joined together!"

Instead, that one cassette is all that remains, and listening to the full feast does not unearth any further gems; in fact, aside from "Madman" and "Sleeping Next to You," the number with which the pair closed the TV show, they seemed simply to be messing about, improvising around whichever riff most recently came to mind. The pleasure, then, lay in second-guessing what might have become of these snatches, had the pair only been able to follow through on the project; and in the spider's-eye view of the two chattering amongst themselves. "Thank you, that was David Bowie, and it was the best thing I've ever heard in my life," announces Bolan after one undistinguished riff passes by, and though you know he was joking at the time, who knows what could have become of that riff?

Bowie attended Bolan's funeral, sharing in the distaste of all the other mourners as an army of fans and photographers descended upon the crematorium, genuine sorrow mixed with sheer excitement; and then he returned to the promotional mill.

He talked of a world tour to be launched the following year, one that would finally allow him to put his past behind him through the perspective of his most recent releases; and, while his audience scratched its head in wonder, unable to imagine how "Art Decade" and "Moss Garden" could ever translate into a gripping live performance, Bowie turned his attention to rewriting another element of his recent past, as he linked up with Pop to "produce" the American's next album, the *TV Eye Live* document of the two 1977 tours.

Except, perhaps, *produce* was not the word that they had in mind, as Pop selected eight tracks from three American shows, themselves taped with less regard for sonic fidelity than any conventional live album of the age might have been, and turned them over to Edu Meyer, one of their West Berlin–based friends, to rough up. In fact, the two producers never even touched the tapes as the record was put together. But they certainly approved of the noise they heard on them.

Meyer explained, "Jim . . . had organized someone to tape [the shows] with a tape deck with two built-in microphones. We worked on it with filtering and editing on a two-track," to transform what was already a lo-fi experience into a rumble that, to unexpectant ears, made even the original *Raw Power* tapes sound like a crash course in clarity.

"As *TV Eye* was coproduced by David Bowie, of whom all things are possible" warned the *New Musical Express* review of the album, "one thought still nags. Maybe [the awful sound] is deliberate. Maybe he and Pop have spent weeks in the studio creating this audio documentary. Or maybe their intention this time was to present Pop, the macho demigod, writhing in the Pop band's cruel embrace. Or maybe it was just a rush job, anything to feed the punk market while it lasts."

There had, after all, been no shortage of opportunistic Pop releases over the past twelve months, as all three of the Stooges' original albums returned to the shelves, there to be joined by the newly salvaged and remixed results of Pop and James Williamson's ill-fated 1975 collaboration. *Kill City*, said Williamson, "is probably, as far as I'm concerned, the best album we ever did."

Pop, after hemming and hawing on the subject for a few years, finally found himself in full agreement. "I stand by the music and I stand by the themes. When it comes on, I feel good. I have a little meter inside me and I can't get anything by it. Either it'll go *woo* and the needle will go right up, or it'll flop. With *Kill City*, it always goes *wooo*." Plus, if you listen to the title track "and then play an Ice-T track from fifteen, eighteen years later, I said it all, right there, right then, before anybody else saw it coming."

TV Eye Live, on the other hand, hung so uncompromisingly stark and raw that, almost twenty years later, with the rest of Pop's catalog long established on CD, *TV Eye Live* remained on the shelf. "You like that album?" he asked incredulously, when the subject was raised. "I've not been able to reconcile myself with that one. A lot of other people don't like it either."

But he didn't think much of it at the time, either. Pop had no doubt that RCA had signed him simply to keep David Bowie sweet, particularly with the post-MainMan fallout still to settle. Even after *The Idiot* made the U.K. Top 30, the company seemed to have little regard for Pop. They proved that when *Lust for Life* was allowed to disappear from view almost before the accompanying tour was over. *TV Eye Live* was Pop's way of thanking them for their lack of support, with a contract-filling live album that they could do whatever they liked with, while he swung off to a new record company.

What they did with it was—well, of course they buried it. But somewhere in the back of somebody's mind, the notion surely lurked that, for the third time in as many years, and for the third time from the same musical and cultural direction, one of the biggest record companies in the world had been handed an album that so defied contemporary attitudes toward what a rock record *should* sound like that it was surely worth more than the lackadaisical flap of disinterest that ultimately greeted it.

Alongside *Metal Machine Music* and *Low*, *TV Eye Live* stands as an album that is so far out on a limb, so disdainful (deliberately or otherwise) of what its audience might think of it, that it cannot even be viewed as a regular LP. It is an artifact, a frozen moment that is merely biding its time before making its purpose felt. On this occasion, however, that would be a long time coming—even *Metal Machine Music* was rehabilitated in the critical mind before *TV Eye Live*, even if that rehabilitation did only arrive at the end of some long and bitter battles. *TV Eye Live*,

Pop once boasted, cost him $5,000 to make, and it netted him $90,000. It was worth so much more than that.

The time they devoted to listening to what became *TV Eye* were the last weeks Bowie and Pop would spend together for two years. They enjoyed Christmas 1977 at Bowie's Hauptstrasse apartment, surrounded by West Berlin friends and further-flung associates. But Bowie's upcoming tour, together with the shorter but no less effective guerilla outings that Pop was scheduling throughout 1978, ensured that their paths rarely crossed— not at all while Pop recorded and toured his next album, *New Values*; and then only briefly the next time around, as Pop sequestered himself away in Rockfield Studios to record his final true masterpiece, *Soldier*.

Bowie stopped by to listen in on the progress and add his own unique imprimatur to one solitary track, "Play It Safe." Then, assured that Pop was not playing it safe, he departed again, leaving Pop to try and salvage an album that had just been completely revitalized. James Williamson was producing the sessions, just as he'd done for *New Values* before it, and with the same instructions as well; to create a record that would get Pop on the radio.

But Bowie's intervention made it crystal clear that the relationship was no longer working. Williamson walked out the moment Pop and Bowie contrived a new song about the Queen of England's sister and her much-rumored love for John Bindon, a lowlife London gangster with the biggest dick in the city. They would never, Williamson warned them, get on the radio singing rude songs about Princess Margaret, and over in New York, Clive Davis could not help but agree with him.

Veteran music biz hand that he was, Davis had had his fill of Iggy Pop the last time their paths crossed, when Columbia signed the Stooges from Tony Defries and were rewarded with the unsaleable monolith that was *Raw Power*.

Davis had moved on since then. In 1974, he started his own label, Arista, and around a shockingly bland catalog of big selling bubblegum merchants (the Bay City Rollers and Barry Manilow were both early Arista artists), he also trusted his staff to develop a roster that would appeal further across the board.

In 1975, Arista beat everybody else to the Patti Smith Group, and essentially ignited punk rock that fall with the release of Smith's *Horses* debut. The following year, when Lou Reed broke away from RCA, Arista were waiting, and while Reed promptly rewarded them with the dreadful disappointment of *Rock 'n' Roll Heart*, Davis was smart enough to know that this wasn't the first time Lou had had an off year, and it wouldn't be the last. He bounced back from *Sally Can't Dance* with the taut dynamics of *Coney Island Baby* (albeit via the sonic mulligatawny of *Metal Machine Music*). He'd bounce back from *Rock 'n' Roll Heart* as well.

But would Arista rebound from the London office's latest signing? Davis apparently flipped when he discovered that his U.K. wing had signed Pop; would have loved nothing so much as to nix the signatures before the ink was even dry. Of course he couldn't do that, but he did make one pledge. The Europeans could do what they wanted. But Arista's American label was never going to release any Iggy Pop records in the U.S. He was true to his word, as well. Lou Reed, on the other hand, was a wizard, a true star, and Davis knew that if he could only tame the savage beast, he could make Reed a million dollars.

Reed was probably further out on a limb in 1976 than he'd been since the Velvet Underground. Except it wasn't an especially good limb. A year that opened with his twisted, bug-eyed portrait staring out from the cartoon front cover of the maiden issue of *Punk* magazine, and the sometimes savage beauty of *Coney Island Baby*, quickly developed into an even ghastlier horror show once he got back into the studio with the notion of making a disco-jazz record. But Davis was right. Reed did recover, and dramatically, too.

He kicked off 1977 by donating some Rapidograph drawings to *Punk*. They appeared in issue seven, and anybody hoping that Reed's visual art might open a fresh window into his soul was left grasping at straws once again—his art did to the eyes what *Metal Machine Music* did for the ears. Clearly, Reed was growling again; and then roaring once more as he followed through with the brilliantly titled and even more brilliantly framed *Street Hassle*.

Punk had more or less passed Reed by. He was aware of it, but he didn't care. "I'm not in competition with anyone, least of all myself. All I want to do is communicate a certain explosive, fun, rock 'n' roll quality that I've liked since I was nine years old, and I want the listener to hear what I heard, the thing that makes me think it's so great."

He acknowledged the obeisance with which the Velvet Underground were now regarded only as something he'd been due for a decade. It amused him to hear of this band or that (usually Brits, but no surprise there) claiming "Waiting for the Man" was the song that got them started, or blasting through "White Light White Heat" as though the Spiders from Mars had never happened. Without Bowie, a growling voice in the back of his mind reminded him, a large slice of the Velvet Underground might well have been forgotten. He'd spent the best part of the last five years fighting that fire with further fuel, all those B-movie rehashes of "Sweet Jane" and "Heroin." Now it was time to reclaim his legacy and really show these punks who was who.

He picked up on Patti Smith's recent exhumation of the Velvet Underground's old show opener "We're Gonna Have a Real Good Time Together."

He riffed on the critics who harped on about the last album's jazzy soul preoccupations with "I Wanna Be Black."

He looked back to a bunch of demos he'd taped around the time of *Coney Island Baby*, and pulled out "Dirt" and "Leave Me Alone."

He mourned the slowly decaying remnants of the life he'd shared with Rachel, as it drifted toward its end. And, best of all, he penned the urban epic he'd been threatening since "Waiting for the Man," "Street Hassle."

Igniting a fascination with spontaneity that his last few albums had allowed the studio to quash, Reed was still touring *Rock 'n' Roll Heart*, dragging that dispirited carcass around Europe through spring 1977, when he conceived *Street Hassle*. Dismantling the programmed set that taunted audiences elsewhere around the continent ("Sweet Jane" as a duet for horns and funkiness? Give us a break!), Reed instead instructed his band in a clutch of new songs—"Shooting Star," "Gimme Some Good Times," "Real Good Time Together," "Leave Me Alone," "Dirt"—and then sent them out for a gig in Ludwigshafen, with the tapes already rolling.

Four days later in London, with a few of the new songs still in the set, he named the new album for the first time in public; and, back in New York in time for the summer, he took the tapes into the studio.

Richard Robinson, whom history for so long had regarded as the ill-judged producer of *Lou Reed*, back in 1971, was recalled to produce; and when label head Clive Davis turned up in the studio one day and suggested that the already sprawling "Street Hassle" title track be made even longer still, Reed agreed. He'd known the song, a down-and-dirty beggar's opera shot through the unrelenting filter of the city that never sleeps, was a masterpiece. Now he believed it was even better than that.

Which nevertheless did not make for a happy session. Fights with Robinson culminated with the producer walking out. Reed was forced to change studios midway through "because we had a fight there," and then Davis returned and told Reed to scrap everything he'd done so far and start again. Reed ignored him. "The record came out and I wasn't crazy. They were just stupid. The head of Arista was stupid."

Street Hassle bears Reed's confidence out, although no matter how great the bulk of the album was, it was always going to be mauled by its title track, a three-part mini movie centered around a slow fuck on a kitchen table, a sordid street-smart drug death, and the ensuing uncertainty regarding what to do with the body. Angelic chorales and insistent cello powered the performance, and there was even a cameo from Bruce Springsteen, five years now into a career that repaid David Bowie's early interest by establishing himself *not* as one of the handful of performers who had arisen with at least one eye on Lou Reed's example, but one of the precious few who actually pulled it off.

"He was in the studio below," Reed explained, "and for that little [spoken word] passage I'd written, I thought he'd be just perfect because I tend to screw those things up"—he'd never forgiven himself, recording "I Found a Reason" for the final Velvet Underground album, for all but desecrating that song's midriff recitation. "I'm too much of a smart-ass. But I knew Bruce would do it seriously because he really is of the street."

Springsteen was radio's golden boy at the time, but of course even his presence could scarcely clean up "Street Hassle" sufficiently for any kind of airplay, even after Reed pulled a mildly less abrasive version out of the hat for a memorable *Don Kirshner's Rock Concert* appearance. Reed shrugged diffidently. "The Velvet Underground were banned from the radio [and] I'm still being banned, for exactly the same reasons. Maybe they don't like Jewish faggots.

"No, it's what they think I stand for they don't like. They don't want their kid sitting around masturbating to some rock 'n' roll record. They don't want their kid ever to know he can snort coke or get a blow job at school or fuck his sister up the ass. They never have. But how seriously can you take it? With or without the radio, I'm still dangerous to parents."

Resplendent in the gritty swagger that hallmarked the new album, Reed embarked on his next tour in spring 1978, kicking off with a week of shows at the Bottom Line in New York, and astonishing everybody with the sheer dynamism of his performance. Looking chunkier and healthier than he had all decade, and more relaxed too, he let the preshow tension rise to fever pitch by deliberately taking the stage late, and then throwing himself into a "Sweet Jane" that veered so close to a stand-up routine that even Reed described the ensuing live recordings as "a comedy album. Lou Reed talks and talks and talks."

He railed against critics ("give me an issue, I'll give you a tissue—you can wipe my ass with it"); he punctured his own pomposity ("what a snotty remark," he admonished himself after informing the audience that an earlier comment was a literary reference); and so on. A few audience members listened for a while, then walked out complaining that it was rubbish. A few more smiled knowingly and made gestures toward their nostrils—although, if Reed was speeding at the time, you couldn't help wishing a lot of other performers would take the same stuff. And, when the best of the shows were released as the double live *Take No Prisoners* album, he wrapped the whole thing up in a cartoon sleeve that reminded you of all the reasons you loved Lou Reed in the first place.

No matter that the set list simply screamed "greatest hits...again" at you. From the moment the show began in earnest, with Lou assaulting the audience from the word *go*, and the crowd, graciously and gratifyingly, howling back at him, it was clear that Reed was out for blood, more talkative than he'd ever been before, but darker and more savage too, slicing open the humor of his remarks with a viciousness that certainly did not involve hitting people with flowers.

But when he looked out into the crowd, the audience was loving it, his friends were lapping it up, and even Andy Warhol was enjoying himself. "I was proud of him," Warhol told his diary later. "For once, finally, he's himself. He's not copying anybody. Finally he's got his own style. Now everything he does works."

The Bottom Line show went out on the road, sweeping audiences nightly from the manic speed rap that disfigured some songs to the timeless beauty that had always permeated others—"Berlin," "Satellite of Love," and, best of everything, "Street Hassle." "I think of it as a contemporary urban blues album," Reed said of *Take No Prisoners*. "After all, that's what

I write, tales of the city. And if I dropped dead tomorrow, this is the record I'd choose for posterity. It's not only the smartest thing I've ever done, it's as close to Lou Reed as you're probably ever going to get."

While Pop teased his talent with *Soldier*, and Bowie somehow followed up *Low* and *"Heroes"* with the most anodyne concert tour of his pre–*Let's Dance* life (all bets are off thereafter), the abomination that he then preserved on the so-abysmal *Stage* live album, Reed had crowned the decade he helped design with an album that said everything his audience had been waiting to hear, in a voice that may not, to contradict Warhol, have been more unique than any other he'd employed, but which certainly was unlike any other you'd ever heard.

Still looking good, hale and healthy, Reed arrived in London on April 9, 1979, to play his first British concert in almost exactly two years—that was how long had elapsed since a dull-as-dishwater showing on the *Rock 'n' Roll Heart* tour. That was how long his U.K. fans had waited to hear the revitalized live show that kicked into position with the birth of *Street Hassle*, and which only gathered greater strength with *The Bells*, a new album that caught Reed collaborating—surprisingly, but very effectively—with Nils Lofgren.

The demented energy that created *Take No Prisoners* was absent from Reed's performance at the Hammersmith Odeon that night, but the show was spectacular regardless, and watching his old friend and sometime rival hurtle through a set that gazed upon almost every phase of his career—including a five-song midsection devoted wholly to *Berlin*—David Bowie could not deny that Reed was leaving the 1970s sounding stronger than he had in a long time.

The Velvet Underground seemed to fascinate Bowie yet again during 1979. In New York in March, he joined John Cale, Philip Glass, and Steve Reich onstage at Carnegie Hall to add wired viola to "Sabotage," the most traumatic of the songs then dominating Cale's live performance. Later in the year, he and Cale would hook up again to record a couple of songs together at New York's Ciarbis Studios. "Yeah, that's Bowie howling away in the background," Cale smiled when a fan played him the tape a few years later, which itself was an indication of just how un-Bowie-like (and, indeed, un-Cale-like) "Velvet Couch" and "Pianola" were.

He dropped by one of Nico's rare New York shows as well, hovering at the back of CBGB with the Talking Heads' David Byrne, but infuriating his hostess by not staying to say hello. She would avenge herself by covering "Heroes," and imbibing it with all the passion, power, and—for it was largely absent in David's original—*loss* that the lyric demanded.

The renewal of relations with Reed, however, had both history behind it and a wealth of possibilities. For all their musical strengths, Reed's last few albums had neither sold as well as his reputation would ordinarily have demanded, nor thrilled audiences in the same way as his earlier releases. Even *Street Hassle* had its critics, deluded deaf men though they might have been, and some people simply took themselves way too seriously to ever appreciate *Take No Prisoners*.

The suggestion that Reed might want to look back toward his earlier releases and pull a producer out of his past was one that Arista had raised on several occasions. Bowie, of course, was their number one choice, and the word on the street was that negotiations had progressed a lot further than anybody realized.

So when Bowie and Reed made their way from the Odeon to the Chelsea Rendezvous, a tiny restaurant in nearby South Kensington, the posse of journalists who accompanied them at least expected to come away with a word or two on that subject.

Instead, they witnessed its destruction.

All seemed calm at the outset. Allan Jones, of the weekly *Melody Maker*, recalled the pair deep into "the old pals act, heads down and toasting each other with Irish coffee." They could have been two former school friends, reunited to mull over past times; they could have been two old ladies, sipping tea and comparing medical experiences.

And then, chaos, Reed lashing out furiously at Bowie, cracking him over the skull and demanding, "Don't you *ever* fucking say that to me!"

No fewer than nine men, minders for the two superstars, leaped to separate the warring pair, whisper soothing words, pat down ruffled feathers. And for a few minutes all was peace and love again. Apologies had clearly been made and accepted, and the pair were talking quietly once more. It wasn't the first time they'd had a public battle, after all—keen memories still recalled their drink-spilling confrontation in New York five years before.

But whatever Bowie said the first time was obviously still on Reed's mind...or maybe Bowie, unable to recognize the warning signs, simply said it again. Because suddenly Reed was on his feet once more, his hands whacking Bowie around the head, while he bellowed, "I *told* you never to say that." And this time, when he was dragged away, he stayed away. The evening ended in stunned silence, embarrassed shock. A photo session that Reed had scheduled for the following morning was canceled without notice, and he flew straight to the next show, in Dublin that day.

Bowie, too, slipped from view, and it was only later that the grapevine, after speculating upon every imaginable cause for the ruckus, finally settled down to repeat the most likely offense.

The pair were indeed discussing the possibility of Bowie producing Reed's next album. They were indeed formulating a plan of attack that could transform his fortunes back to the heights he'd enjoyed at the time of *Transformer*. But Bowie laid down one condition that Reed apparently found impossible to accept.

"Only if you clean your act up first."

Only if you clean your act up first.

"How ironic," Nico smiled when the story made its way back to her. "The whole reason David wanted to work with Lou in the first place, and Iggy as well, was because he hadn't cleaned up his act. Now he was telling him to do it. No wonder Lou hit him. I would have as well."

EPILOGUE

Why end the story there? Why not continue on, through Bowie's internationally chart-topping revision of "China Girl," and the enduring loyalty that saw Bowie include further Pop songs on both *Tonight* (1984) and *Never Let Me Down* (1986)? The full-scale reunion, conspiring to create Iggy's own first hit record, 1986's *Blah Blah Blah*?

Why not chase through to 1997, and his live reconciliation with Lou Reed, replaying their Save the Whales performance at a Madison Square Garden party, at the end of Bowie's fiftieth birthday bash? Or forward a few years more, to Bowie contributing some vocals to Reed's *The Raven* album, a collection of verse built round Edgar Allan Poe?

Why not cover the Velvet Underground reunion in 1992, or the Stooges' reformation in 2003? Mott's return in 2009? Bowie's self-revitalization in the years around the millennium? There have been so many highlights in the last thirty years, there must be a chapter or two to wring out of them?

Maybe there is. But that's all it would be, a wringing-out of detail and document, a hop-frog through a series of incidents that may each have a tale to tell, but which really aren't a story. Not this story, anyway. "China Girl" was massive, but it was also embarrassing. *Blah Blah Blah* was a hit, but it was horrible as well, the worst record Iggy Pop had ever put his name to—and coming hot on the heels of Bowie's worst ever, the truly execrable *Tonight*, was anybody surprised at that?

The reunions were great if you don't care about age, and the fact that a band matters most because it exists in its own time and place, *not* because the members are thirty years older and still remember the tunes. Nostalgia exists so that we can all relive our distant pasts. But memory is intangible for a reason. You can never go back, not really.

Oh, and Madison Square Garden? Lou Reed was there, but Iggy Pop wasn't, and neither was anyone else with whom you'd associate the birthday boy. A cynic might look at the lineup, in fact, and wonder whose benefit it was all *really* for? Bowie's? Or the cable TV cameras that were broadcasting it live, and wanted to make sure there was some star power showing, to justify breaking in to their scheduled programming?

All three men have made some great records in the years since that night at the Chelsea Rendezvous. True, the 1980s were uniformly bad, and if anyone can listen to Lou Reed's "Little Red Joystick" without gagging a little, then we'll play you Iggy's "Candy" immediately after. Followed by Bowie's "Day In Day Out."

Slowly, however, the worms turned. Reed was first, winding up that hateful decade with his finest album since *Street Hassle*, and maybe even better than that. *New York* was more than a return to songwriting form, it was a return to meaningful observation as well, and across the albums that have flowed since then, you get the feeling that he has finally settled into life as Lou Reed; that he no longer feels the need to compete with kids who are three generations younger than him, and who will always look better on YouTube than he does. He makes records for himself these days, and people don't even shy away from the unexpected ones.

In 2007, Reed released *Hudson River Wind Meditations*, an album of tai-chi–inspired mood music that was as pastoral as *Metal Machine Music* was grating. But nobody called him a madman for doing so; nobody accused him of ripping off the kids. It was what it was, and if the world has learned any one thing over the past three decades, it is that an artist is *always* worth more when he follows his own heart than when he does what everyone else says he ought to. And it was Lou Reed who taught it that lesson.

Iggy was next to cast off the cobwebs. *American Caesar*, in 1993, was a jewel, stepping back from the hackneyed rent-a-Pop noises he'd been making since *Blah Blah Blah*, and again letting his songs speak louder than the sounds. He can still be crass when he wants to, and leading the reunited Stooges into the studio to record the abysmal *The Weirdness* was proof that even the greatest intentions have their dark sides.

But the reunion brought Ron Asheton some joy through what turned out to be the last years of his life—shortly before he died in January 2009, the old trouper looked back on the days of the original Stooges and said that they felt like a dream. Now he was reliving that dream, and friends were convinced that he'd never been happier. Maybe *The Weirdness* prevented the rest of us from sharing that emotion, but it doesn't really matter now, does it? James Williamson slipped in to fill the late Ron's shoes, the *Raw Power* album is back on the stage boards, and at the present pace of events, the band should be ready to self-destruct *Metallic KO* style sometime around the year 2012.

Bowie was the slowest to crawl out of the abyss, because he had the furthest to climb. *Let's Dance* in 1983 finally transformed him into the all-purpose superstar that Tony Defries once envisaged, and how ironic that Bowie waited until then, a year after their contract finally expired, before proving that he could write songs as commercially world-beating as Defries always said he could.

But having reached the top, he hated the view. Ambition, after all, is a wonderful thing, but only if it's really what you want to do, and Bowie was never going to be happy joining the rest of the throng chasing minor royalty around Studio 54 while snorting coke with whichever MTV star was closest. He cut two more albums in a similar vein, then retreated back into his shell of reinvention, first via the excoriating exorcism of the Tin Machine noise machine; then through the subtle peaks of *The Buddha of Suburbia*.

He made one more pop record because his label paid him a lot of money to do so, but *Black Tie White Noise* barely registered on the fan base, and he was back with Eno before you could say "liver salts," crafting and casting *Outside:1* upon the world, an album that looked back to the mad peaks of *Low* and *"Heroes"*; forward to the industrial sonics that were then shaking and reshaping the world of pop; and found a happy land somewhere in between.

Earthling followed, all jungle drum and bass—and then a sudden realization that he didn't need to do that anymore. Once, Bowie led the field because he stepped where nobody else went. He started lagging behind when he paid more attention to bandwagons. Now it was time to listen to himself and, like Lou Reed with *New York* and Iggy Pop with *American Caesar*, he finally made the album we'd been waiting for for so long. '*Hours…*' from 1999 remains the finest farewell to the twentieth century that any rock star Bowie's age could have made, a record so loaded with sadness and sentiment that you just knew he looked back on the days of his youth as fondly as the rest of us did.

He even started playing "The Bewlay Brothers" onstage! Onstage at the BBC concert where he premiered it in 2002, Bowie declared that he'd never played it live before, and he was right. He hadn't. But sneak a peek at the set list that the William Morris Agency telexed to New York promoter Ron Delsener in February 1972, outlining the composition of the live show that Bowie would be bringing to Carnegie Hall the following month, and there it was, "The Bewlay Brothers," climaxing the acoustic set that closed the first half of the show.

That show never happened. It would be six more months before Bowie came to America, by which time the *Ziggy Stardust* album was firmly in the ascendant. But Bowie remembered, and he also remembered the joy of those early live shows, just plucking out songs from wherever he found them, mixing covers with oldies and unexpected goodies and simply going out there to give the fans a good time. To "entertain" them, as he told the Aylesbury Friars crowd once, and he succeeded with room to spare.

A real heart attack finally slowed the reborn Bowie in 2004, retiring him from the concert circuit that he'd been scouring with so much pleasure for five years, and sending him into a twilight world of subtle guest appearances and occasional TV commercials. Rumor of a new album resurfaces periodically, but right now he is silent and no one can begrudge him that. Like Lou Reed, like Iggy Pop, David Bowie is responsible for some of the most crucial, influential, and utterly indispensable music of the rock 'n' roll era, and most of it was made at a time when half of the world didn't know who these artists were.

The other half, though . . . the other half thought they were gods. And reliving the decade when they were at their greatest peak, it's difficult to argue.

ACKNOWLEDGMENTS

To say that David Bowie, Iggy Pop, and Lou Reed have sound-tracked my life is a little like saying my cross-eyed cat Oliver looks a little strange. It's something I don't even think about; the shelves upon shelves of their music that dominate my CD/vinyl/eight-track collection are as much a part of the furniture as the shelves themselves, and I doubt a week goes by when I don't listen to some music by at least one of them. There was even a time when it was a daily ritual.

This book is not my first investigation of their lives; as both an author and a journalist, I have probably spent more hours writing about the sprawling family trees that emanate from the careers of Bowie, Pop, and Reed than every other artist put together. So the most important thank-you of all has to go to this holiest of trinities, simply for keeping me so happily occupied over the past thirty years; and especially to Iggy and Lou, for the very entertaining interviews that we've conducted over the years.

I also owe a lot to Nico, who once spent an entire afternoon talking with a starstruck fan, providing me with the framework of this book more than twenty-five years before I ever thought of writing it.

And then: Gratitude and thanks for the chat to: Gaye Advert, Willie Alexander, Ron Asheton, Trevor Bolder, Angela Bowie, John Cale, Leee Black Childers, Jayne County, Tony Defries, Gus Dudgeon, Dana Gillespie, Bob Grace, Brian James, Ivan Kral, Jimi Lalumia, Phil Lynott, Phil Manzanera, Lawrence Myers, Peter Noone, Andrew Loog Oldham, Kenneth Pitt, Tim Renwick, Scott Richardson, Mick Rock, Mick Ronson, Susie Ronson, Yvonne Ruskin, Tony Secunda, TV Smith, Scott Thurston, Maureen Tucker, Cherry Vanilla, Mike Vernon, Tony Visconti, Overend Watts, Doug Yule, Tony Zanetta.

I'd also like to thank Ken Sharp and Mark Johnston; Kenneth Pitt, for opening his Andy Warhol archive to me; and Paul Trynka, author of the ever-astounding *Iggy Pop: Open Up and Bleed* biography, for sharing interviews (the Riot Squad, Laurence Thibault, Phil Palmer, James Williamson, and Iggy) and confidences, and for salving my anxieties over the more minute pieces of detail. Paul was writing his own Bowie biography as I completed this book, and I cannot wait to read it.

Mike Edison, Jessica Burr, and Aaron Lefkove at Backbeat Books and copy editor Polly Watson.

Malcontent Pictures for permission to quote from the TV Smith documentary *Uncharted Wrecks of Wonder: The Story of the Adverts and TV Smith*.

And finally, to the family and friends who were around while I cranked *Take No Prisoners* up as loud as it would go: Amy Hanson, Jo-Ann Greene, Jane Hanson, Jenny and James, Linda and Larry, Phil and Paula, Sue and Tim, Deb and Roger, Dave and Sue, Oliver, Toby and Trevor, Jenny W., Karen T., Vaughan Funnell, Anchorite Man, Bateerz and family, Chrissie Bentley, Blind Pew, Mrs. B. East, Gef the Talking Mongoose, the Gremlins who live in the heat pump, Geoff Monmouth, Naughty Miranda, Nutkin, a lot of Thompsons, and Neville Viking.

SELECTED DISCOGRAPHY

The Astronettes

1973 *People from Bad Homes* (Golden Years)
David's little joke. CD compiled from both the Astronettes sessions and a similarly abandoned Ava Cherry album.

David Bowie

1967 *David Bowie* (Deram)
Bowie's debut album has been reissued and repackaged in a multitude of formats, the most notable of which are the double vinyl package *Images* (London) and the CD The *Deram Anthology 1966–1968* (Deram), the former rounding up all of Bowie's released material from this period, the latter adding outtakes and rarities.

1969 *Love You Till Tuesday* (Decca)
Unreleased until the mid-1980s, this set includes material recorded for a projected musical movie, together with other scraps from the era. An accompanying DVD is equally entertaining.

1969 *Man of Words, Man of Music* (Philips)
Bowie's second album, better known under its 1972 reissue title of *Space Oddity*.

1970 *The Complete Arnold Corns Sessions* (bootleg)

1971 *The Man Who Sold the World* (Mercury)

1971 *Live at Kingston Poly* (bootleg)

1971 *Hunky Dory* (RCA)

1972 *The Rise and Fall of Ziggy Stardust and the Spiders from Mars* (RCA SF 8267)

1972 *Bowie at the Beeb* (Virgin)
This two-CD collection of crucial BBC session performances, including the 1971 live concert and seminal Velvets covers, was released in 2000.

1972 *Live at Santa Monica* (bootleg)
One of the first Bowie bootlegs, from a September 1972 radio broadcast, subsequently given official releases on Griffin and, in 2008, EMI.

1973 *Aladdin Sane* (RCA)

1973 *His Master's Voice* (bootleg)
Ziggy's farewell show has since been released officially as *Ziggy Stardust: The Motion Picture*, on both audio and video. Remixing, however, renders both shows a shadow of the original (despite featuring additional material for the show); seek out instead the original vinyl bootleg, taken from a 1974 TV broadcast, for the best of the show, including Jeff Beck's guest appearance, the full farewell speech, and a riveting Ronson guitar solo through "Moonage Daydream."

1973 *Dollars in Drag* (bootleg)
The *1980 Floorshow* broadcast.

1973 *Pin Ups* (RCA)

1974 *Diamond Dogs* (RCA)

1974 *David Live* (RCA)

1975 *Young Americans* (RCA)

1976 *Station to Station* (RCA)

1976 *Thin White Duke* (bootleg)
A dynamic live performance recorded in New York on the *Station to Station* tour. Highlights from the gig were used as bonus tracks on the CD reissue of *Station to Station* itself.

1977 *Low* (RCA)

1977 *"Heroes"* (RCA)

1978 *Live at the Garden* (bootleg)
Bowie's attempts to document his 1978 tour, *Stage*, suffers from a debilitating mix and a castrating rearrangement of tracks. This raw recording from the Boston show on the same tour offers a far better assessment of the outing. It's still pretty drab, though.

John Cale

1970 *Vintage Violence* (Columbia)

1971 *The Church of Anthrax* (Columbia)

1972 *The Academy in Peril* (Reprise)

1973 *Paris 1919* (Reprise)

1974 *Fear* (Island)

1974 *Berlin 4 October 1974* (bootleg)
A rioter's-eye view of the final Cale, Nico, and Eno performance.

1975 *Slow Dazzle* (Island)

1975 *Helen of Troy* (Island)

1976 *The Ocean Club* (bootleg)
Collecting live cuts from 1976 and 1978

1977 *Guts* (Island)
Compilation featuring one unreleased track.

1977 *Animal Justice* EP (Illegal)

1978 *Even Cowgirls Get the Blues* (ROIR)
Collection of live material from 1978 to 1979.

1979 *Sabotage—Live* (Spy)

Wayne County

1974 *Wayne at the Trucks* (Munster)
Released in 2006, the original *Trucks* show, plus additional material.

1977 *The Electric Chairs* EP (Illegal)

1978 *The Electric Chairs* LP (Safari)

1978 *Storm the Gates of Heaven* (Safari)

1979 *Things Your Mother Never Told You* (Safari)

Dana Gillespie

1974 *Weren't Born a Man* (RCA)
Includes Bowie/Ronson's production of "Andy Warhol."

1975 *Ain't Gonna Play No Second Fiddle* (RCA)
The best of the above, plus unreleased Mick Ronson productions, were compiled onto the CD *Andy Warhol*, released in 1994.

Elton John

1970 *Tumbleweed Connection* (Uni)
The CD remaster includes Ronson (as a member of the Michael Chapman Band) rocking Reg's world through an early stab at "Madman Across the

Water," destined to be the title track of Elton's next album, *but not in this vastly superior form.*

Lulu

1974 "Watch That Man" / "Man Who Sold the World" (Polydor)
Single produced by Bowie/Ronson.

Mott the Hoople

1969 *Mott the Hoople* (Atlantic)

1970 *Mad Shadows* (Atlantic)

1970 *Live Fillmore West San Francisco* (Angel Air)
Phenomenal concert recordings.

1970–1974 *In Performance 1970–1974* (Angel Air)
Four-CD box set includes three live shows, including the 1972 Philadelphia gig with Bowie, and a stellar 1974 US date, plus other concert material.

1971 *Wildlife* (Atlantic)

1971 *Brain Capers* (Atlantic)

1972 *Two Miles from Heaven* (Island)
Released in 1980, band-compiled collection of out-takes 1969–1972. The CD includes bonus tracks.

1972 *All the Young Dudes* (Columbia)

1973 *Mott* (Columbia)

1974 *The Hoople* (Columbia)

1974 *Live* (Columbia)
Original single LP since expanded to a two-CD set.

1974 *European Ending* (bootleg)
Recording from the band's final tour with Mick Ronson.

Nico

1968 *Chelsea Girls* (Verve)

1969 *The Marble Index* (Elektra)

1971 *Desertshore* (Elektra)
Above two discs repackaged as *The Frozen Borderline* (Rhino) with bonus outtakes and demos.

1974 *The End* (Island)

1974 *Notre Dame, 13 December 1974*
Nico live, supporting Tangerine Dream at Notre Dame Cathedral.

Iggy Pop

1975 *Kill City* (Bomp)
Released in 1977, the final throes of the Williamson-Osterberg Disintegration
Society.

1977 *The Idiot* (RCA)

1977 *Iggy 1977* (Easy Action)
Four-CD box set comprising three live shows from 1977, plus a disc of so-called
alternate mixes and a radio broadcast.

1977–1981 *Where the Faces Shine Volume One* (Easy Action)
Six-CD box set comprising two shows from 1977, plus one apiece from 1978,
1979, 1980, 1981.

1977 *Lust for Life* (RCA)

1978 *TV Eye Live* (RCA)

Lou Reed

1970 *Lou Reed and Nico* (bootleg)
Informal rehearsal tapes.

1971 *The Velvet Underground: Ultra Rare Trax Vol. 2* (bootleg)
Includes a nine-song selection from Reed's 1971 visits to Richard Robinson's
apartment, plus various VU outtakes.

1972 *Lou Reed* (RCA)

1972 *Lou Reed, John Cale, Nico: Live at the Bataclan* (bootleg)

1972 *Transformer* (RCA)

1973 *Live at the Alice Tully Hall* (bootleg)

1973 *Berlin* (RCA RS 1002)

1974 *Rock 'n' Roll Animal* (RCA)
The first half of Reed's stellar Academy of Music, New York show.

1974 *Sally Can't Dance* (RCA)

1974 *Whatever Happened to Dick and Steve?* (bootleg)
One of the better shows from the *Sally Can't Dance* tour.

1975 *Lou Reed Live* (RCA)
The second half of the *Rock 'n' Roll Animal* show.

1975 *Metal Machine Music (The Amine B Ring)* (RCA Red Seal)

1976 *Coney Island Baby* (RCA)

1976 *Rock and Roll Heart* (Arista)

1978 *Street Hassle* (Arista)

1979 *Live—Take No Prisoners* (Arista)

Mick Ronson

1974 *Slaughter on Tenth Avenue* (RCA)

1974 *Live at the Rainbow* (bootleg)

1975 *Play Don't Worry* (RCA)

1975 *Ian Hunter* (Columbia)
Credited to the former Mott front man, but in truth the sound of the Hunter-Ronson partnership in full flow. The song "Boy" may or may not have been dedicated to Bowie.

1976 *Just Like This* (Burning Airlines)
Released in 1999, the sessions for Ronson's aborted third album.

The Spiders from Mars

1976 *The Spiders from Mars* (Pye)
Trevor Bolder and Woody Woodmansey make the best they can of a bad situation.

Steeleye Span

1974 *Now We Are Six* (Chrysalis)
Includes Bowie's wheezing death rattle sax through "To Know Him Is to Love Him."

The Stooges

1969 *The Stooges* (Elektra)

1970 *Fun House* (Elektra)

1970 *The Complete Fun House Sessions* (Rhino)
Eight-CD box set comprising every note recorded during the album sessions.

1970 *Live at Soldier Field* (bootleg)

1972–1974 *Heavy Liquid* (Easy Action)
Six-CD box set comprising studio outtakes and rehearsals and live material recorded on either side of *Raw Power*.

1973 *Rough Power* (Bomp)
Seventeen-track anthology of alternate/original mixes for the *Raw Power* album.

1973 *Raw Power* (Columbia)

1973 *Double Danger* (Bomp)
Official release for the 1973 Academy of Music show recorded for a possible live album.

1974 *Metallic KO* (Skydog)
Released in 1976, highlights of the final Stooges concert blended with other material from the band's last tour.

Cherry Vanilla

1976 *Live at Max's* (Max's Kansas City)
Various artists collection includes live cuts by Vanilla and Wayne County.

1978 *Bad Girl* (RCA)

1979 *Venus De Vinyl* (RCA)

The Velvet Underground

1966 *Factory 3 January 1966* (bootleg)
The first rehearsal with Nico.

1966 Scepter Studio acetate (bootleg)
The legendary lost mix of the first album.

1966 *Live in Columbus* (bootleg)
The finest document of the Velvets with Nico.

1967 *The Velvet Underground and Nico* (Verve)

1967 *Live at the Gymnasium, New York* (bootleg)

1968 *White Light White Heat* (Verve)

1968–1969 *VU* (Polydor)

1968–1969 *Another View* (Polydor)
Released in 1985/1986, two LPs worth of unreleased material.

1969 *Live 1969* (Mercury)
Two-LP set released in 1974.

1969 *The Velvet Underground* (Verve)

1970 *Loaded* (Cotillion)

1970 *Live at Max's Kansas City* (Atlantic)
The box set *Peel Slowly and See* (Polydor) features all three Verve albums, plus a wealth of live and outtake material. Reissues of *Loaded* and *Live at Max's Kansas City* (Rhino) are laden with bonus tracks.

1971–1973 *Final VU* (Captain Trip)
Four-CD box set comprising live recordings from the post-Lou era.

1972 *Squeeze* (Polydor)

BIBLIOGRAPHY

Ambrose, Joe. *Gimme Danger: The Story of Iggy Pop* (Omnibus, 2004).

Angell, Callie. *Andy Warhol Screen Tests: The Films of Andy Warhol Catalogue Raisonné* Vols. 1/2 (Abrams, 2006).

Auslander, Philip. *Performing Glam Rock: Gender and Theatricality in Popular Music* (University of Michigan Press, 2006).

Bangs, Lester. *Psychotic Reactions and Carburetor Dung* (William Heinemann, 1988).

Biesenbach, Klaus (ed) and Bandy, Mary Lea (curator). *Andy Warhol: Motion Pictures* (KW Institute, 2004).

Blacknell, Steve. *The Story of Top of the Pops* (Patrick Stephens Ltd., 1985).

Bockris, Victor. *Transformer: The Lou Reed Story* (Simon & Schuster, 1995).

Bockris, Victor. *Up-Tight: The Velvet Underground Story* (Cooper Square Press, 2003).

Bockris, Victor. *Warhol: The Biography* (Da Capo Press, 2003).

Bowie, Angie. *Free Spirit* (Mushroom, 1981).

Bracewell, Michael. *Re-Make, Re-Model: Becoming Roxy Music* (Da Capo, 2008).

Buckey, David. *Strange Fascination: David Bowie—The Definitive Story* (Virgin, 1999).

Cale, John & Bockris, Victor. *What's Welsh for Zen: The Autobiography of John Cale* (Bloomsbury, 1999).

Cann, Kevin. *David Bowie: A Chronology* (Fireside, 1983).

Cohn, Nik. *Awopbopaloobop Alopbamboom: The Golden Age of Rock* (Weidenfeld & Nicholas, 1969).

Defries, Tony and Thompson, Dave. *Gods & Gangsters: The Autobiography of Tony Defries* (unpublished/uncompleted 2007).

Devine, Campbell. *Mott the Hoople & Ian Hunter: All the Young Dudes—The Biography* (Cherry Red, 1998).

Doggett, Peter. *Lou Reed: Growing Up in Public* (Omnibus, 1995).

Downing, David. *Future Rock* (Panther, 1976).

Farren, Mick. *The Black Leather Jacket* (Plexus, 1985).

Flür, Wolfgang. *Kraftwerk: I Was a Robot* (Sanctuary, 2000).

Frame, Pete. *Rock Family Trees* (Omnibus Books, various editions).

Garner, Ken. *In Session Tonight* (BBC Books, 1992).

Green, Jonathon. *Days in the Life: Voices from the English Underground 1961–1971* (William Heinemann, 1989).

Guinness Book of British Hit Singles…Albums (Guinness World Records, various editions).

Hanson, Amy. *Kicking Against The Pricks: An Armchair Guide to Nick Cave* (Helter Shelter, 2005).

Heylin, Clinton (ed). *All Yesterday's Parties: The Velvet Underground in Print 1966–1971* (Da Capo, 2005).

Hoskyns, Barney. *Glam! Bowie, Bolan and the Glitter Rock Revolution* (Faber & Faber, 1998).

Jarman, Marshall. *David Bowie World 7" Records Discography 1964–1981* (self-published, 1994).

Jasper, Tony. *The Top 20 Book* (Blandford Books, various editions).

Johnstone, Nick. *Lou Reed Talking* (Omnibus, 2006).

Marshall, Bertie. *Berlin Bromley* (SAF, 2006).

Matheu, Robert & Bowe, Brian J. (eds). *Creem: America's Only Rock 'n' Roll Magazine* (Collins, 2007).

Mayes, Sean. *Life on Tour with David Bowie: We Can Be Heroes* (IMP, 1999).

McNeil, Legs & McCain, Gillian. *Please Kill Me: The Uncensored Oral History of Punk* (Grove Press, 2006).

Melly, George. *Revolt into Style: The Pop Arts in Britain* (Penguin, 1970).

Murray, Charles Shaar. *Shots from the Hip* (Penguin, 1991).

New Musical Express 1973 Annual (Fleetway, 1973).

New Musical Express 1974 Hot Rock Guide (Fleetway, 1974).

New Musical Express Greatest Hits: The Very Best of NME (IPC, 1974).

Nilsen, Per. *The Wild One: The True Story of Iggy Pop* (Omnibus, 1988).

Novick, Jeremy & Middles, Mick. *Wham Bam Thank You Glam: A Celebration of the 70s* (Aurum Press, 1998).

Paytress, Mark. Bolan: *The Rise and Fall of a 20th Century Superstar* (Omnibus, 2002).

Paytress, Mark & Pafford, Steve. *BowieStyle* (Omnibus, 2000).

Pegg, Nicholas. *The Complete David Bowie* (Reynolds & Hearn, 2004).

Petrie, Gavin (ed). *Pop Today: A Disc Special* (Hamlyn, 1974).

Pitt, Ken. *Bowie: The Pitt Report* (Omnibus, 1985).

Pop, Iggy. *I Need More: The Stooges & Other Stories* (2.13.61, 1997).

Reed, Lou. *Between Thought and Expression: Selected Lyrics* (Hyperion, 1991).

Roberts, Chris. *Lou Reed: Walk on the Wild Side: The Stories Behind the Songs* (Carlton, 2004).

Rock, Mick. *Blood & Glitter* (Vision On, 2001).

Rock, Mick. *Raw Power: Iggy & the Stooges* (Omnibus, 2005).

Rock, Mick & Bowie, David. *Moonage Daydream: The Life and Times of Ziggy Stardust* (Universe, 2005).

Rock File Vols. 1–5 (New English Library, 1973 etc.).

Rolling Stone Cover to Cover: The First 40 Years (Bondi Digital Publishing, 2008).

Seabrook, Thomas Jerome. *Bowie in Berlin: A New Career in a New Town* (Jawbone, 2008).

Sewall-Ruskin, Yvonne. *High on Rebellion: Inside the Underground at Max's Kansas City* (Thunder's Mouth Press, 1998).

Simmons, Sylvie. *Too Weird for Ziggy* (Grove Press, 2004).

Stein, Jean & Plimpton, George (ed). *Edie: An American Biography* (Alfred E. Knopf, 1982).

Strong, Martin. *The Great Rock . . . and Psychedelic Discography* (Canongate Books, various editions).

Thompson, Dave. *Beyond the Velvet Underground* (Omnibus, 1989).

Thompson, Dave. *Children of the Revolution—Gum into Glam 1967–1976* (self-published, 1985).

Thompson, Dave. *Glam Rock: 20th Century Rock & Roll* (Collectors Guide Publishing, 2000).

Thompson, Dave. *Hallo Spaceboy: The Rebirth of David Bowie* (ECW, 2006).

Thompson, Dave. *Ignatius Pope—The Iggy Pop Story* (unpublished manuscript, 1978).

Thompson, Dave. *Moonage Daydream* (Plexus, 1987).

Thompson, Dave. *To Major Tom: The Bowie Letters* (Sanctuary, 2002)

Thomson, Elizabeth & Gutman, David (eds). *The Bowie Companion* (MacMillan, 1993).

Tobler, John and Grundy, Stuart. *The Record Producers* (BBC Books, 1982).

Tremlett, George. *David Bowie: Living on the Brink* (Century, 1996).

Tremlett, George. *The David Bowie Story* (Futura, 1974).

Tremlett, George. *The Marc Bolan Story* (Futura, 1975).

Trynka, Paul. *Iggy: Open Up and Bleed* (Broadway Books, 2007).

Various authors. *Mojo David Bowie Special Edition* (2007).

Visconti, Tony. *Bowie, Bolan and the Brooklyn Boy* (HarperCollins, 2007).

Warhol, Andy. *The Philosophy of Andy Warhol (From A to B and Back Again)* (Harcourt, Brace, 1975).

Warhol, Andy & Hackett, Pat. *Popism: The Warhol Sixties* (Harvest Books, 1980).

Watson, Steven. *Factory Made: Warhol and the Sixties* (Pantheon Books, 2003).

Whitburn, Joel. *Top Pop Singles . . . Albums* (Record Research, various editions).

Witts, Richard. *Nico: The Life & Lies of an Icon* (Virgin, 1993).

Wrenn, Mike. *Lou Reed: Between the Lines* (Plexus, 1994).
Wrenn, Mike. *The Velvet Underground & Lou Reed* (Babylon Books, 1982).
Young, James. *Nico: The End* (Overlook Press, 1993).
Zak, Albin III. *The Velvet Underground Companion: Four Decades of Commentary* (Schirmer Books, 1994).

Plus individual issues of the following publications:

Alternative Press, Circus, Classic Rock, Creem, Daily Express, Disc & Music Echo, Disco 45, Goldmine, Interview, Live! Music Review, Melody Maker, Mojo, National Rock Star, New Music Express, Q, Record Collector, Record Mirror, Rolling Stone, Sounds, Spin, Street Life, The Daily Mirror, The Guardian, The L.A. Times, The New York Times, The Observer, The Sun, The Word, Uncut, Vox, ZigZag.

INDEX